THE THOUGHTFUL TEACHER'S GUIDE TO THINKING SKILLS

Gary A. Woditsch

with
John Schmittroth

LEA LAWRENCE ERLBAUM ASSOCIATES, PUBLISHERS
1991 Hillsdale, New Jersey   Hove and London

Lawrence Erlbaum Associates, Inc., Publishers
365 Broadway
Hillsdale, New Jersey 07642

Library of Congress Cataloging-in-Publication Data

Woditsch, Gary A.
    The thoughtful teacher's guide to thinking skills / by Gary A. Woditsch with
John Schmittroth.
        p.   cm.
    Includes bibliographical references and index.
    ISBN 0-8058-0289-4. — ISBN 0-8058-0290-8 (pbk.)
    1. Thought and thinking—Study and teaching.   I. Schmittroth,
John.   II. Title.
    LB1590.3W63   1990
    370.15′2 — dc20   90-42928
                                                                           CIP

Printed in the United States of America
10 9 8 7 6 5 4 3 2 1

If anyone finds gain herein, it is due to the sacrifice of loved ones, especially my wife and mother.

G. A. W.

CONTENTS

CUI BONO?

Who can expect to profit from this guide? This book deals with how instruction, at any level from K to graduate school, can be shaped to improve thinking skill, so it is clearly a book meant for teachers. As it unfolds, it raises thinking skill issues appropriate to elementary, intermediate, secondary, and collegiate levels, and it deals with those issues in turn.

But there appears to be a problem. Moving through instructional levels suggests that only part of the book will suit any given teacher. Of what interest is a section on elementary instruction to someone who handles college classes, and why should the secondary teacher care about either collegiate or elementary issues? Even more worrisome is the receding likelihood that such a book would have much to do with an individual teacher's practical classroom concerns.

Fortunately, appearance here is misleading. Every page of this guide aims at classroom impact, regardless whether that classroom happens to serve a college, a kindergarten, or something in between. That impact is meant to flow from the reader's strengthened grasp of what constitutes and what advances skillful thought.

It happens to be very difficult to achieve this new understanding from the vantage of any single instructional level. Skillful thought and the things that nurture it change as thinking matures and grows more practiced. Moving through the chief levels of instruction lets us profile that change. We see unexpected jumps and gradual shifts in the growth of skill that no amount of prodding from a single level would reveal.

As this sense of how minds grow begins to firm, it casts new light on classrooms. Problems that once seemed unique to a given age or grade level turn out not to be. Some thinking weaknesses and biases that seem to cry out for the attentions of formal schooling reveal themselves as products of such schooling. Challenges we once would not have dreamed of imposing on students begin to seem prudent. All this because we've gone past the mind's momentary performance (the usual view from an accustomed grade level) to its deeper, more abiding imperatives.

In the process of gaining this sense, you will witness what teachers from levels other than yours face and do in classrooms. The utility of that exposure could come to astound you.

Minds frequently harbor a surprising mix of strengths and weaknesses. Sometimes, to truly advance the capabilities of a mind, you need to treat one part of it as though it were the unsteady implement of a preschooler, another part as if it belonged to a doctrinaire sixth-grader, and yet another as though it were ripe to conquer college prelims. You will encounter minds whose composite challenge crosses all manner of instructional levels.

For that reason alone it is wise to always covet insight about what teachers at other levels do. Unlike our educational systems, skillful thought often does not advance in predictable increments tuned to a calendar. A college teacher cannot be sure that her sophomores will arrive with their sixth-grade thinking skills intact. Some of her quite clever sophomores will have avoided developing sixth-grade skills, getting by instead on strategies that counterfeit them. If the college teacher can't discern that lack and instruct to overcome it, those sophomore minds will grow—if it can be counted growth—only more accustomed to their limitations.

In one sense thinking skill instruction asks us to defer a powerful teaching instinct. It is natural for teachers to beckon, to draw students to their lore, their insight, even their skill. But thinking skill instructors must first take care to discover where students stand before they beckon. Students cannot advance to new thinking skill from capabilities they are *supposed* to have—only from capabilities they actually do have. The trick to teaching thinking skill is to meet minds where they in fact are—not where grade level presumes they should be—and to lead them hence.

That suggests a workable summary of what this guide is about: how to meet minds where they stand and how to lead them hence. Any teacher inclined to do such things in any classroom can look for profit in this book.

There is profit here for the administrator as well. Administrators strive to encourage and enhance the best efforts of their staffs. The thoughtful administrator can come away from this guide with a reasoned view of what distinguishes "best effort" from merely "lots of effort" in developing thinking skill. It takes that view to decide what needs more and what needs less program emphasis and resource if we want students who truly think more skillfully.

IN MEMORY

John Schmittroth and I planned to write this book together. The prospect pleased us. There was special exhilaration for me; I would be writing to a consummate teacher, and with an unequaled friend.

The early chapters were mine to draft. Lengthy phone conversations insured that John had already incisively touched the drafts he received. When I shipped off Chapter 8, the mails brought me John's review questions for Chapter 10, plus six pages of notes for what would have been his Chapter 9. And then he went to hospital.

I hoped it would cheer him to receive my version of Chapter 9, which incorporated all his notes; the sentences, wherever possible, intact. I envisioned the superb composition teacher's vigorous nods, both affirming and negating, his sharp wit and his salvaging pencil all at work from that hospital bed. But John never got to read Chapter 9.

Although John left this life, he didn't leave this book. Too many years have ingrained him as my idol in this profession of teaching. It is hard for me to shape a phrase about instruction without wondering how his sparkling, demanding mind might respond. He would often surprise me, and so I cannot be sure how he would feel, in detail, about the portions of this book he did not see. But his inspiration extends truly to those portions, and I wager he would stand by me in them as he stood in those he did read. You are with me, John, in each instance of the pronoun, first person plural. We have finished us a book.

GUIDELINES

Pick up a guidebook to some special activity, like scuba or sky diving, and you'll see that it usually begins with a preview of requirements and equipment. What abilities and attitudes will the venture call upon, and how do you select the best gear? It's a reasonable approach, even to the business of teaching thinking skills.

Let's begin with equipment. Basically, a teacher requires a thorough grasp of the subject matter to be taught coupled with a sense of how to convey it effectively to students. You will need to know just what thinking skills are, how they work, and what you can do to improve them in your students.

You might try to assemble this equipment by teasing the necessary insights out of the vast cognitive development/thinking skills literature, but if won't be easy. You will face mountains — still rising — of material. And apart from heroic stamina, you will need a very sharp eye to sort the productive leads from the dead ends. Some key insights — we'll point them out when we get to them — won't even turn up there. The literature holds rewards for the person conscious of the issues and experienced in dealing with them, but it's a difficult place to start.

We've decided, therefore, to put all the necessary equipment in this book. We don't try to report everything that's been said about thinking skills. As a matter of fact, we deliberately avoid much of what's been said. We convey only what the past 20 years of teaching, researching, and experimenting have shown us to be important. Much of this could be pieced together from the literature, but some of what we think is helpful you only encounter here.

Examples are another useful kind of equipment. We don't just explain;

we also show where we can with exercises and even some lesson plans for various levels of instruction. There are two basic approaches to thinking skill instruction. The overt approach is to shape a course of instruction that concentrates explicitly on thinking skills. The covert approach involves reworking the pedagogy of established courses so that they heighten the use and growth of thinking skills. We provide samples of both strategies for you.

There is one final, important piece of equipment you will have to fashion yourself, though we can help. You will need a better grasp of your own thinking skills.

We can describe this need best by considering, for a moment, the question of ability. The odds on developing a skill we don't have ourselves in someone else are not good. When we contemplate teaching thinking skills, most of us wonder if we have what it takes. Well, rest assured. The chances you do are overwhelming.

Any competent teacher is, in at least one context, a formidable thinker. The business of mastering a discipline sufficiently to instruct in it prompts extensive use of higher order thinking skills. But having a skill is not quite the same as being able to impart it. While the good teacher has thought long, hard, and well, nothing in her preparation or her practice demands that she be aware of how she manages to do these things.

We generally come to the skills of thought tacitly, by modeling what more accomplished thinkers do until we ourselves have the knack. Once we have the knack, the fact we have it tells us precious little about what it is. How much does having a good throwing arm tell you about the dynamics of nerve, muscle, bone, and sinew that make it work?

Another reason we don't come to conscious terms with our own thinking skills has to do with a corollary of effective behavior. The more adept we are at any complex behavior, the less conscious we need to be about it. Once our breast stroke or golf swing of sense of syntax or skill at statistical analysis is "in the grove," habit takes over and sends deliberation off to seek new work.

The dominance of habit is especially strong in the case of thinking skills. Having never risen to full consciousness, both the skills and weaknesses of thought slip easily into the domain of habit. One troublesome consequence of this is that our best thinkers are often least able to speak usefully about their skill. For them, a complex series of mental operations has come to feel like a flash of seamless insight. What they perceive they do in solving a problem can be a very poor guide to what the less practiced thinker must in fact do.

For such reasons, the typical teacher is not well versed about his or her own thinking skills. This doesn't, usually, matter at all. He or she can go forth and teach English, algebra, or history brilliantly. But it matters a great deal if he or she wants to develop thinking skills explicitly in others. If your aim is to teach others to think well, it's important to be on good terms with how *you* do it.

This is the tricky part. You need to come to an understanding of how *you* do it, not just "how it is done." There are thousands of descriptions of how good thinking is done; hundreds of different theories, schemata, and thinking skill rosters. A few of them are pretty good; most of them are not. But none of them can take the place of your own increasingly discriminate understanding of what it is you do when you think well. Familiarity with your own mind's work will give you that sharp sense — so useful in the classroom — of what student minds are doing and what they need. You'll use that understanding to judge competing theories and thinking skills approaches. As your vision of what works in you improves, so will your aim in choosing and devising classroom ventures that make it work better in others.

If you don't develop this consciousness of what you do when you think well, you'll simply have to teach thinking skills the way others tell you to, and take their word for it.

How can you come to this heightened awareness of your own thinking skills? A good way is to follow a dual agenda as you read this guide. Read it first to grasp what it has to say about thinking skills and how they can be taught, very much as you would read any textbook. But at the same time, probe it for what it reveals about your own thinking. You will, for instance, find methods discussed that aim at making students more conscious of their thinking processes. Try them on yourself. Test insights you uncover; play with them at appropriate points in classes you now teach.

If you do, two things will happen. You will begin to see that your own good thinking, which seems so automatic, is really an integration of distinct mental operations. It has phases, or parts, which you blend so deftly that you aren't aware of them. Next, as you grow able to discern those parts, or phases, you will see that they occur again and again as components of good thought. Conversely, when thinking is slipshod, some of these phases are significantly absent. You'll be identifying the allies and enemies of effective thought — critical intelligence for the thinking skill instructor.

So use this guide to explore your own thinking. In one sense, *you* are the real thinking skill text. You contain all the requisite skills and considerable experience in using them. Consider this guide a tool to help you decipher that text.

Save for one item, that fairly well exhausts our equipment list, and we've seen that there is little doubt about your ability to teach thinking skills. What about attitude?

In class, while you're leading students toward growth in their thinking ability, you'll need conviction that the job is doable and confidence that you're able to do it. The best way to end up with sound conviction and solid confidence is to start with neither. Approach all prophets of thinking skill instruction, including us, skeptically. Be receptive, but wary. Take as little as possible on faith.

Why should you be skeptical? For two reasons, really. First, because there are weighty criticisms of the very idea of attempting to teach thinking skills, which you should consider thoughtfully as you approach your own commitment. We discuss some of these in the first chapter.

Second, you should be skeptical because there are many approaches to thinking skill instruction, some very slickly packaged, that could have an impact on students that you might find undesirable. Just about any organized, sustained teaching effort *will* have an effect on students. The difficult question, often glossed over, is whether the effects it will produce are in fact the ones we prize.

That's why good teachers always weigh innovative teaching proposals critically. They consider the proposal's rationale, look at its assertions and ask, "How does this fit what I know about students?" If the fit isn't good, it leaves the teacher uneasy, thinking about modifications, adjustments, alternatives. If the fit is good, the teacher might be inclined to try it. Sometimes, even if it feels right, it doesn't quite work right. Then the teacher modifies her approach, or her understanding of students, or both. The good teacher is perpetually experimenting in light of her deepening grasp of the human learner.

Which brings us to your final piece of required equipment. You will need to surface your own assumptions about the human learner, and compare them to the ones that motivate this guide. Everything you read here is based on what we consider well-evidenced views about learner capabilties, what keeps them fallow, and what makes them grow. We say just enough about those views in the next chapter to make our assumptions clear. As we progress, we examine and ply these assumptions even further, so you should be in no doubt where we stand. But the key point is that you should view our stance — and any other about thinking skills — in light of what you know about learners.

There's a special reason for keeping your finger on the learner's pulse, and it has to do with the fact that it's easy to misread the real promise of the thinking skills focus. That promise is sometimes seen as flowing from clever new instructional techniques — keen insights about how teachers can be more effective in class. That isn't so. Ad agencies long ago proved you can be clever and effective in pursuit of the trivial. If the thinking skills focus holds real promise — and we certainly think it does — that promise is rooted in a more penetrating understanding of the learner, an understanding that is a reprize of old and new insights regarding the anatomy of student ability and motivation. If we can teach thinking skills better today, it is only because we have better insights about students.

Using This Guide

At first, it will seem that this guide moves through the various instructional levels in a linear fashion, addressing primary, then intermediate elementary, then secondary and collegiate student needs. Actually, appearance here is misleading on several counts. The guide really advances in a cumulative rather than linear fashion, and that means it really won't serve you best if you read only those chapters that address the level at which you teach.

Perhaps that seems inconsiderate, but we feel it is critical to see any thinking skill instructional effort in light of the overarching agenda. The kindergarten teacher will comprehend his thinking skill mission better when he sees how it anchors later intelligent performance, and the college instructor will gain as she sees her performance targets in light of their pedigree. Teachers who work late in the instructional sequence will meet students who have avoided growth appropriate to the earlier years, and knowledge of earlier approaches can serve them well.

In addition, the cumulative design lets us keep the size of this guide manageable. We avoid having to frequently redevelop and repeat key insights about thinking skills at each instructional level. With a few cues and reminders, we can leave it to the attentive reader to carry these forth.

So for maximum gain, you will have to read the whole guide at least once. Then you can appeal to those sections that seem most relevant to your instructional challenge.

All right. Now that we have some notion of the equipment you need to assemble, let's begin.

CHAPTER 1

THINKING SKILLS
AT ISSUE

Forethought

This book is about to examine thinking skills and ways of developing them, but is that a sensible thing to do? After all, teachers have been sparking, guiding, and striving to advance student thinking for thousands of years. Why should there suddenly be a "thinking skills" movement? An imposing number of reasonable educators aren't at all sure there should be.

It will help sharpen our focus if we inspect some of the whys and wherefores, pros and cons of the thinking skills emphasis. A clearer sense of the problem, they say, is an almighty step toward its solution. For us, the step is critical; it can help us avoid approaches that strive to fix things that aren't broken.

TEACH THINKING? . . . DON'T BOTHER

Without trying very hard, you can find any number of attitudes and orientations in the world of education that do not take kindly to the notion of teaching thinking skills. Arguments that conclude it is pointless or even damaging to try come in great variety, but they tend to reflect any or all of three main positions: (1) You can't teach thinking skills; (2) we've always taught thinking skills; (3) even if you could teach thinking skills, you shouldn't.

1

Because these positions influence a good deal of educational practice and policy, and because each contains more than just a grain of truth, we give them a closer look.

YOU CAN'T TEACH THINKING SKILLS

The toughest attitudes to combat are the ones so deeply rooted they are seldom expressed. We have those in education, and one in particular determines a great deal of what we as teachers think we can and cannot do. Put simply, it is the belief that the learner's abilities are fixed before he or she ever enters a classroom. Students come, the assumption goes, gifted, average, or substandard. The teacher can exercise whatever abilities the student brings, but the abilities themselves are impervious to instructional change.

The ability to think, this view continues, is the basic fixed attribute. The Intelligence Quotient is often thought of as signaling a genetically defined mental limit. And if this is the case, the attempt to significantly improve anyone's thinking skills would be as productive as trying to cram 2 pints of water in a 1-pint cup. The proper task of an educational system, under this view, is to determine native student aptitude as early as possible so the student can be "matched" to an instructional program suited to his or her ability

This clear and simple view is, unfortunately, too clear and too simple to fit the evidence. Undoubtedly, students arrive at school with differing aptitude and ability, but research suggests that suitable instruction can make vast changes in this input profile. Stable IQ gains of 30 points and more have resulted from a semester's careful, yet not overly demanding, instruction.[1] Nevitt Sanford recently expressed the conviction that there are "no dispositions of personality that cannot be changed through education . . . ,"[2] and mounting evidence presses us to include the disposition to think effectively.

There is much at stake on the issue of whether education can or cannot influence core abilities. If you conclude it cannot, education in some ways becomes a more comfortable profession. The best a teacher can then do is

---

[1]There are numerous heartening studies of gains in cognitive aptitude as a result of planned instructional intervention. In the course of making its case, Arthur Whimbey's excellent *Intelligence Can Be Taught* reviews several of these. Each review rewards consideration but see especially Whimbey's treatment of the Milwaukee Project (pp. 42–47), which dealt with instructing preschoolers, and the pivotal Bloom and Broder work with college students at the University of Chicago (pp. 53–59).

[2]Nevitt Sanford, "Foreword," in Arthur Chickering and Associates *The Modern American College* (p. xx).

embellish what is given. You can acculturate students and immerse them in subject matter, but you can little influence their capacity to function. Although teachers do some good from this perspective, it is specially reassuring that they can't do much damage.

But if basic abilities are maleable and can be influenced by instruction — if, for instance, what a teacher does can leave dormant, expand, or shrink one's capacity to think — then teaching becomes a different proposition altogether. It becomes a key determinant of human possibility. The character of society can rise or fall by what teachers choose to do or leave undone. Teaching suddenly becomes a high-risk industry with a much greater potential for both good and harm.

The signs, you will be happy or sorry to hear, are that the teacher can have extensive impact on basic student ability. Much of the scope and extent of a student's lifelong performance hinges on what does or does not happen in classrooms.

The basic error in the proposition that thinking skills can't be taught lies mostly in an antiquated view of human development, but it gains support also from a tendency to confuse various impediments to good thinking with the notion of a fixed limit on cognitive ability. We know there are profound psychophysical maladies that short-circuit effective thought, but we are learning that the vast bulk of weak and unproductive thinking is the result of relatively simple, bad, and correctable habit, quite often unconsciously reinforced in the classroom. On the other hand, we never have had nor foreseeably will have a measure of the limits of anyone's cognitive ability. To get such a measure, we would have to display a mind whose developmental limits had been reached, and as yet no mind has been shown incapable of further growth. Highly resistant, maybe, but not incapable.

Whereas the general proposition — you can't teach thinking skills — is hard to defend, it is often used to imply other more defensible propositions, such as: "You can't teach thinking skills *easily*," or "You can't teach thinking skills *that way*." You find arguments of that kind in this book, and you will judge them on the available evidence. But for "You simply can't teach thinking skills," there is no evidence.

WE'VE ALWAYS TAUGHT THINKING SKILLS

This proposition is especially difficult to refute, because it happens to be true. Schooling always has developed thinking skills. The real issue has to do with *which* thinking skills it develops.

Memorization, recall, and iteration are among a set of thinking skills researchers have come to call *respondent*. You might think of them as "passive" or "reactive" skills employed to absorb and play back information, as well as to apply learned rules and formulae when called upon.

Another set of skills are called *operant*. These are employed in analysis, synthesis, and comparison; they "operate" on information rather than simply retain and reiterate it. These are the skills that build and test ideas, create analogies, and solve unprecedented problems.

It happens that the bulk of schooling fosters "respondent" skills. One study of college classroom instruction suggests that the typical freshman/sophomore student is likely to engage in the type of higher level cognitive activity that employs operant skill very infrequently during any classroom period, and not at all in better than half of them.[3] Classroom time is overwhelmingly time for respondent skills.

In one sense, it might be said that a good deal of schooling develops a certain kind of thinking skill too well. Students become so thoroughly versed in memorization and reiteration that they are not only unskilled in, but reluctant to employ, operant thinking. They've grown comfortable with copying and mimicking, and are ill-at-ease with real inquiry.

Schooling of *any* kind does exercise and develop tools of thought. What's troublesome is that crowding the kit with inferior tools can actually hamper student performance, rather than extend and strengthen it.

EVEN IF YOU COULD TEACH THINKING SKILLS, YOU SHOULDN'T

One good argument for not doing a thing is that doing it would detract from something more important. Many very capable teachers tend to resist any new instructional objective, including thinking skills, on just such grounds. And their case is compelling.

If you believe that the teacher's essential task is to impart a disciplined body of knowledge to the student, it is easy to conclude that schooling today has endangered this priority by adopting too many nonessential missions. In addition to the babysitting, policing, and counseling that apparently must go on in school, more and more of the classwork itself is spent in addressing supposed student growth needs and wants, less and less on mastering a subject.

Begrudging the considerable time and effort spent — with indifferent result — on remedying the physical, psychological, socioeconomic, political, ethical, and cultural shortcomings of students, teachers now hear a call to do something about thinking skills. Add this new brand of developmental

---

[3]Keeley, Browne, and Haas, *Cognitive Activity in the Classroom: A Comparison of Three Kinds of Raters, Using the Cognitive Activities Ratings Scales (CARS).*

therapy to the six or seven kinds education already sponsors and there remain still less time and resource for the task of teaching a discipline. Little wonder many good teachers resist adding "thinking skills."

Where thinking skill becomes another "tacked on" special focus for the curriculum—a little instructional detour every student must take—your authors stand four-square with the opposition. Better not to raise the thinking skills issue at all than to address it that way.

However, it is rather silly to view thinking skills as an issue outside the curriculum trying to get in. Reflect once more on the essential task of the teacher and look carefully at what our best teachers do. You will find thinking skills already very much on the inside.

Good teachers will insist that you never confuse the task of imparting a disciplined body of knowledge with the business of dispensing facts and information. A body of knowledge is alive; otherwise it would be called a corpse. What's vital in a discipline is what thought has made, is making, and will make of its subject matter. More than anything else, a discipline *is* systematic thinking, and to convey the discipline means to engage students in its modes of thought. We would be more accurate and could make our point more easily if we called academic fields "disciplined bodies of thought" rather than "disciplined bodies of knowledge."

Good teachers go to great lengths to spark in students the kind of thought that animates their chosen discipline. They model critical thinking and problem solving and the precise use of language for their students, and they tease and challenge students toward the use and mastery of those skills. Such teachers are already up to their elbows in the thinking skills business.

Anyone can choose whether to accept or reject a given thinking skills package or curriculum. But, for good teachers, there is no choice about whether or not to teach thinking skills. Enlisting and developing such skills is the only path available.

The issue that remains open to choice is one of method and approach. One option is to continue to do what good teachers have usually done, which is to follow their instinct and intuition. The tradition doesn't talk about teaching thinking skills; it talks about teaching subject matter. Consequently, you teach subject matter and grope quietly by yourself for artful ways to excite and harness student thinking.

The alternative is to take the implied but seldom-voiced thinking skills goal out of the closet and make it explicit. Keep using your instinct and intuition but inform them as fully as possible about the quirks and foibles of thinking skills and their development. Doing so will clarify and multiply your options, expand your teaching repertoire, improve your aim, and generally enhance your control over the outcome of instruction. It will also help you separate promising new instructional approaches from seductive but fruitless educational fads.

We think any really useful thinking skills approach should start here, on the inside, assisting the committed teacher with the work she or he already has in hand. Teaching fads and fashions—including many that address "thinking skills"—often seem to be saying, "Drop everything! Here's what you should do and how you should do it." It isn't surprising that many teachers, experienced in and quietly committed to the business of maturing minds, should resist.

We've briefly looked at three positions that characterize much of the wariness about teaching thinking skills. But we will understand more about the root of that wariness if we go back to the second position and probe just a bit further. We said that schooling can and does develop thinking skills but happens to favor the respondent ones. Why has schooling traditionally emphasized the passive rather than active mental abilities? The answer can lead us to a new perspective on the thinking skills issue.

THE PASSIVE SKILL BIAS

If you have a job to do, it seems obvious you would prize those skills best suited to doing it. When it comes to mental skills, however, there's a problem. We have conflicting views about what the mind's job is.

If, for instance, we assume that the business of the mind is to simply receive and mirror what is real, our premier set of skills (call them Set *A*) will be those that emphasize information acquisition and retention—the relatively passive "intake" or "respondent" skills. If, on the other hand, the mind is seen as *selectively shaping* the constructs we employ about our world, the skills seen as critical become postacquisitive, *construcural* skills. These are the active or "operant" cognitive abilities (call them Set *B*) by which we process information—decompose and recompose it—so as to better model experience given our purposes.

The basically Aristotelian, commonsense core of western civilization sanctions the former job description. The world is crammed with things, and we tend to think the mind achieves knowledge by carefully depicting, camera-like, what is there. We consequently have a deep cultural bias toward viewing the respondent skills (set A) as the principal weapons in the mind's arsenal.

But the leading scientific and philosophic minds of this century, with such rapidly maturing disciplines about human performance as anthropology and linguistics, insist on the latter job description. The world isn't just crammed with things; it's overwhelmingly rich, and most of the wealth is obscure. No end of snapshots could ever reveal its hidden structures. To cope with this bottomless universe, the mind doesn't just take pictures; it selectively *makes* them. It *constructs* ideas, insights, and explanations—

shapes, tests, and reshapes them—in order to win some grasp and control of the real. Our cultural heritage is a collection of man-made constructs that have worked. Progress is an effort to devise and adopt constructs that will work better. For this kind of task, operant skills (set B) are clearly the mind's premier tools.

Actually, we know the mind needs both set A and set B skills to handle what's on its plate, but there is another factor that tends to bias us even further toward set A skills.

It would be horribly wasteful if each new mind had to construct, from scratch, its own sense of itself and its world. Better to give it the hard-won insights of other minds and let it begin its own "making" from there. Thus was education born, the original "head start" program launched in prehistory. And what this ancient and hallowed mission of transmitting culture asks most of new minds is *respondent* skill. The young mind must first be docile to the knowledge we already have; *then* let it begin its own building.

This seems a reasonable prescription, but it simply isn't workable. We have more knowledge to transmit than any mind could conceivably receive. Throughout this century, endless debate has swirled through educational councils about what should be transmitted and what left out, but the "essential core" keeps growing. Much of the innovation in schooling has aimed at transmitting more knowledge faster. For students, this has meant their respondent skills have had to stay in harness longer, now bearing nearly all the load from K through graduate school. The day of the operant skills just never quite seems to dawn.

Finally, the respondent skills enjoy a natural bias that grows apparent when we contrast skill set A with skill set B. It happens that respondent skills set A comprises abilities that develop at a chronologically earlier age than those of operant set B. Set A skills are precisely those that acculturation requires of the child, and so they take shape quickly. But the problem with set B skills is not just that they develop later. It is that they need not develop much at all.

Operant skills are on one hand frighteningly optional and on another frighteningly essential. They are optional in the sense that an individual can wend his or her way convincingly through present-day society without them, whereas the absence of Set A skills is immediately and painfully evident and constitutes an overt handicap. The absence of Set B skills, however, can go long undetected. In a world crammed with preprogrammed roles, "Receiving, Retaining, and Reiterating"—the *real* three R's of much of our schooling—can get you by. Routine behavior requires little more.

But Set B skills are essential from a societal point of view. Societies develop fatal dysfunctions, grow suicidal, and collapse without sufficient wielders of Set B skills. It should come as no surprise: If knowing is mirroring what is around you, the skills of the mimic are focal. The trouble with a mind whose attributes are those of the photocopying machine (copy, hence preserve, thus iterate) is its inability to assess the fitness of what it duplicates. Like the magic salt mill, it grinds on and on till sweet waters turn bitter.

ADJUSTING THE BIAS

Good teachers have long sensed that knowledge does not transmit well to the passive mind. They tend to transmit knowledge along with a demand to employ it. First the student is confronted with, or reminded of, some facts, some data, some assertions. Then comes a puzzle, conundrum, or problem that requires that this information be used. Such teachers intuit a profound truth about the mind: It resists owning knowledge it can't use, and it is anxious to claim knowledge it can. Igniting a *need* to know is the good teacher's secret trick, and at her most devious, she will even hook the student on a problem for which she hasn't supplied the required information. Students then have no recourse but to ferret out the information themselves, thereby doing some of the teacher's transmission work for her. Meanwhile, the wily teacher monitors the birth pangs of newly self-motivated learners.

In doing this, the good teacher sets a tempo that especially invigorates the maturing mind. It isn't simply that the mind now uses both operant and respondent skills; it's that these skills interact in a way that best suits the psychology of cognition. The mind's operant skills, busily at work, call upon the respondent skills for more precise and pertinent information. The respondent skills reply with insights that inform but also extend and enrich the problem. The two sets of skills no longer need an external goad; they are briskly triggering each other. When the mind achieves some resolution of the issue at hand, it has actually accomplished several things. It has used some of the knowledge it possessed, thus enhancing the value of its holdings. In the process, it generated new knowledge, thus expanding its base of insight. And the mind, having demonstrated the utility of its own skill, is more prone and more able to go to work again.

If there is promise in the thinking skills movement, it lies in amplifying and extending this dynamic of instruction, in making it the conscious model of effective schooling rather than the private insight of a scattering of teachers. To achieve this, the movement will need to concentrate on fostering the operant skills—we are already well versed in exercising the respondent ones.

We come to grips with operant thinking skills in the following chapter, but it might be useful in closing this one to emphasize a key characteristic of the mind implied by what we've said so far.

The mind does not come prepackaged with all its skills set and idling, just waiting to be employed. The mind fashions its skills as it confronts tasks that require them, much as we fashion or acquire other tools as the need arises. The mind shapes higher order skills only when higher order performance is demanded. It is perhaps easier, from this perspective, to understand why many capable minds do not exhibit higher order skills. It also becomes easier to see the teacher's role in shaping thinking skills. More than we've been accustomed to think, minds are what their mentors make of them. Teachers who don't believe thinking skills can be taught will tend to sanction and confirm the condition of the minds they confront. Teachers who believe such skills can be taught will tend to transform those minds.

We conclude this, and all other Chapters, with The File. In most cases, The File is — and unless you do something with it, remains — a blank page. It is there for those of you who want to extend, or confound, or otherwise make note of thoughts raised as you considered the chapter. We think any record of your *operant* responses to what you've just read will eventually prove useful.

The File

THE FILE

THE FILE

THE FILE

CHAPTER 2

THINKING SKILLS

Forethought

It is time now to identify the thinking skills we wish to develop, and that is the single most critical task anyone who seeks to teach thinking skills faces. How you solve that problem—how you make the selection—will determine just about everything that follows.

Unfortunately, this is the job that the literature on teaching thinking skills does most poorly.

We noted before that our culture—any culture, for that matter—supports a kind of superficial notion of what the mind's job is; what you might call an ordinary, commonsense view. By "superficial," we don't mean the commonsense view is necessarily wrong; we mean it isn't very deep or very precise. It is too thin to sustain much probing and too weak to support sound elaboration. Commonsense views are good enough for everyday use—mentioning this, referring to that—but they tend to break down as explanations of how things really work. The average, off-hand view of a combustion engine wouldn't let you build one. We have these handy, commonsense notions about what thinking skills are. And, surprisingly enough, most thinking skills approaches do build directly on them.

If you were to survey, as we have, the thinking skills literature and extract from it a "standard" or "dominant" view of what the thinking skills are and how they should be developed, the result would paint a superficial and seriously distorted view of the mind's abilities and how they mature. Let's take a look.

THE COMMONSENSE/THINKING SKILLS MOVEMENT APPROACH

The first thing you will notice on entering the literature is the bewildering array of thinking skills it calls to your attention. Here is part of one man's selection, clustered as instructional objectives, K through 12:

K–4

Association
Observation/description
Comparison: figural
Classifications: grouping
Estimation
Figural analogies
Convergent thinking
Verbal sequences
Conservation
Deductive reasoning
Translation: shapes
Spatial perception

5–6

Definition of terms
Comparison
Classification: verbal
Inductive reasoning
Figural sequences/patterns
Verbal analogies
Space–time relationships
Experimenting
Simple logic: inference &
    probability
Applications to related areas

7–8

Reasoning by analogies
Prediction
Deductive reasoning: formal
Concept building
Control of variables
Operational definitions
Cause & effect
Beginning synthesis
Inferences
Extrapolation
Generating hypotheses
Structure & operating analysis

9–12

Application to different
    situations
Synthesis
Model building
Clarifying concepts
Statistical reasoning

These are presented as the general category of thinking and reasoning skills; there are 56 other skills proposed at three higher levels, and this list is presented, asserts the author, to clarify what is misleading and confusing in the thinking skills literature.[4]

---

[4]Martinelli, Keneth J., "Thinking Straight About Thinking," *The School Administrator* (Vol. 44, No. 1), 1987.

Under three major headings and six subheadings, another view—sustained by a nonprofit regional research center,[5]—lists 19 thinking skills:

Attaining concepts	Evaluating evidence
Identifying relationships	Evaluating value
Recognizing patterns	Elaborating
Proceduralizing	Problem solving
Recognizing context	Inventing
Storing and retrieving	Attending
Memory frameworks	Setting goals
Categorizing	Monitoring attitudes
Reasoning analogically	Self-evaluating
Extrapolating	

In simply presenting these lists we do not, of course, do justice to their authors, who have reasons for their particular selections and explanations for how the skills they nominate interrelate. On inspecting the literature that accompanies the second list you would, for example, see that it embraces most of the behaviors identified in the first list, perhaps in a more summary, hierarchic way. Our point is to simply show you two not immediately compatible thinking skills lists. There are hundreds.

Several questions keep occurring as one examines such lists. How do their authors know these are *the* thinking skills? Are the named skills really discrete? So many of them seem to overlap and contain one another. Some lists are short; some are long—are any complete? The different lists assign different priorities and different developmental sequences to what appear to be very similar items. Who's right?

We will leave the thinking skills lists for a moment and turn to another peculiarity of the thinking skills literature. On one hand we have a jungle of nominated thinking skills. But when we turn to the vehicles of thought— those apprehensions about experience that the thinking skills employ—we face an almost featureless desert. Very seldom are there more than two words used to describe those things with which the mind does its work. Most of the time, the thinking skills literature doesn't explore the constructs employed by the mind at all; when it does, it almost always limits itself to talk of "ideas" and "concepts."

In short, the thinking skills literature, hardly quibbling anywhere with common sense, tends to generate a picture of the mind as burgeoning with a great variety of skills used to manage a single class of objects called

---

[5]Marzano, Robert J., & Hutchins, C. L. *Thinking Skills: A Conceptual Framework*, Mid-continent Regional Educational Laboratory, 1985. A summary listing of the skills appears on the back cover.

"ideas" or "concepts." We glean an astonishingly different picture when we consider what might be called the view of the critical epistemologist.

THE EPISTEMOLOGISTS' APPROACH

We here paint you another composite picture of a very complex domain. *Epistemologist* is a term that describes people involved in the theory of knowledge. They investigate what it is we know and how we come to know it, and they arrive at this inquiry from a broad range of academic backgrounds. The picture we sketch draws on many investigators, among them men like Lev Semenovich Vygotsky, Jean Piaget, Willard Van Orman Quine, Jerome Bruner, and Claude Lévi-Strauss.

The image that tends to emerge from the work of such men is remarkably different from that suggested by the thinking skills literature. What is astonishing about it is that this discrepancy has gone so long unnoted. The mind that the critical epistemologists depict seems to have relatively few basic skills, and these are used to deploy quite a range of different constructs. We look first at the thinking skills portion of this view and then consider how it treats mental constructs.

THE MEAGER BASIC SKILLS

Several people—Quine among them—have occasionally taken what might be called a reductionist's approach to understanding cognitive ability. To grasp this approach, take as an example the seemingly infinite range of visible color that strikes the human eye. The search for three irreducible primary colors out of which those countless others can be fashioned is a reductionist's search. The quest is for the basic elements in a complex phenomenon that, when understood, help us account for all the rest.

Approaching the capabilities of the mind this way, epistemologists come up with a very skimpy list of core abilities. The precise number might differ somewhat, depending on such things as where you draw the line between cognitive and sensory activity, but basically there appear to be about three. There is an ability to store and recall signs or symbols of events, what we call memory. There is an ability to distinguish like and unlike, what Quine calls employing a similarity standard[6]. And there is an ability to join things: to predicate, to affirm something about something else. And that's about it.

The mind has only three or so abilities? It doesn't seem possible until we

---

[6]See Quine, W. V., "Natural Kinds," *Ontological Relativity and Other Essays* (pp. 117 through 125).

reflect on a characteristic these basic abilities share. We can easily label this characteristic, but it may take a moment to grasp what the label signifies. It is simply that these core abilities function recursively.

We find recursiveness at work in a variety of places. A mathematical function, you may recall, is recursive if, when fed its own product, it produces a new product. Take $(n + 1) = n'$, start with $n = 0$, and when you solve the equation put the product, n', in place of n and run it again. Keep cranking this function and you will generate the whole infinity of positive integers. In linguistics, recursive rules explain how, with a limited vocabulary and a small set of semantic and syntactic axioms, speakers of a language can generate and understand an infinite number of sentences. In a purely figurative way, you might see a trace of recursion in how those primary colors mix to form the endlessly varying hues our eyes detect.

In similar fashion, the root abilities of the mind are recursive in that they operate on their own products to generate new products. In so doing, the root abilities interact and combine in new and more complex ways, and then in sequences of ways, and then in sequences of sequences of ways. The result is an increasingly powerful articulation of new capabilities the mind can bring to its work.

What this view gives us, among other things, is a clue to understanding what all those profligate and confusing thinking skill lists mean. Look carefully at the previous two lists and note that they make more sense when viewed not as skills, but as mental *activities*. They are important kinds of jobs we can catch the mind doing. We observe someone classifying, or producing verbal analogies, or engaged in deductive reasoning. We decide it is a significant activity people should be skilled in doing. We add it, as another "thinking skill," to our growing list.

Nowhere in this process have we actually touched the underlying abilities the mind employs to do these various jobs. We've simply captured the outer manifestation of a hidden process. The skills employed in deductive reasoning, evidence suggests, are also at work in classification and in generating verbal analogies, but differently configured. Most thinking skills lists point to frequently used recursions of those few underlying skills. They would be more accurately described as thinking activity lists.

We gain a better sense of the mind's recursive functioning if we now turn to the other end of the epistemologist's view and see what it has to show us about the vehicles of thought.

CONCEPTS AND THEN SOME

Anyone familiar with the literature in developmental psychology knows that the path a child takes to concept formation is a complex one. There are numerous preconceptual constructs the child employs in dealing with his world, and it will help us if we briefly recall Vygotsky's[7] analysis of these.

All the child's early constructs are concept *surrogates*. They lack the concept's capacity to sustain logical relationships and to reference univocally, but they are *selective* representations of experience and the child uses them for purposive communication and action. First, the child binds together different objects and sensations solely on the ground of their co-occurrence in immediate perception. The bonds of these conglomerates are highly subjective and unstable, but the child nonetheless employs these "heaps" (to use Vygotsky's term) in organizing its affairs. "Mother" for the young child may signal a wavering construct comprised of sensations of sight, touch, smell, security, food, caress, and satisfaction, while for the adult it signifies maternal agency. The two may coincide somewhat in their referents, but not at all in their meaning.

Beyond *heaps* there emerge various levels of "complexes" (Vygotsky distinguishes five types[8]) by means of which the youth identifies groupings in terms of bonds actually existing between objects. For example, toy blocks, spheres, and triangles are treated as one kind because they share the same color. Because the various types of complexes identified by Vygotsky are built of relationships perceived by the adolescent mind to inhere in a world outside itself, complexes mark a giant stride toward objectivity in thought. But the referent bonds that cement lower order complexes are themselves haphazard and fragile, and hence these complexes organize experience only transiently.

As youthful thought evolves through the various types of complexes, and as adult language ratifies some as more useful than others, these surviving bonds increase in stability. The child comes finally to associate certain experiential objects under one unwavering criterion and arrives at the highest form of complex thinking. Vygotsky labels it the *pseudo-concept* because it appears to exhibit an abstract specifying characteristic that enables us to tell which things in experience it applies to and which things it does not. Unfortunately, appearance here is only skin deep. In the child's mind, the characteristic is still bound to its concrete objects, and the pseudo-concept cannot sustain activities involving generalization.

As the child moves from *heap* to *pseudo-concept*, she in effect articulates new ways of making connections between discrete events in experience. Simultaneously, there is growth in her capacity to attend selectively to some characteristics of experience and ignore others. When a fixed connection

---

[7]No one interested in how the mind matures can afford to miss Lev Semenovich Vygotsky's *Thought and Language*. His work is an important enhancement and corrective to Piaget's.
[8]Ibid., pp. 61–67.

encounters a well-formed capacity for selective attention, the seed of full-fledged abstraction and bona fide concept formation germinates.

We need to draw a few things from this minicourse in concept formation. First, notice that this entire process, from heap through pseudo-concept, is a cognitive enterprise, an effort to "know." And all this knowing, although it falls short of conceptual adroitness, serves the child remarkably well. It is a mistake, then, to think of all productive thought as conceptual. *Cognition* and *conceptual thought* are not equivalent terms.

Second, we need to ask what effects this growth in the mind from facility with heaps through pseudo-concepts to concepts. We know that purpose stimulates it; the child's need for more refined, more adept, and more effective ways of grasping and managing its experience. But what brings about the transformation to higher order constructs is the recursive exercise of the mind's root abilities. The child *recalls* a sequence of heaps. She notes *likenesses* across that sequence. She *joins* those likenesses in a new representation of experience, a representation more durable and wieldly because it leaves out extraneous sense data. She has formed a complex. When better constructs arise in the mind, it is because the mind has *fashioned* them; not because some new, till-then-dormant insight was genetically triggered.

We can, with these two observations, dispel a misleading impression that the thinking skills literature has not roused itself to challenge. The impression is that thinking skills are what humans employ exclusively to resolve the difficulties they encounter in life. There is a sense here of "inner" abilities we call on to deal with "outer" situations. The world presents us with a problem, and we use thinking skills to resolve it. That impression is no more than half right.

We *do* use thinking skills that way, but if those same skills had not worked nonstop long before the world handed us what we normally think of as a problem, we could not see the world at all, let alone its aggravations. We need to acknowledge and understand all that behind-the-scenes labor. The mind first builds the constructs it employs to interpret the world, then it returns to the world revealed by those constructs to deal with the problems thus exposed. Interestingly enough, the mind's prime way of dealing with problems when they emerge is to continue doing what it did from the first, which is to build better constructs, more probing insights, more useful conceptions about how to advance in its journey.

Unfortunately, most of the thinking skills literature based on the work of the developmental psychologists introduces an unwarranted assumption that leads to a superficial view of the mind's postdevelopmental task. We look at that assumption in the next section, and our examination goes far toward defining the thinking skill instructor's mission.

THE MIND'S UNRULY STABLE

It is an axiom of developmental psychology that the stages of cognitive development unfold in necessary sequence from simple to more complex; first facility with heaps, then complexes and pseudo-concepts, and finally with concepts. Unfortunately, there is an overwhelming tendency to adopt an unwarranted corollary: once concepts, no more pseudo-concepts, no more complexes, no more heaps. And that corollary sustains the pervasive and damaging myth of the homogeneity of adult thought: the presumption that all thought is conceptual.

It is understandably a difficult myth to penetrate. Cognitive constructs of all kinds share a common currency of exchange in language. Because the vast majority of uses to which language is put in day-to-day affairs is ostensive — merely pointing to this, directing attention to that, or recalling events — nearly any underlying construct will do. This surface similarity and parallel utility for ordinary purposes, engendered so well by language, obscures the deep-rooted ways in which cognitive constructs differ.

The evidence suggests that we do not begin with heaps and end with the space from cranial wall to cranial wall aswim with scientific concepts. Remember that the elements of thought are *constructs*, shaped by the mind. Each is formed not as well as it *might* be, but as well as it *need* be, given the abilities and purposes of the cognizer and the vicissitudes of his interactions with his world. Where the complex suffices — or seems to — the complex remains. Hence heap, complex, and concept coexist, and cognition is best seen as a business of rearing and managing a heterogeneous stable of cognitive forms.

The different denizens in this stable do different work. All of them convey meaning, but their capacities for meaning differ. Heaps organize and recall our affective reactions to sensory experience. Complexes capture some of the surface structure of that experience. Concepts go farther and convey underlying, deep, remote, dependable characteristics of the passing scene. Each type of construct requires and responds properly to different handling. Only concepts, for instance, support fully logical manipulation. Many of our troubles come from treating these chickens, pigs, and cows as though they were all one kind of animal.

Speaking of animals, the mind is very much like a certain proverbial one. It is important, particularly for teachers, to realize that you can lead a mind to concepts, but you can't, so to speak, make it drink. You can't simply *give* someone a concept. You can give someone a term, which in your mind labels a concept, but until the receiving mind explores the relationships and specific denotations that fix the concept — indeed, make it what it is — that mind will not possess it. Attentive teachers experience this. They know that writing the definition on the board is but the first step. Getting students to use the concept — clumsily at first, but with increasing precision as they discover what things it is like and what things it is unlike — is what makes it theirs. Concepts are *functional* constructs, building blocks in our view of the world, and use is what proves and defines them. Recalling a concept is recalling how it *works*. Unless, by being employed, it has expanded your insight or somehow clarified your experience, you don't have it. It is quite true, in this sense, to say that the only constructs a mind has at its disposal are those it has built itself. The forming may be prodded and guided, but the mind must make; it can't simply take.

This may help us see how young minds, immersed for 12 years in the rich conceptual domains of the various disciplines, can arrive on college campuses having never engaged in sustained conceptual thought. Developmental psychologists time and again note the capacity of earlier forms of cognition in the sequence of emergence to "mimic" the operations of later forms. For most of the storage, retrieval, and heavily cued performance tasks that constitute the bulk of schooling — for that matter, the bulk of life — complex thinking coupled with short-range memory serves nicely. The mind makes concepts when it needs them. Otherwise it will settle, economically and easily, for less.

CONTRASTING VIEWS OF THINKING SKILL INSTRUCTION

Let's look in summary fashion at the two views of the mind we've explored, this time with an eye for the teaching task they imply.

The commonsense/thinking skills literature view sees the mind already possessed of concepts. Perhaps it doesn't have the right ones, but concept acquisition is not a problem to this view; concept manipulation is. It identifies a lengthy roster of concept manipulation skills, and the task of the thinking skills teacher is to drill students in the employment of the skills on that roster.

The critical epistemologists' view sees the mind equipped with a small set of core abilities that, recursively employed, shape increasingly precise and powerful constructs about the world as the need arises. Concept acquisition, or better, concept *generation*, is very much a problem. Concepts, in this view, are a principal product of mental skill, not commodities passively received and held in storage. The teacher's first task, from this vantage, is to stimulate complacent minds, satisfied with their preconceptual grasp of things, to employ core abilities in achieving a higher order, conceptual grasp of things.

We might stop here a moment and notice that this job description is very much like the one good teachers already implicitly follow. But what about concept manipulation from this point of view? Once you get minds to achieve concepts, aren't we at the same point at which the commonsense view begins? Do we not now face the same task of drilling students in concept employment skills? No, but to see why not we have to make explicit something about the epistemologists' view of mental skill that we've so far left implicit. It is simply that the skills of concept formation and the skills of concept manipulation are basically the same.

The mind builds a concept by manipulating the prior constructs it already has on hand. There are 16 red objects on a table, and the mind forms a complex of these as "the group of red things on the table." Someone picks up one of the objects and carries it away. It doesn't alter the complex, which still references what the senses apprehend as "the group of red things on the table." But the mind can be brought to recall the one red thing removed, affirm its likeness to the things still present, and generate a new construct — "red things" — which it can now apply to a great deal more than sits before it. Ask a child with the former construct where all the red things are, and he will simply point to the table. Ask the child with the new construct, and she will remind you of the piece taken away and perhaps include your tie.

It is by compelling the mind to manipulate its store of constructs that new constructs emerge. It is also by compelling the mind to manipulate its constructs that problems are solved. Building new constructs is, in fact, the mind's archetypal *problem*, so building new ideas and solving problems is very much the same kind of activity, employing the same core abilities.

The task of the thinking skills instructor, from this vantage, is not one of drilling the student in some hundred or more different skills. It is rather the task of acquainting the student with the small set of core abilities *already* at his or her disposal and encouraging their use in varied ways across a broadening range of situations. As successful employments of those skills increase in number and variety, so will the student's inclination to use them and adeptness in doing so. That is the way the mind's capabilities grow.

All this intensifies our original question: What *are* the core abilities a thinking skill instructor needs to trigger, guide, and emphasize? We have enough background now to approach a working list.

GENERIC THINKING SKILLS

An especially good way to grasp the value and importance of a skill is to look at what happens in its absence. Psychologists who analyze item failures in IQ tests and other mental performance tasks do this, and they are among the researchers who have done most to identify behaviors that attend effective thinking. IQ tests, for instance, confront students with a variety of types of problems. In fact, the range of problems is broad enough to call upon virtually all the kinds of mental activity named in our first two "thinking skills" lists. Here are some of the more recurrent forms of *behavior* that accompany problem-solving failure in tests of this kind:

1. Subject exhibits random attention; unable to sustain focus on the critical variables of the problem.
2. Subject scans haphazardly; does not probe a complex problem until all its components are identified.
3. Subject fails to test known relationships (prior knowledge) against potential relationships in the problem; does not analogize.
4. Subject guesses chronically; jumps from the first "lead" to an answer without incorporating available data.
5. Subject fails to check solution; does not review problem to see if solution constructed (a) works and (b) is the best alternative.

These "failure prone" behaviors emerge again and again across a broad spectrum of problem types. It is important to note that they are exhibited by subjects of all ages; you will find them in doctoral candidates as well as students in early elementary. They are strikingly similar to the kinds of behaviors Vygotsky and his colleagues clinically observe in preconceptual children who think in heaps and complexes. The lack of focused attention and chronic guessing are hallmarks of thinking in heaps. Incomplete scanning, disuse of prior knowledge, and no review impulse characterize various modes of thinking in complexes. The converse behaviors, on the other hand, characterize both the emergence of conceptual thought and what psychometricians have come to call "high IQ":

1. Selective attention: the ability to control the class of stimuli that receive conscious attention.
2. Sustained analysis: the capacity to probe a complex situation until all its components are identified.
3. Analoging: the capacity to test known relationships for similarity with those potential to a new situation.
4. Suspension of closure: the capacity to assess all available problem factors before positing a solution.
5. Autocensorship: the capacity to test a solution covertly, before affirmation.

It is important here to reflect on what we have in this list. Are these the core abilities of the mind? No. Recall that we identified only a few core abilities. The mind can remember, it can identify like and unlike, and it can predicate. All three of these core abilities are at work in each of the five behaviors just listed. What we have in each of these behaviors is a characteristic interaction—recursion—of the core abilities that the mind employs whenever it tries its best to deal with one of two tasks. The first task is building a better construct with which to grasp some aspect of experience—you might call it striving for a better understanding. The second task is solving problems; reducing the discrepancy between what we seek and what is. Whenever we want to wring meaning out of experience or solve problems, these behaviors are critical.

We should consequently note that these five behaviors—in whose employment the mind can gain increasing *skill*—are not critically important to a good deal of what the mind does. The passive tasks of reception, retention, and reiteration do not draw heavily on them. But they appear again and again wherever the mind actively strives for better insight and tries to resolve difficulty. Sustained conceptual thought would be impossible without them. We decided the two "thinking skills" lists presented earlier in this chapter were really lists of important mental activities. Doing anything on those lists consistently well requires the employment of all five of these behaviors.

What these five behaviors represent is a set of archetypal ways the mind deploys itself when it effectively does its most important work. They are ubiquitous behaviors; they go on wherever the mind does this work well. Their omnipresence in good mental work leads us to think of them as generic, so we call them generic thinking skills.

It is also true that the absence of these skills—and it is astonishing how often they are disused or employed erratically—correlates with poor mental performance. On the other hand, these skills represent very basic mental behaviors. They are not so complex that they can't be found and strengthened in the early elementary child; they are not so automatic and ingrained that you can count on them in the doctoral candidate.

So now we have, at long last, a set of targets for the thinking skill instructor. Thinking skill instructors could not do better initially than to set their sights on improving the skills of selective attention, sustained analysis, analoging, suspension of closure, and autocensorship, skills that support those core abilities of the mind to remember, discern, and predicate.

We get to know these skills better as we consider, in the next chapter, some overall guidelines on how to develop them.

THE FILE

THE FILE

CHAPTER 3

LEARNERS AND HOW THEY TICK

Forethought

We've just moved through different ways to conceive and identify thinking skills. It would not be surprising if the reader came away a bit short of breath and not quite sure how it all applies. Fortunately, there is a rallying point when confusion rises about the thinking process. Just set aside the abstractions and skill lists for a moment and reflect on how learners behave. Put yourself in the learner's shoes, and if you do this carefully enough, you'll be in a good position to see where theory fits.

THE RELUCTANT SKILL

Often, when exploring how learners think with a group of educators, it is useful to gain some sense of how the group tends to view the way minds work. One question, in particular, provides that insight quickly, and frequently we ask it: "What is the first thing you do when you encounter a problem?"

You generally receive answers like these: "Well, first I define it — see what kind of problem it is. . . ." ". . . I break it into parts. . . ." "I think what would count as a good solution." Or, more humorously; "I call the repairman." "I route it to the appropriate department."

Perhaps individuals in such audiences have entertained the correct answer, but none has yet volunteered it. The first thing most people do when they encounter problems is try to ignore them. You behave, if you can, as though the problem isn't there. And there is, in this tendency, an important clue to the dynamics of skilled thought.

This initial tendency to ignore problems may seem at first a sign of

23

laziness, but it is not. It is actually a shrewd survival tendency. Human beings are organisms with limited resources and energies. Life is filled with anomalies and problems—things that deviate from or frustrate our expectations. If our *first* reaction was to try resolving these as they appear, the organism would quickly exhaust itself. And it happens that a great percentage of our perceived difficulties, when ignored, go away on their own. There is some wisdom—perhaps misdirected—in the man who couldn't repair his roof when it rained and didn't need to when the sun shone.

So first we ignore problems—perhaps they'll go away. But some problems persist and elicit our next response, which is simply to acknowledge the problem. We complain and go on trying to ignore it. If the aggravation continues, we often call on a strategy familiar to anyone who has raised children. We complain *to* someone; we try to get someone else to solve it for us, and this frequently works.

If no one is there to help and the problem persists, emotion sometimes leads us to gestures—symbolic solutions—like yelling or kicking or thumping with a wrench. The odds here are not good, but aside from relieving tension, sometimes it seems to work. If we've solved the problem before, or have seen it solved, we'll pattern our behavior from habit or memory, and the odds here are much better. If none of these or a variety of other stratagems works, we can either despair or settle down, really face the problem, and think about it.

The point of this progression is that the full, attentive, conscious employment of the mind tends to be a last, and not a first, resort. Each individual has a rich repertoire of less demanding responses to life's situations; responses that often suffice. In some cases the individual is so clever at deploying these responses that he or she has little need to call on higher order cognition. Such a person may even come to view people who do exhibit careful thought as plodding, cumbersome, or unstylish.

As employers of higher order cognition, we tend to be conservative and at times even reactionary. Good thinking is hard work, and until we become habituated to it and sensitive to its unique rewards, our tendency is to avoid it, using lesser skills where we can. We are wily copyists and mimics, and much that passes as a product of our thinking is really the product of someone else's. We also—each of us—have a finely tuned sense of the odds in matters that concern us, and we tend to guess a lot.

This may seem an unappealing view of mankind, and we think of examples that belie it. All of us have known the bright, precocious student with the questioning mind, given to precise thought and clear expression. Such students are a delight and a gift, but we mislead ourselves if they shape our expectations. There is a tendency to feel that this is the kind of student we deserve. It is a bad tendency for two reasons. First, it leads to continual disappointment. Second, it removes all motive to grasp the psychology of the really normative mind, which is more practiced in avoiding thought than in thinking. And we do need to grasp this psychology if we want to lead the normative mind past its usual performance to real thinking skill.

There are, then, two characteristics of typical learners that warrant the thinking skill instructor's attention. Both of them contribute to a kind of inertia regarding higher order thought—an unconscious bias *against* the employment of operant thinking skills. We've already suggested the first characteristic. It is a natural and reasonable impulse toward economy of effort, a tendency to meet most demands with the least dislocation and expenditure of energy.

The second characteristic seems simple and surmountable, until we reflect on how much it is culturally reinforced. It is the learner's uncertainty about how to do higher order thinking. Of the vast array of behaviors we model and role-play on our way to maturity, operant thinking is the least accessible. Thinking is a personal activity, but society makes it a far more private matter than it need be. The learner has to make headway in a culture that is mute about the component behaviors in operant thinking. We are well exercised in the respondent skills of copying, memorizing, and recitation, but there is very little clear modeling of higher order cognition. What clues we do receive are often misleading. We are taught not to move our lips, not to count on our fingers, and in other ways led to the impression that thinking is some kind of hidden "flash of insight" happening.

So learners couple a tendency to avoid operant thinking with an uncertainty about how to do it—an uncertainty they are conditioned neither to recognize nor to voice. These are your standard handicaps as a thinking skills instructor facing the typical learner, and overcoming them will be a large part of your task.

It was important to form this initial image of the learner, because in a moment we look at what kinds of teaching strategies it takes to move such learners toward thinking skill. But part of the picture is still missing. We need a clearer view of where we want to take such learners, so let's first look at a simple example of good operant thinking.

THE CAPABLE THINKER

We are going to present Joanne[9] with a very simple problem, ask her to step before the class, and solve it out loud. But before we do, you should know some things about Joanne, and about the problem.

---

[9]Joanne is a pseudonym, but I first encountered the problem-solving style of this very real young lady during Arthur Whimbey's presentation at a cognitive skill task force meeting held November 6th and 7th, 1975, at Bowling Green State University, Ohio. A tape of Whimbey sharing the protocol at that time is still in hand, but he has since committed it to print. It may be found in Whimbey and Lockhead, *Problem Solving and Comprehension*, (pp. 23–24). All the parenthetical statements on pages 26 and 27 are taken directly from that source and location.

Joanne is an exceptionally capable graduate student. As an undergradu-
ate, she majored in both physics and literature, and for a time aimed at
teaching the latter at the college level. After completing a Master's degree in
Comparative Literature, she shifted careers because of poor job prospects.
And at this time she is an exemplary medical student.

The problem we have for Joanne hardly ranks as a problem. Not only is
all the required information present, but so are clear instructions on what to
do with the information. It is a completely unambiguous, trick-free,
single-answer problem. Nevertheless, a handful of students in any average
freshman class usually manage to come up with a variety of wrong answers.

These three figures are drawn on the blackboard in careful proportion:

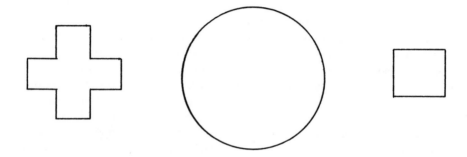

Joanne is called to the front of the class and handed the following typed
problem statement: "If the circle is taller than the square and the cross is
shorter than the square, put a K in the circle. However, if this is not the
case, put a T in the second tallest figure."

We ask Joanne to solve the problem, and here is what she says and does:
Joanne gives the blackboard a long glance, skims the problem statement,
and then begins to read the problem aloud: "If the circle is taller than the
square and the cross is shorter than the square, put a K in the Circle."

"Let me start again." "If the circle—I'll put my finger on the circle—is
taller than the square . . . Yes, the circle is taller than the square."

"And the cross is shorter than the square. . . I'll move my finger from
the cross to the square and compare them. This part is false. The cross is not
shorter than the square."

"Put a K in the circle."

"So I shouldn't put a K in the circle. Part of the statement is false. I would
only write K if both the first part and the second part were true."

"I should read the whole sentence again and see if my conclusion is
correct."

"If the circle is taller than the square . . . Yes . . . and the cross is
shorter than the square . . . No . . . Put a K in the circle . . . I didn't.
That's correct."

"I'll continue on the next part of the problem."

"However, if this is not the case. . . And it isn't the case. . . put a T in the second tallest figure."

"The second tallest figure is the cross so I'll put a T in the cross."

You would have to know Joanne to realize that this little protocol runs true to form. She is very precise, careful, and explicit in all her work. Let's examine a little more closely what she's done.

Because you weren't present that day, you'll have to take our word for the first noteworthy characteristic of her performance. As she stepped briskly to the board, she did not check her hem, blush, fidget, or otherwise express consciousness of the sometimes uncomfortable business of being in front of a class. She was already anticipating the problem about to come up. There is a preliminary form of selective attention at work here; a disposition, based on proven competence, to seek out and identify problems rather than retreat and be cornered by them. Good thinkers are confident that their minds can do good work, and they begin concentrating as soon as the game is afoot.

After skimming the problem, she begins reading aloud but curiously stops after the first sentence. She's recognized (analoging) that what she has is an imperative sentence, a complete direction. She concentrates (selective attention) on this, bracketing out the rest of the problem. Less facile problem solvers often try to work the whole problem statement at once, many times tangling elements in the two sentences that then have to be unsnarled. But having segregated the first sentence, Joanne begins a *sustained analysis* of its components. She uses available aids (her finger on the blackboard) to make sure she identifies each and every element of the problem. This process reveals to her that the cross is not shorter than the square.

Students who get this problem wrong do not go to such lengths. A number of them admit to misreadings. Having placed the K in the circle, they grimace and say, "I thought it said 'if the cross is shorter than the *circle*!'" This is the kind of thing Joanne intends to avoid.

Remember that analoging is the skill of bringing past insights to bear on the present situation. Joanne is familiar with "If . . . then" statements. She knows that if an element of the conditional clause is not true, the consequent does not follow, and she tells us so. Another group of wrong-answer students, when debriefed, revealed that they saw the cross was not shorter than the square but put the K in the circle anyway, because the first part of the conditional was correct.

Joanne is now pretty sure she has it, but she *suspends closure* even before going on to the next element of the problem. There is a chance she could have transposed proportions, misread, or missed something. So she goes through her solution (autocensorship) to this point again. Wrong-answer students seldom do this. Many right-answer students whose initial reading was faulty save themselves by doing it.

Joanne goes now to the final part of the problem and seems rather quickly to get the *T* in the cross. She gives no vocal evidence here of suspending closure or autocensorship. But reflect again on what she brings to this stage of the problem. At this point, her extreme prior care has given her a clear, intense, and proven (she checked) facility with the elements of the problem. She's already absorbed that the cross is the second tallest figure, so she inserts her *T* there. The less facile problem solver, however, would have been wise to suspend closure and check again, thus avoiding another class of wrong-answer students. This bunch, having spotted the relationships correctly, fall short at the finish line by misreading again. Having put a *T* in the circle, they moan, "I missed 'tallest' . . . I thought it said 'put a *T* in the *second figure*.' "

You may wonder why we asked an outstanding grad student to solve a simple follow-the-directions problem one might expect a good sixth grader to do. Capable sixth graders, bent on securing a correct answer, will in fact generate protocols very much like Joanne's. There may be differences in tempo, pattern, and sequence, but the same generic skills will identifiably be at work. We picked Joanne, however, to underline several things. First, proven brilliance, experience, and maturity bestows no exemption. Joanne did, and had to do, just what an able sixth grader or anyone else has to do to generate a solution in which she could have maximum confidence. We would be more accustomed to the sight of Joanne stepping to the board, studying the problem for a moment, and without a word placing a *T* in the cross. But her processes of mentation, though unobserved, would have been essentially the same.

The problem we set Joanne was perhaps trivial, but nothing about her performance was. She did what was necessary to delineate the problem's elements, determine their relationships, and respond to the problem's constraints. We witnessed her employment of selective attention, sustained analysis, analoging, suspension of closure, and autocensorship at a very rudimentary level and so have only a glimmer of how empowering these skills are for her. A full protocol of her facing a complex, real-life issue (working with extensive but perhaps insufficient information toward not one but a range of plausible solutions, having then to select a "best") would likely fill this book with its recursions and deployments of those skills. But we have seen that even trivial problems leave no option but to use these skills, and even trivial problems defeat those who do not command them, or who tend to use them indifferently.

Here is our goal for the learner unaccustomed to skillful thought. We want a confident proficiency in, and an inclination toward the use of, generic thinking skills. We are in a position now to explore what a teacher can do to bring the reluctant and uncertain thinker to such a state of skill.

TEACHING STRATEGIES: SEVEN AIMS AND AN INSIGHT

Here we talk about the broad aims of the thinking skill instructor. Later we'll look at the various proven ways these aims can be met in the classroom: the instructional techniques. To make that discussion even more concrete, we will look at them in the specific light of what can be done at the elementary, secondary, and collegiate levels.

But even at this broadest, most general level there is a question of the teacher's overall orientation that affects all later issues about technique. You would likely deduce this orientation from the following discussion of aims, but it might be best to bring it out firm and clear at the beginning. The orientation of the effective thinking skills instructor is very much the orientation of the good coach.

As you know, there are coaches and there are coaches. Some get by on the ability to pick already skilled players. Others have the knack of transforming initially clumsy and sometimes reluctant stock into credible, even excellent, performers. It's this last kind of coach we want to keep in mind; he or she faces a situation almost indistinguishable from the one a thinking skill instructor faces. Both need to motivate the novice, both demonstrate components of good performance, leading the novice through the "moves," and both oversee practice like a hawk.

The first overall aim of the thinking skill instructor is to build the student's confidence in his or her thinking ability; yes, even when the student doesn't appear to have much and even before he or she has employed any. The effective thinking skill instructor exudes confidence in the poor thinker's coming transformation. There simply isn't any doubt; "of *course* you can do it." The student will need that confidence to survive mistakes and continue despite them, like the tennis novice who needs to get past the first several dozen awful serves.

The second aim is to open a window to the student's thinking processes, so that they can be observed by the instructor, the student, and the student's peers. This is the point at which the thinking skill instructor has it tougher than the average coach. Before he or she can do anything to improve the student's thinking behavior, that behavior has to be made visible and explicit for everyone involved. There are techniques that will enable you to do this — Joanne's "vocalization" of her thinking is one, along with various special ways of writing — and we explore these later. But this aim goes beyond issues of technique. The problem is to make a whole class of hidden behavior — thinking — public in a way that is sanctioned, acceptable, and productive for students.

The task is to socialize students around examining their attempts at operant thinking, thereby making a hitherto tacit dimension of student performance explicit. This is really not hard to do, and once it's done, a certain dialogue about thinking habits, glitches, problems, strengths, and styles is sanctioned. It is not, however, a free-ranging, ego-embellishing dialogue — a "rap" about thinking. It is a dialogue kept on track, bound to the immediate evidence of a thinking task well or poorly executed. The point of it is, of course, to make students explicitly conscious of their own thinking processes. What the student grasps about his or her thinking behavior, the student can modify.

You might, as a model, think about the good coach with his team in the locker room following scrimmage. He monitors what team members say to each other: "Man, why you hit that back so high? You try to tickle his chin?" "That end left his shape in the astro. You really plucked ankles." "Sam, you passed right *by* him. You lookin' for cheerleaders?" A lot of performance assessment takes place; it gets heard and it gets processed. There's no surprise and very little offense taken. The same words from a stranger in a lounge, on the other hand, could start a brawl.

The third aim is to concentrate on the student's thinking *process*, not the product. A right answer is never, by itself, a guarantee of capable thinking. Mimicking and guessing often produce right answers. Good coaches are most infuriated when a bad serve gets the ball across the net in play, as though bad habits were thereby justified. Bad serves that don't work are easy; they speak for themselves.

The fourth aim is to maintain progression: Keep a careful pace. The general goal is to move students from using their skill on simple, unambiguous problems toward using them on muddy, confusing, real-life ones. The thinking skill instructor's first concern is to make certain that each student, at a rudimentary level, understands and can employ the generic skills. It is surprising how often some students, for instance, reveal by performance that they never sustain analysis or suspend closure. Clear-cut, "trivial" problems like the one we handed Joanne are very good for diagnosing and remedying such thinking difficulties. They reveal process cleanly because they are simple and seldom contaminated by emotion and bias. But once those generic skills are in place, the instructor's task is to move those skills toward work in increasingly complex and ambiguous situations.

The fifth aim is to avoid, wherever possible, doing the students' thinking for them. In teaching any discipline, there is need to organize information and insight and deliver it to the student, but we tend to overdo it. It is often better to disorganize things just enough so the student has to work for resolution and insight. Whenever possible, ask rather than tell. Instead of "These are the three major consequences of the Battle of Plattsburg," try "What do you suppose the three major consequences are?" The latter tugs on operant skills whereas the former sidesteps them. For a time, curriculum innovators were getting hefty test score gains by underlining key sentences in paragraphs for students and making them pop up on cathode ray tubes.

They were also obviating the students' need to think. When you can, let students find and underline their own key sentences.

The sixth aim is never to confuse teaching thinking with teaching *about* thinking. A history of Wimbledon will do little to improve a novice's court performance, and discourse on thinking skill theory or recitation of the field's jargon won't improve student thinking. You will need to do things like label skills, but as a general rule, avoid labels until students have practiced and are conscious of the subject skill. Let the students' *need* for terminology trigger your supply of it.

The seventh aim is to maintain an open window on your *own* thinking processes. Reveal—vocalize—your own thinking and problem-solving behavior regularly. What you model in the classroom will have the dominant impact on students. And above all, when you model, model truthfully. Not like the algebra teacher who, having spent 2 hours on a proof the night before, has it slickly on the board and explained in 5 minutes. Students tend to read such performance as normative, despair of duplicating it, and give up. If you are an especially skilled performer, explain why. Point to the years of training, the practice. Make mistakes and recover from them in class. If you want students to employ aids in thinking, use them yourself. Draw diagrams, count on your fingers, move your lips, pace the floor, let them know the things that help you concentrate and achieve precision.

These seven aims are best seen as durable tendencies on the part of the thinking skill instructor, who will adapt and interweave and apply them in a thousand different ways as instructional techniques are chosen or devised and class sessions planned. The point is simply that the effective thinking skill instructor will be predisposed to these aims; traces of them will appear again and again in his or her work. You will be reminded of them all from time to time in the chapters to come.

Finally, there is an important insight about learners you would do well to tuck away at this point. Recall our general description of the learner's tendency to be conservative in the use of higher order skills. This is an accurate view of the learner's tendencies, but there is one important exception. There is a class of behavior in which creatures often use their capabilities with abandon, far more intensely than a sober assessment of the situation would seem to justify. It's called play. Play often seems a sheer delight in employing capabilities, and it is an important way for both young and old to come to know what they can do, as well as exercise their skills. There are many ways thinking can be play, and the clever teacher will not ignore occasions for the student to take delight in the use of his or her mind. We touch on this now and then up ahead.

THE FILE

THE FILE

THE FILE

CHAPTER 4

THE PRIMARY AGENDA

Forethought

At the primary level (Kindergarten through third grade) the approach to thinking skills needs special care. We should keep ourselves in check for a variety of reasons, and it will help to mention some of the major ones.

These are, without doubt, the student's most malleable and forma- tive years, and so the proponents of any educational or doctrinal objective are tempted to lay siege on this period of growth. If it is true that well-shaped intervention by the teacher in these years can do the most lasting good, it is also true that ill-conceived intervention can do its most lasting damage.

And the primary learner's sponge-like susceptibility to instruction makes it difficult for the teacher to assess her true impact. Students respond without discriminating between instruction that truly enables and instruction that merely indoctrinates. In later life the student may sense the distinction, but in the primary years the teacher must make it if it is to be made at all.

Unfortunately, this is the best time for the zealous yet indiscrimi- nate teacher to indoctrinate the student in thinking skill schemata and problem-solving methods that can produce remarkable performance without in fact advancing the operant skills. Very complex perfor- mances can be conditioned and trained, and the resulting display can be quite stunning. Remember, however, that the point of operant skill *is to produce effective behavior* in lieu *or even* in spite of *conditioning.*

Trained performance is one route to doing things well; good thinking is quite another.

Finally, there is a good deal of evidence that primary education is at present doing its job more sensitively and effectively than any other level of formal education. In part this may be due to its avowedly developmental mission, but in any case the health of the venture suggests that thinking skills instructors should contemplate modifications with special empathy for the good work underway. At times, the most effective advance in the development of primary thinking skills may require no more than a slight change of emphasis and a sharpened focus on the teacher's part.

TWO CAUTIONS

Keep two cautions in mind as you approach teaching (coaching) generic thinking skills at the primary level. The first is *Move with Restraint.* Examine carefully what is currently taking place in the classroom. You may find that generic thinking skills are already being called forth. If they are, gratefully and graciously recognize the fact. If you do anything, make sure it builds on and doesn't damage what's already there.

Second, *Don't Pursue an Integrated Use of the Generic Skills.* This is not the time to emphasize comprehensive problem-solving behavior—not because it *can't* be done, but because there are better things to do.

GENERIC SKILLS AT THE PRIMARY LEVEL

We can grasp and employ these cautions better after we've translated the generic thinking skills into terms more closely related to primary student behavior. First we'll establish our terms and then we'll explain them:

Selective Attention = "Point Out"
Sustained Analysis = "Take Apart"
Analoging = "It's Like"
Suspension of Closure = "Another Way"
Autocensorship = "Try Out"

"POINT OUT"

Whenever the young student fixes on one event in the passing flow of experience and sustains that focus despite distraction for some time—

however briefly—he or she is exercising selective attention. The young mind is engaged with—often lost in—something it has picked outside itself. Indiscriminate scanning and the passive reception of whatever the world sends one's way ceases. All except the focused event is ignored, bracketed out.

If this bond between mind and object is fragile, the press of happenings will quickly break it. An itch, a bouncing paperwad, a rude noise may be all it takes. Once again the mind is the world's puppet, dancing whatever tune it plays.

But when the bond is strong, the world must grudgingly let the mind have *its* way. Only when the mind *points* to some discrete thing in the wash of experience and figuratively lifts it *out* of the overall deluge can real thinking begin. Now, with focus, the mind can test significance, try meaning, assign value.

As teachers, we are forever "pointing out"—calling for the student's exercise of selective attention. We are seldom overwhelmed by our success. To students passively inclined and of weak attentiveness, our call is just one more of the world's intrusions, particularly aggravating because it demands response. If the goal is developing thinking skill, our "pointing out" is not what counts. The student's capacity to "point out" does.

There can be inherent pleasure and intrinsic reward in the child's act of sustaining focus. It is the first step toward wonder and the great riddle of what things are and how they work. There is no adventure without focus. The young mind can form a distinct appetite for it, even a hunger, and that should be a principal goal of thinking skill instruction at the primary level.

"TAKE APART"

We placed especially heavy emphasis on nurturing the young child's capacity to "point out"—sustain focus—because the strength of that generic skill gives impetus to the others. Strong focus binds the mind to its object with an almost irresistible urge to explore. The mind wants to possess in the only way it can, by knowing, and it knows by penetrating, noting likenesses and distinctions, shaping the object's unique place in the store of all else it knows. Much less than this can satisfy a weak focus. A simple cataloging of the object as something already familiar will often suffice. A glimpse of a thin, shiny, blue thing against a wall might elicit nothing more than "just another bike".

We encourage cataloging at the primary level, for good reason. It gives the young child a way of ordering the limitless furniture of her world. But in the process we run the risk of submerging the impulse to explore. The child can be lulled into a sense that the mind's business is maintaining a master file, where events find their right labels. Minds rooted in this view can come to view exploration as an awkward, untidy, and troublesome thing.

It is possible, however, to pursue even the cataloging in a way that encourages the impulse to take things apart and strengthens the skill of sustained analysis. The young mind's discovery that things *do* come apart in different ways, and that in taking them apart we gain new intimacy with and mastery of them, has to be the baptism of its thinking career. And as "Take Apart" skill grows in the primary student, the "Point Out" appetite naturally increases. There is now a growing reward for focus, called discovery, and that reward can come from focusing on even the most ordinary things. Note a happy rule at work here: The primary teacher who works carefully on abetting the "Take Apart" skill has unleashed a hidden ally—the recursive nature of the generic thinking skills. Really strengthen one generic skill and you are likely to stimulate them all.

"IT'S LIKE"

Analoging—likening things—is the mind's primary way of grasping the unfamiliar. I've never seen a real camel, but in pictures it seems like a funny horse, and that leads me to expect some things of it. Sure enough, when I finally see one it walks, runs, and eats grass, but it also spits and it doesn't whinny or smell like a horse. In these two brief sentences, there are at least seven comparisons, seven checks on likeness. It is difficult to imagine a chain of thought that owes nothing, at least implicitly, to an act of gauging similarity. Every time, for instance, you use the word "again," you are noting or anticipating a likeness.

We mentioned earlier that without this root capacity for likening things we would not be able to discriminate our world at all; we simply couldn't know. To what it doesn't grasp, the mind can only bring what it grasps, and then explore how the two are alike and how they differ. The process sounds tame, but it can be dynamite, at times suddenly and unexpectedly reshaping the entire landscape of what we thought we knew. Science gives us an interesting history of such upheavals.

But if likening things is such a seminal part of thinking, why should the primary teacher worry about it? Because, however much an unconscious part of thinking analoging is, it is optional as an active, conscious approach to experience. When we encounter the unfamiliar, strange, or confusing, our reaction is more likely to ignore, reject, or shrink from it. Teachers encounter the terminal "I don't know" far more often than the tentative "I'm not sure, but it's like. . . ." We are better at conditioning young minds to the likenesses their culture has drawn for them than we are at building their own "It's Like" skills.

Although it's not difficult, it does take deliberate effort to get young minds to hunt for, shape, and employ analogs. But the effort pays off, for as those skills grow, so does the ease with which the child meets — even seeks — newness in experience. Again, it isn't hard to see how "It's Like" skills increase the scope and power of "Take Apart" and "Point Out" skills.

"ANOTHER WAY"

Suspension of Closure is a subtle skill, and a tough one for the young mind given its leanings. Adults seem so pleased and are so magnanimous with rewards when you quickly give them the right answer. When problems are simple and familiar, leaping at answers becomes a satisfying game. But as problems grow more difficult, things begin to fall apart. The answer may be unclear, but you still leap at it, guessing more now, or even, in desperation, using an answer that you remember won acclaim for some other child facing a totally different question. And now, what you deliver is labeled wrong. No one's face lights up. Problems are hard, and tricky, and they bite back. They aren't much fun anymore.

Suspension of Closure is a conscious act of stopping the action — interrupting the natural thrust of the mind toward resolution — to take inventory of how and where things are going. It is motivated by a desire for precision and effectiveness in the outcome, and this desire in turn is rooted in the experience of our own fallibility as problem solvers. We know that inattentiveness and lack of care can easily lead us to failure. The careful thinker uses Suspension of Closure regularly, whenever there is the slightest cause to doubt that progress is as sound as it could be. This self-monitoring of the thinking process can begin the minute the problem arises — "The problem is such-and-so. Is it really? Did I put that right? Is there a better way to set it up?" — and it can occur at or retrace to any phase of the deliberations. This is a very tall order for the young mind at the primary level.

But laying the foundation for Suspension of Closure is very much a desirable primary goal, and there are two crucial steps the primary teacher needs to take in building that foundation.

The first step is to build in students a capacity to sense and work with alternatives. Is there another way you can draw a cat? Is there another way you can answer the question? In addition to breaking "single" and "right" answer fixations, cultivating "Another Way" sensibilities conveniently focuses the student on his or her on-task performance. Having responded to a task with multiple products, the student can be led by the teacher to examine which product is "better." The idea of relative rather than absolute performance is broached, and the seeds of self-monitoring, on reasonable grounds, are sown.

The second step is more difficult because it goes against dominant teaching convention. Yet the first step can hardly succeed without it. A good way to put it is, "favor the *considered* answer over the *speed* answer wherever possible." Usual teaching tempo favors the speed answer. "Whom did we fight in the War of Independence?" asks the teacher. Several hands shoot up and the teacher points to the first. "The British!" snaps Johnny. "Very good, Johnny!" says the teacher. Contrast this scene with the following:

"Think about this for a minute, class. Whom did we fight in the War of Independence?." Eventually hands raise. The teacher picks one; probably not the first. "Well, we fought the British, but a lot of the colonists were called 'loyalists' and fought with the British, so I guess a lot of the time we were fighting each other." The teacher in this class has been cultivating and favoring the *considered* answer. Speed answers exalt rote, memory-fueled responses. Considered answers require thinking.

"TRY OUT"

Autocensorship, though it embraces the business of checking your solution to see if you have the right answer, should not be confused with that business. Checking by yourself to see if your computations are correct is only a very special and limited case of autocensorship. The real business of autocensorship is to determine whether your solution or decision, *before* you offer or employ it, will in the broadest sense really be useful and effective. It entails exploring the consequences of your decision before you act on it.

The capable adult, after insuring that his or her solution is internally sound, asks next if it is practically and contextually sound. Will it work? My economic analysis, quite accurate, proves that we *must* close Lincoln Elementary. The voters can't fault the analysis. Nor can they govern their fear of what will happen to their children and their section of town if Lincoln Elementary does close. By itself, my economic analysis might only intensify the problem.

Envisioning, in light of the information I have and can reasonably get, the consequences of my decision—that is the heart of autocensorship. Reversing a computation (i.e., checking) is one way to do this. Projecting causes and effects in one's own mind is another and generally more useful way. The careful "gedankenexperimenten," or thought-experiments by which leading scientists envision theoretical consequence, is perhaps a prime example of this, but the writer who needs to communicate effectively with his audience is always doing it too. My words may meet my needs, but how will they meet the needs of other minds?

At the heart of Autocensorship is the motive and skill to "Try Out" decisions and seek the consequences. Obvious ways to let students try out ideas come quickly to mind. There are all the "What would happen if . . . ?" questions: "What would happen if Humpty-Dumpty was as light as air?" But there are deeper pedagogic possibilities, too. Try to give questions and problems — even (perhaps especially) arithmetic ones — a context where the quality of the answer makes a clear difference to the young mind. Too often the student can see no use at all for what we call a right answer. If the answer can be tried, and the *consequence* allowed to define right or wrong, better or worse, the student has cause to rethink and even think ahead.

TWO CAUTIONS AGAIN

We now have a checklist for our careful (*Move with Restraint*) walk through the existing primary program. Does the program exercise and strengthen attentiveness ("Point Out" skills) where it can? Does it encourage the child in analysis ("Take Apart" skills)? Does it get the child to explore and apply her own experiences ("It's Like" skills)? Does it provide room for alternative performance on task ("Another Way" skills). Does it let them explore the consequences of their answers and solutions ("Try Out" skills)?

But keep one important distinction in mind as you walk. If, on your inspection, you attend mostly to the curriculum materials, your answer to the preceding questions stand a good chance of being "Yes." The better workbooks make a real effort to capture the child's attention. They are loaded with carefully paced analytic tasks. There is no end to their call for the child to discriminate — note likenesses and differences. Even alphabet recognition and letter forming is cleverly couched in noting what is common and uncommon among shapes. Yet it is possible to lead children through such workbooks without achieving any of our primary thinking skills objectives at all.

A sole dependence on the workbooks in class will confirm these skills as "what you do in workbooks." Worse, it can confine the skills to exercise in an activity that, when experienced by the child as tedious and boring, reflects on the skills themselves as tedious and boring. And make no mistake; even the cleverest, glossiest workbook can become boring. Well-designed material might spark interest, but only active, inquisitive minds can sustain it.

We stub our toe here against a great instructional truth. In developing thinking skills, curriculum material can never be more than auxiliary. It can be helpful in exercising skill, just as workouts help the sportsman or woman, but it cannot teach or coach them. To gauge the quality and effectiveness of an instructional program, you *must* look to what teachers in it are doing. We know that an individual can work through material with remarkable gain on his or her own. But that is an instance of *self*-teaching, not mere exposure to material, and it requires durable motives and capabilities uncommon at the primary level.

So as you walk through the primary program with our list, ask these kinds of questions. How often do teachers actively model the five skills? Do they model them in everyday contexts that have nothing to do with workbooks? If the teacher uses these skills only when the book is open, that is when students will expect to use them. Do teachers convey their own delight and fascination in employing the skills? Do they make room and wave the students in so they can try and taste that delight and fascination? Do they, for instance, somehow get across the notion that a skill is like a prized object, only hidden inside yourself, and that you can do with skills what kids do with prized objects — play with them?

This is a good time to bring up our second caution, which was *don't pursue an integrated use of the generic skills*. Aim the primary years at discovering and enjoying the generic skills as and when circumstances call on them; they can be orchestrated later. Premature orchestration can throttle them for good. Remember that each of our generic skills is a disposition to use the mind in a certain way. You root these dispositions best by letting the child discover that these are, in their own right, pleasing and rewarding ways to use the mind. When the skills we've outlined become a private source of satisfaction to the student, you've largely won. Our mark is to give the child a feel for and a satisfaction in using the skills. "All right, children, remember: First we Point Out, then we Take Apart, then we do our It's Like, then we look for Another Way, and finally we Try Out," is just the kind of thing that could obliterate the mark. Concentrate on eliciting the individual skills. Let the children bridge and integrate them on their own. You'll be surprised how well they do.

If, after your examination, you don't think the existing program is addressing some of these goals well, here are some suggestions and examples for a revision. If you feel the bases are already solidly covered, you will probably find a good deal that is familiar in what follows.

TEACHING "POINT OUT" SKILLS

We know the primary child's attention is easily distracted, and as teachers with an instructional mission, we tend to find this worrisome. Don't fight it. Instead, make it work for you. Set yourself to becoming the dominant distraction in your classroom.

For example, either before class or with your back turned to it, pin something outlandish to yourself, like a green paper cat. Proceed as you normally would until the reaction builds. Then ask someone what's the matter. Let the student(s) direct your attention to your new decor. Ask "How did that get there?" As you pretend surprise, begin questioning. This is the class's chance to teach you.

"I can't see it from here. What is it?" "A Cat? What color is it?" "What is it made of?" Lead the questioning where you choose, including into the class material, but try to make mistakes the class can catch and set right. If this is a spelling period, for instance, you might say, "Oh, if it's a cat, I know how to spell that," and put B–A–T on the board. If you are naming colors, you might try, "I don't think this is green. This is blue. No? Well, then, show me something blue, so I can see." When you've gone as far as you wish (there really is no "end"—you could be exploring cats the children have or have known), unpin your green cat. But think what you might be able to do if there turned out to be a smaller red mouse, or something else, underneath.

This is a simple, and seemingly silly, example, but consider what you've achieved. You've sparked, not demanded, attention. You've led children to feed their own attention by using what they know to correct mistakes you've made with the object of their focus. Handled carefully, your questioning can lead them to understand that object better when they're through than when they began. It is a useful gimmick to play "dumb" from time to time. The trick is transparent, but the students like it anyway. It gives them a chance to play-teach, and whether you play-teach or real-teach, you come away with a clearer grasp of your material.

You can sharpen attention while you're reading by playing the "Be a Word" game from time to time. "Johnny, you can be 'dog,' Clare, you are 'cat.' " When those words occur during your story, the child waves, or shouts it, or holds up a card on which she's printed it. Others will be listening for those words, too. After awhile, you can put a list of words on the board before your story and let the children pick their own. Variations of this can work with arithmetic. Assign children numbers and ask the answers to stand up.

Any number of "Finding" games help. Break the class into team A and team B. Each team has to find things in the other team. You ask team A to find blue shoelaces, or a flower or horse (on someone's print shirt or dress). Keep a team score, and every once in awhile ask for something that isn't there. When they don't find it, say "that's right," and give them a point. You should play, too. Ask a team to huddle and name something for you to find. Make your search out loud, make it long, and almost don't find what you're looking for, modeling good search behavior all the while: "First I'm looking at all the shoes. Oh, there's Bobby's new cowboy boots, and see

Jane's shiny ones? they're called patent leather. . . . No, no I don't see it. But you wouldn't expect to find it on shoes, would you?" Etc., etc. This can help children see the kinds of things one does when being attentive.

"Show and Tell" is a popular activity, but often too little is made of it. You can easily build the day before and the day after into excellent thinking experiences for the children and a valuable source of intelligence for your future instruction of the class. You stand to gain a profile of each student's strongest focuses — the things they like best and hence have attended to most.

After you've set guidelines on what can be brought, ask the children to make a choice but keep it secret. On the day before the show, let the class guess what each child in turn will bring. (Recall we said guessing was a bad way to resolve inquiry. It is, however, often a fine way to start it and stimulate focus.) Voting is a good way: "How many think Charles will bring A? How many say B?" When you've tallied the votes, Charles can reveal who's right. Ask Charles why he chose what he did. Then ask him what he would bring if he could bring anything in the world he wanted to.

For you, the questions will provide a useful profile of Charles' interests — his special areas of "expertise" — which you can weave into your teaching in a variety of ways. You've also mapped out compatible interests and common grounds for the rest of the class, as well as heightened anticipation of the big day. As for Charles, you and the class have affirmed, supported, and sanctioned his interests. In a variety of ways, you've announced that "to be interested" is a good thing.

On "Show and Tell" day comes the chance to give your "Point Out" function to the students. Encourage each presenter by yourself being an attentive, questioning listener. Help the child explore the object, yes, but help especially to explore the child's *interest* in it: What sparked that interest and fostered it.

On the day following "Show and Tell," you of course have the full richness of the prior day on which to exercise the students' "Point Out" skills. Kindergarteners can name and talk about the things they liked best, were frightened by, or were most surprised to learn; older students can write about them.

As a matter of fact, "Show and Tell" is almost too rich an instructional event to simply cram into a few days. Think how you might stretch the benefits by making it a showcase feature every few days, with only one or two presenters at a time.

"Catch the Teacher" is tailor-made fun for students and a sure way of keeping them alert. It will work with any subject matter and at any level of difficulty suitable to your students, from very simple to very subtle. Begin by clearly tipping your hand: "I'm going to tell you a story and I'm going to make a mistake. See if you can catch it . . . "The lazy cat lay in the shade, carefully licking its feet until it finished all five of them.' " As students gain experience in catching you out, you can telegraph less and hide your errors more cleverly. The golden day will come when they catch an error you weren't aware you were making. Building errors into instruction with a commission for students to uncover them is useful for a special reason. At first, striking and attractive events tend to be the ones that easily win attention. But the most productive kind of attention (the kind that leads to spotting and assessing problems effectively) is the kind that is tuned to what is anomalous — what doesn't fit — in experience. The habit of identifying rather than ignoring error is critical to effective thought, and approaches like "Catch the Teacher" will help establish it.

In General: Plan your "Point Out" exercises and enticements so that your young students develop a robust appetite for spotting things. That appetite will only become truly durable and healthy when it grows capable of feeding itself, and this self-feeding involves use of the other generic thinking skills. We've cautioned against efforts to train students in systematic use of the generic skills at the primary level, because emphasis on system can prematurely abort the young mind's process of discovering, "tasting" and trying its own abilities. But the generic skills do naturally call upon each other, and here the teacher should be willing to let nature have its way. When "Pointing Out," in conjunction with other skills, pays the student off in discovery, better insights, and satisfying solutions, it will become a tried and trusted disposition of the learner. One of the skills "Pointing Out" will enlist most often in achieving this disposition is that of analysis. What captures the mind's attention, the mind will want to "Take Apart."

TEACHING "TAKE APART" SKILLS

It would be difficult to avoid calling upon student "Take Apart" skills. The teacher would have to abandon all questions save those that call purely on memorization. Whenever you require a student to extend a performance — to elaborate, revise, or make it more precise — you call to some degree on the skills of analysis. "You said the pirate was bad, Johnny. Why was he bad?" You've asked the student to "research" a predication he's made, to discriminate, perhaps more carefully this time, what led him to affirm one thing of another. Analysis is always a call to examine an event more carefully, to pass it through a finer screening of likeness and distinctions.

Strangely enough, the fact that even a new Kindergartener comes with an extensive history of having roughly analyzed things turns out to be a handicap in developing analytic skill. Parents often — and others almost always — condition the child toward quick, superficial, one-step analyses as the proper coinage in social exchange. The extreme example is the familiar,

"Why? Because." Much more common is the simple throw-away reason, like "You can't. It's bad for you." Adult conversation is itself loaded with trite formulas that are the merest shadows of real inquiry and analysis. "How are you?" "I'm fine." It should not surprise us that analytic behavior for the child is often no more than a search for the first satisfactory rote response.

This conditioning can be troublesome. The child who tends to be rewarded for glibly mimicking casual adult usage elsewhere finds that it doesn't satisfy the teacher. At best this can be confusing; at worst it can build resentment. Don't try to fight such ingrained behavior head-on by challenging superficial explanations. Move the child quickly into new contexts where interesting real analysis can occur and count.

"Unscrambling" is a good stimulus to analytic skill. It initiates a quest for correct relationships and right order. You have separately cut out the body, head, tail, and legs of a paper dog. You inform your class that you are going to pin your friend on the board, but you put the parts in wrong and ridiculous places. Let the students object and guide you in "taking apart" the mess and assembling it correctly. Even a ploy as simple as this can awaken new levels of discrimination. When told that "the legs go at the end and point down," put the front legs on the back end. The students will create revised and more accurate instructions. By now, the principle is familiar: You make errors that the students can detect and that require employment of the target skill to set right.

"Unpacking" will trigger the kind of analysis we sometimes call deductive. You might assign a small group of students an imaginary "mystery box." You can divide the entire class into groups, each with a box, if you wish. The group has brought the box to school and it contains everything we need for a good picnic, or everything we need to go fishing, or all the parts we need for a tricycle. The group's task is to "unpack" the box by drawing, perhaps on the board, pictures of all its contents. After you've done this a few times, you can add a further requirement. Request that the contents be laid out in some appropriate order. For instance, you can ask that the things we need first be taken out first. You can have contests for which team takes apart and lays out their box most competently.

Questioning, as we've indicated, is your primary stimulus for "Take Apart" skills. Never resist the impulse to launch a "How?" or "Why?" that will stimulate a student to unravel the dynamics of a thing, event, or situation. There is hardly a better time to ply the Socratic trade than when you have your class engrossed in a story. You are all sharing a special, simplified world that careful questioning and weighing of response can only enrich.

Reading is a good context in which to pursue another goal that you have slyly set in the interest of building "Take Apart" skills. You want to increase the student's appetite and aptitude for questioning. It will take considerable care because you need to avoid pointless questioning, but you can begin to selectively transfer your own role as questioner to students. Begin by announcing that you will stop a time or two during the story so that anyone can ask a question. Stop only and briefly at those peaks of interest or excitement in the story that are likely to produce questions. As students grow used to this, stop now and then at a suitable point and say, "I know a good question to ask right here. Can anyone guess what it is?" Gradually do this when you are handling other parts of the curriculum as well. You will be modeling considerate, issue-oriented questioning — the kind that leads people to initiate use of their own "Take Apart" skills.

But do be selective about using this technique. Limit it to a small portion of your readings. The majority of student reading should be left uninterrupted, so that students come to experience it as a personal process of embuing and enjoying the whole.

Writing exercises are an excellent context for stimulating a very special "Take Apart" skill, and the primary years are a good time to begin calling on it. That skill is giving examples. Giving examples is the way one "takes apart" a generality and, in speaking as well as writing, gives worn, everyday phrases the precision and impact they need. Make it a point to prompt examples in writing and even hold example exercises or contests, with extra points for the good ones. For instance, write "It's a cold day" on the board and ask the class what tells us it's a cold day. "I shiver." "There are icicles on the roof." "The wind blows right through my jacket and gives me goose-bumps." "The sink froze and my Dad's car wouldn't start." "My breath makes smoke." If this were a contest, the one about goose-bumps would get more points than the one about shivering because it's more specific: It "takes apart" further. What we have in giving examples is another form of "unpacking."

In General: This is a good place to step back and regain perspective on our thinking skills mission. We are looking at various ways to directly stimulate use of the generic skills in class. Meanwhile, there is a course syllabus in place, and we need to integrate our thinking skills efforts with our established syllabus objectives.

You have noticed, from our examples thus far, the strong symbiosis that "Pointing Out" and "Take Apart" skills share. Any sound exercise of "Pointing Out" is likely to ignite analysis. Any effective act of "Taking Apart" will produce a new array of things worthy of selective attention. Instructional planning for the thinking skills instructor is a matter of selectively enhancing and resisting these tendencies to suit the instructional mission. Yes, this means there are times when you will draw reins on a healthy student impulse to good thinking, if only to shift direction.

A sound strategy at the primary level is to ignite an appetite to use these skills whenever you can, with exercises and games of the type we've suggested. If a "Point Out" exercise you've initiated sends the class eagerly off into analysis, fine. Feed that appetite. But never quench it. While sparks are still in student eyes, direct those skills toward the established syllabus. Avoid continuing a thinking game to the end of student enthusiasm, and then turning sated minds to the remaining classwork. When you are all back in classwork, draw parallels: "We're going to work some problems, and what we do with them is the same thing we did with the paper dog. . . ." We've warned against forming the impression in student minds that thinking is what goes on in workbooks. The impression that thinking has its place only during the teacher's "special" times would also be unfortunate. The impression we need is that thinking is good *any*time. The goal of the artful teacher is, of course, to so integrate the class experience that any distinction between thinking skill exercises and established classwork will be trivial.

Nothing will help the student integrate his or her own life and classroom experiences more than a healthy command of our next skill.

TEACHING "IT'S LIKE" SKILLS

Your class is divided into two teams. Each team will strive to build a list with 10 items on the board. The items will have checks next to them, and the team with the highest number of checks wins. You raise your pencil and say, "I want you to name something that is like this, and you have to tell me the ways what you name is like this pencil." A member of team A says "pen," which gets written under their list on the board, and adds that it's like a pencil because it writes. That earns one check. Other members of team A get to add likenesses. Pens are shaped like pencils. Another check. You carry pens in pockets like a pencil. Another check, and so it goes. When each team has all its items and checks, team members get a chance to make extra points by adding checks to the other team's list.

The "It's Like" game, in all its many variants, helps students to expand their sense of likeness criteria. They will quickly move from obvious criteria like shape, size, and color to less obvious ones like ingredients, purpose, function, and value.

Is it bigger than a bread basket? Take a cue from the game shows and count your student winnings in increased analoging skills. The key is to avoid guessing games that count on simple recall. Shape yours so that the clues require finding likenesses and noting differences. You might start a "Guess What I'm Thinking About" session by saying it's like a car. Students can then ask you whether it has any of the characteristics a car has: "Does it have a motor?" "No." "Does it have wheels?" "Yes." "Does it carry people?" "Yes." After any question about a characteristic, students are allowed one guess: "It's a soap box!" "No." After a wrong guess, the rule is to ask about characteristics again. "Does it have a steering wheel?" "No." "It's a bike!" "Bingo!" As students adjust, let them host the guessing games.

Classroom readings, reading assignments, or stories told in class are ready-made opportunities for students to search out likenesses in their own experience. "Have you ever done anything like that?" "Have you ever been happy like that?" Have you ever been frightened like that?" "Have you ever seen anything like that?" Projecting one's own experience into other people's situations is a crucial form of analoging. All empathy is based on it, as is the capacity to shift point of view. These, in turn, are essential ingredients of effective conceptual thought.

Acting is an excellent way to extend these critical analoging capabilities of empathizing and shifting point-of-view. "What kind of face would the mean giant make, Sally?" "How would that man with a stiff leg walk, Tim?" The effort to perform "like" someone or something reveals a good deal concerning what the performer perceives about that someone or something. Discussions and comparisons of such performances can reveal still more to student minds about the objects portrayed. And, of course, analysis and selective attention have to be employed to gain this sharpened sense of likeness.

Another excellent game for the "It's Like" skills is "What kind would *you* be?" "What kind of dog would you be?" "What kind of tree would you be?" "What kind of car would you be?" In a sense, this gets the analoging skills to work in reverse. The child will pick the "X' that is personally most attractive, often without knowing the criteria she has used. But she *has* compared her choice with others of its kind, and it has more of what she admires. It's a natural for the teacher to enlist the "Take Apart" skills here and ask the child why she made her choice. The explanation will give you the criteria that the chosen item best suits and is most like. You use this same dynamic when, while studying careers in social studies, you ask, "What would you like to be when you grow up?"

In General: The key value of "It's Like" skills is that they cause the student — more effectively than anything else — to draw upon the experience, knowledge, and skill he or she already has. When possible, affirm this truth to the analoging student. Compliment them on what they make of their sensibilities. Knowledge, experience, and skill that proves useful generates pride and becomes valued. It establishes a taste for more knowledge, skill, and experience.

Think about prompting the "It's Like" skills whenever a student becomes bogged down or uncertain of how to proceed. Often, tying the unfamiliar to the familiar is the most enabling thing you can do for a student in difficulty. "This problem is like the one you just solved, Greg, with one important difference. Can you tell me what the difference is?. . . ." Whenever possible, don't lead students out of trouble. Help them find their own way out.

TEACHING "ANOTHER WAY" SKILLS

"Another Way" skills seem so simple they are usually overlooked, but they are so important they should never be. Consider the psychology for a moment. Whenever the student is doing something under the conviction that it is the only way it can be done, the task is clearly controlling the student. Whenever the student is doing something under the conviction that there is another way, but in this case he's chosen the better one, he is in control of the task.

Arithmetic is one place where we too often make it seem there's only one way. Stretch a bit whenever you can to show where there are alternatives, and you will find you are teaching better math. Take the relationship between things and numbers, for instance. Put 16 objects on a table and ask the students how many different ways they can make four. Among other ways, they can pull out random little groups of four things, they can push things into four different-sized piles, they can even have four piles of four things each. You've even conveyed a little set theory.

We've already mentioned the use of "What If" questions to stimulate a sense of alternatives. Story time is again an excellent setting. "What if you were that little girl, Jenny? What would you do?" Building alternative worlds is good practice for discovering alternatives in the one we inhabit.

When students are on task, regularly request alternative products. The key demand here is, "Can you do it another way?" That's a nice house. How else can you draw it? " "I like your story about destroying the rock monster. Could you write one where you had to make friends with it?" One valuable consequence of alternative products is the opportunity it gives a student to compare his own workmanship. It can be an easy and profitable introduction to self-assessment.

In General: we've said "Another Way" skills will lead to the capacity to suspend closure on task, to reflect on performance while underway. As students approach this happy outcome, "Another Way" skills will accustom them to view the world as responsive to their considered choices rather than as dictating behavior. It very much favors the acquisition of skill to see that how I choose to do something makes a difference.

TEACHING "TRY OUT" SKILLS

We've argued on other occasions that the queen of analytic behavior is assessment — evaluation. It is the most demanding form of cognition because it requires, in addition to the best possible grasp of its object, an estimate of the object's consequences. If you want to pick the truly capable thinker, pick the one who can best assess self and situation. That person will be a master of autocensorship—projecting the consequences of an act before acting.

Building "Try Out" skills can look very much like building "Another Way" skills, with one important difference. "Another Way" skills look for a different product or procedure. "Try Out" skills look for the different consequences of a given solution.

We've mentioned that "What If" questions are a good preparation for the "Try Out" skills. They lead young minds to test causal chains and imagine consequences. Changing the data during story time is an obvious way to do it. "What if the little Dutch boy had found a stick by the dike?" Entice students to explore alternate paths. Such encouragement will heighten their sense of what makes a story work.

"Let's Suppose" is a next and slightly more focused step. You concentrate here on a definite student suggestion or solution and push it toward its consequences. "Suppose we *do* give Prince all the candy he wants to eat, Daryl. What would happen?" Lead the student to plausible events and circumstances that will "test" the solution and tease out its limits. "Suppose he doesn't have a toy to give her. How will he make friends then?"

"Jane brought three oranges and Kevin brought two apples. How much fruit did they have?" When Timothy says "four," you can say, "No, that's not right. Anyone else?" Or you can say, "Let's pretend these are four pieces of fruit, Tim. Give back Jane and Kevin what they brought." Trying out wrong answers is an excellent way to help a student see what went wrong. Do it tangibly, with physical things and physical demonstrations when you can. The next step is to ask them to "imagine" part of the demonstration. Finally, you can ask them to "imagine" the whole test. All the while those "try Out" skills are gaining strength.

Your modeling as teacher is always important, but it is especially important here. Don't solve problems and give conclusive answers without yourself employing your "Try Out" skills openly and clearly. Showing students how you test answers—and that you *do* test them—will do more than anything else to sanction "Try Out" skills. Again, it will help to occasionally test answers that are wrong, and to discover that error through your testing. After awhile, you'll find the students more than willing to help.

In General: In working on "Try Out" skills, strive for a class atmosphere in which answers are a stimulant to further thought. Remember the distinction between considered answers and speedy ones. In some classes you can sense that the apex of performance is the quick right answer. Far less frequently you find a class that views right answers as stimuli for assessment and further inquiry. When you do find such a class, you will find that its teacher is specially sensitive to *how* students achieve their answers. Consider for a moment; an answer is the termination of a sequence of thought. Celebrate the process of thinking in your classroom, not its termination. Among the praises you bestow on students, "good thinking" should rank higher than "correct."

THE PRIMARY AIM, IN SHORT

Friendly acquaintance and enjoyable, productive work with the generic skills — these are the things the primary years should provide — not self-conscious learning skill jargon and not rote thinking protocols. From the student's point of view, the most rewarding moments of the primary experience should be moments when these skills were alive and working. You've helped young minds find and stretch their capabilities. That will be a tough act for the rest of the educational system to follow, and an impossible one to beat.

Note that this time we haven't left The File empty. We want to nudge you to use it. We've examined some classroom exercises in this chapter and seeded The File with still more. We hope it will prompt you to begin building your own trove of useful thinking skill ideas and approaches. We haven't much room, so suggestions in "The File" will be synoptic and brief, for you to unfold as you see fit.

The File

Following are suggestions for games and activities designed to exercise thinking skills. Use them, modify them, adapt them to your own needs. Add them to your own file of activities for each of the five thinking skills.

Pointing Out (Selective Attention)

1. Where does the light come from?
   Car (headlights, taillights, backup lights, fog lights, dome light, spotlight, light reflected from chrome, etc.)
   Star
   Candle
   Day
   Night
   Christmas tree

2. My Musical Instrument.
   Pantomime for the class "your" musical instrument and try to make

the pantomime complete. If the instrument is usually carried in a case, you must remove it before playing. If it needs to be prepared in a special way, you must prepare it in that way. Note that one usually plays a piano seated. Note that an acoustic guitar must always be tuned before it is played. Note that the bow of a violin must be resined. If your instrument is such that you carry it in your pocket or purse, you must remove it from your pocket or purse.

Piano	Harmonica	Drums
Guitar	Comb and tissue paper	Trumpet
Violin	Flute	Trombone

3. The class is divided into teams of three or four, each team with a captain. One of these teams *judges*. The others are instructed to discover among themselves the most unusual thing seen by a team member on the way to school. If there is a disagreement, the team captain decides. And when time expires, the captains present their "discoveries" or ask other team members to do so. The judging team listens, takes notes, and, under the direction of their captain, designates the winner.

4. In an ensuing class the following (more interesting) game may be played. As before, the class is divided into small teams one of which is to judge. This time the teams are asked the most unusual thing that *might* be seen on the way to school.

   Here the teacher may want to limit the choices to real things in the realm of probability. Or she may want to open things up and make no limitations. In either case she should instruct the class and the judging team. Finally, she may want the class to "meet" fictional or historic characters who are doing something (e.g., three pigs picking up bricks, the pied piper practicing a rock song on his "pipes," Buffalo Bill looking for buffalo, Robert Bruce watching a spider spin its web).

Take Apart (Sustained Analysis)

Your favorite sandwich. Your favorite Dessert. Breakfast. Dinner. A Big Mac. A fishing rig. Your favorite outfit to wear; shoes, socks, everything seen. A favorite story, into three action segments. The contents of a purse into three or four groups of things. The observation, "It's cold outside." A flashlight. One dollar a) into dimes, b) into nickles, c) into quarters, d) into half dollars, e) into pennies, f) into the fewest number of all coins, but including each denomination.

It's Like (Analoging)

1. Try 20 Questions as a team game. (For youngsters, this is a game in which you have 20 questions to uncover a hidden topic.) Two teams, A and B, are in competition. Team C, perhaps with the teacher as a member, selects the topic from the accompanying list or from similar ones that the team might suggest and responds to the questions. The first question goes to the winner of a coin toss.

   That team (lets say A won the toss) can ask questions until it receives a "No" answer, or passes to team B. At this point, team B begins and continues until it receives a "No."

   If one team cannot phrase a question in a reasonable time or asks a question not capable of a yes or no answer, that team receives a "No." and the questioning goes over.

   Clearly, the team that deduces the answer within 20 questions is the winner. If neither of the competing teams solves the problem, the teacher may a) declare the C team winner or b) declare A or B a winner on the basis of fewer No's. Topics:

   Empire State Building (or a prominent building in your area).
   Big Bird
   Window
   VCR
   Oak Tree
   Sesame Street (the street, not the program)
   Bruce Sringsteen
   A sportscaster

2. The M-T Game: The owner of a Mystery Thing gives a solid though often oblique clue to the class and answers each question honestly and fully. Questioners try to discover similarities between the Mystery Material and things that they know. Questioner, for example, may ask, "Is your M–T like a Car?"

Topics	*Possible Clue*
Skis	I go fast on these.
Ice skates	These make me taller.
My Dog Ruffy	This has twice as many as I have.
Teacher's desk	I'm mostly on one side of this.
Bar of soap	Mom makes me grab this.
toothbrush	This makes it hard to talk.
traffic light	This tells my Dad what to do.
fingernail file	Mom carries this.
comb	This is like your mouth.

3. Dune Buggies and Camels:
   The following vehicles are most like what animals?

Golf cart	747	power boat	pogo stick
bicycle	large truck	ocean liner	dune buggie
sled	sports car	destroyer	

Another Way (Suspension of Closure)

If you couldn't brush your teeth, what are other ways (even though inferior) to take care of them? (What "other ways" do dogs and cats use?)

If you couldn't live in the state in which you're now living, which state would you choose?

If you couldn't watch TV, how would you fill in the time?

If you couldn't use a pen or pencil in your writing hand, how would you communicate in writing?

If you could make only one rule that all the class members would have to observe, what would it be?

If you could have 10 dollars to spend today, what would you spend it on? Make a list with the most important (though not necessarily the most expensive) thing first.

Try Out (Autocensorship)

What if;
Cats could fly?
Cars ran on milk instead of gasoline?
The Three Little Pigs built their first house out of bricks?
We were allowed only 4 hours of sleep a night?
School were in session only in the morning — 12 months a year?
Canaries had long, rat-like tails?
We never learned how to read?
The temperature in your part of the country were 10° warmer year
    round?
Milk were pink? (Note all products made with milk.)
Recesses were abolished?

THE FILE

THE FILE

THE FILE

CHAPTER 5

TRANSFERENCE AND RECORDING

Forethought

We insisted earlier that thinking skills mature recursively, and we've come to a point where it will help if we can see a bit more clearly what this assertion implies.

So far, through the primary years, we've concentrated on getting students to call up and exercise their "Point Out," "Take Apart," "It's Like," "Another Way," and "Try Out" skills. Once we've shaken out these skills, our next job will be to employ them in thinking skillfully.

Now we're talking about developing "good thinking skills" and "skillful thinking" as though they were two different things. Admittedly this sounds like a play on words, but it isn't. There really are two different goals here. First we want to make sure that students do possess and can exercise the generic skills. This is our good thinking skills goal. Next, we want to be sure they can orchestrate and apply these skills efficiently on task. This is the skillful thinking goal. First we help students draw the equipment and make sure it's in working order. Then we see if they can regularly hit bullseyes with it.

Suppose we do both jobs well. Students do exercise the generic skills, and then they do come to apply them skillfully to task. The consequence we are most likely to notice when this happens — the one that earns the cheers — is that the task is successfully accomplished; the bullseye is hit. The consequence usually least *noticed, but especially prized by the thinking skill instructor, is that the skills employed have themselves gained strength. Skillful thinking enhances the good thinking skills. In this sense, generic thinking skills have much in common with muscle. Skillful use enlarges them, expands their utility and durability. Here lies the key to the recursive process that the thinking skill instructor does her best to foster. Good thinking skills found a basis for skillful thinking. Skillful thinking matures good thinking skill. Matured skill enables more skillful thinking, and so onward.*

Much of what you do as a thinking skill instructor will be defined by the need to keep this recursion going; to do each of two jobs in a way that enhances the other. You will develop good thinking skills to prompt skillful thinking. Prompt skillful thinking to develop better thinking skills. In this chapter, we consider some issues that rise as we approach this process.

SKILL TRANSFERENCE

Our aim in the primary years is to bring the five generic skills to bloom in the student. We strive to cultivate their vigor in the classroom and root them in the student's personal inclination and satisfaction. The intermediate years will continue this nurturing, but they also initiate something new. This is a time when we begin a careful transplanting; a shifting of the thinking skills into the full light of the student's own consciousness.

There are two reasons for wanting students to be conscious of their own thinking processes; one long range, and one much more immediate. The long-range reason involves the issue of ownership, and it requires a reprise of the thinking skill instructor's goal.

Strictly speaking, good performance does not require process consciousness. It is, for instance, possible to improve all kinds of student thinking performance without requiring that the student understand the processes he or she is perfecting. As long as you—the coach—recognize good thinking performance and know ways to trigger and exercise it in your students, you can often get that performance out of students without bothering with their introspection. Why, then, should we bother?

In the jargon of learning theory, we bother because we want to improve skill transference. This simply means that we want our students to think effectively in situations other than those we design and control in the classroom.

There is an important but frequently overlooked feature of this transference issue. Effective behavior can never simply be transferred from a learned to an unlearned situation. Imagine that you have just successfully taught a youngster to hammer a 3″ nail. She's good at it, and can sink those nails without leaving hammerhead marks on the 2 × 4. So now you hand her a ¾″ brad.

Disaster will be the inevitable result if she simply transfers her 3″ nail-pounding skill to the ¾″ brad. She must modify her hold, her swing, her force, and her wrist action if she's to sink the brad properly. So it is with every skill that moves to an unlearned situation: To be effective, the performance must be modified.

To modify performance, you need control of its components. This is relatively easy where the components, as in nail hammering, are visible, tactile, ostensive. It is not so easy where the components, as in thinking, are normally hidden and left undistinguished. If we want students to transfer their thinking skills effectively, we need to help them discriminate good thinking behaviors well enough to control them. Keep in mind that the capacity for transference is tied to the capacity for control.

When developing thinking skills in students, it's a good idea to now and then ask yourself who really owns the skill. You may bring students to a high degree of performance in some mental task, but if they arrive there solely by following your performance instructions and examples, they are using your skill; ownership remains with you. If, on the other hand, they get there by modifying their own performance in light of an understanding you've helped them achieve about its components, they come to own the skill. The good thinking skill instructor is not satisfied to simply coach good thinking performance. This is the point where our coaching analogy breaks down. The thinking skill instructor's ultimate goal is not to coach players, but to coach self-coachers, capable of taking on any game in town.

The second, more immediate reason we want students to be conscious of their own thinking processes is to improve your access to those processes. Usually, the instructor has to *infer* (*guess* is often the better word) what those processes are from student products — exams, papers, and the like. But as we bring students to better discriminate and express their own thinking processes, your access to those processes — and your ability to assess and direct them — is enhanced.

The thinking skill instructor will invoke two new techniques during the intermediate years that are especially suited to introducing students to their own thinking. Vocalization — thinking out loud — is the first, and we treat that extensively in the next chapter. The second technique involves writing of a special type. We call upon this special writing in the next chapter as well, but a careful look at it now will help us gain perspective.

WRITING

What we are about to say may cause you to stiffen in your chair, so we hasten to assure you that the consequences are not as bad as they might at first appear.

As a thinking skill instructor, you will have an intense concern for and involvement in student writing. You will employ student written work in basically two ways: first, as a means of exposing and exploring student thinking processes, and second, to involve students in one of the most effective behaviors for strengthening thinking skill — intelligent writing.

Odds are, we realize, that you do not teach composition classes and are not a member of an English department. What we've just said in no way handicaps you, nor will it require crash courses in composition or attendance at writing workshops. On the other hand, if you *do* teach composition and *are* an English department member, it will require that you examine your trade from a less usual perspective.

We want to consider writing within the context of fostering thinking skill, and from that perspective it is useful to divide writing into two kinds. There is writing that records, and there is writing that composes.

Of the two kinds, composition is by far the more demanding form, embracing almost all the art and craft of writing as we usually think of it. We devote Chapter 9 exclusively to composition and its function for the thinking skill instructor. You will discover there (happily, we think) that the biology or math teacher with very little literary impulse can, after getting a few distinctions clear, pretty well put composition through its major thinking skills paces.

This leaves us with composition's humble sibling: recording.

RECORDING

You would not be wrong to think of the kind of writing we call "recording" as simply making or taking notes. Recording *is* note-making, and making notes appears to be such a simple, obvious, menial task that it usually receives no attention at all as an object of instruction. It is seldom ever thought of as an instructable form of writing.

As a thinking skill instructor, however, you will come to see that recording is a critical tool for anyone who wants to understand his or her own thinking processes and styles. Beyond this, recording is itself a more complex and powerful behavior than we usually suspect. In its mature forms, the process of note-making calls on all five of our generic thinking skills.

To grasp the value of note-making more clearly, we need to reflect on a special feature of thought.

The food for all thought is experience, and it's important to note that experience, so far as we think about it, quite literally rests in the past. The vast majority of what our minds work on lies between two boundaries: the instant and the distant past.

Imagine, for a moment, an event that happens right now. This instant, my face is slapped. The past (long hours with an unslapped face) informs me that this is an unusual and unexpected event. In tenths of microseconds I'm evaluating that slap and reacting to it. I may slap right back, I may decide I deserve it, I may aloofly turn and walk away. And though I'm convinced I'm dealing with the here and now, in actual fact I'm responding to something already past, with only its fading sting left in my "now." The great bulk of our consciousness is spent dealing with the instant past. The present is merely a source: It hands us new experiences, new pasts to deal with.

Even when my thoughts are on the future—when I try to foresee, imagine, sketch possibilities, control forthcoming events—all those untasted futures are projections from past livings, talkings, readings. I can predict and even prepare for an expected slap, but only by dredging and sifting experience. Our thoughts are always shapings and reshapings of what *has* happened.

For thought to exist at all, then, it must have access to experience, and the mind's sole access is memory. There are other kinds of access to experience, like instinct and habit, but conscious thought requires memory, and the quality of that thought depends significantly on the quality of the memory. Given two minds of equal ability confronting the same task, the one with the better stocked memory respecting that task—able to call on more comprehensive and relevant experience, to offer more precise and useful information—will likely do the better job.

Memory, however, is by itself a limited and chancy repository for experience. Sometimes deliberately, more often by inattention and mischance, we forget. So we bolster memory by recording experience.

Our earliest attempts are efforts to record on ourselves; in effect, to enhance what is often called long-term memory. We connect sounds and repeat them until an extremely complex psychophysical performance becomes automatic—we speak a language. We tick all seven points off on our fingers to make sure we don't forget one. We recite the list ("milk, bread, eggs, TV guide . . . milk, bread, eggs, TV guide. . . . ") on the way to the store.

But history suggests that memory, even when bolstered in these ways, does not by itself lift us very far into culture and society. It was one particular aid to memory, the knack of recording events symbolically—in effect, writing—that gave us a sufficient grip on experience to assure our climb.

Making notes is a brilliant and shockingly simple solution to a profound problem. It captures experience while leaving our memory untaxed and lets us return to an unchanged record so long as the carved tablet or script on paper lasts. Cognition now has access to an expanding universe of experience memory alone could not begin to capture.

By enabling us to fix and store great quantities of experience, note-making multiplies our power to compare and contrast happenings. We spot likenesses and differences that the small stock of unaided memory would never disclose. That is why there could be no science without note-making.

Theory may animate science, but its body is built of endless recordings — notations about how phenomena important to the science behave. Whatever command science wins us over its subject matter, it gains by carefully making, gathering, and manipulating those recordings.

Similarly, we amplify command of our own experience to the degree that we can store it more precisely and make it "hold still." Johnny recalls merely that he spent Saturday afternoon studying in his room. A careful timetable of that afternoon would have shown him that he actually spent a total of 18 minutes on his chapter. Because the three chapter exercises require about 15 minutes apiece, a brief activity log might have told him something important — and correctable — about his study.

Note-making requires and enhances taking notice, which is another way of describing selective attention, and that is why it is a behavior thinking skill instructors want to encourage and sharpen.

First, encourage students to record on their own neurophysiology. Show them how to use their bodies to help their minds. Whenever you, as a teacher, can usefully back a thought with a physical act, do it. Count on your fingers, repeat important points and insights aloud, make hasty sketches on a blackboard and correct them as the issues grow clearer, pace the floor when you're struggling with a tough point. Where it is helpful and not distracting, encourage students to do the same. The idea here is to help students identify the ways they can use themselves to heighten their own attentiveness. Perhaps a given student will decide that sitting stock-still in a soundproof room is most conducive to thought, but let that be a trial-and-error discovery. Talk about your own physical style for thinking and encourage students to search for and develop theirs.

Next, you will want to encourage and improve student recording on paper, and there are several things to consider here.

It helps, in the student's mind as well as yours, to realize that there is a big difference between recording and composing. Writing that *records* aims simply to capture what is salient (useful, relevant) about experience so that the mind has secure and ready access to it. Writing that *composes* seeks to convey a *designed experience to a reader*; it intends to spark in a reader just those insights and sensibilities that the writer means to convey.

You can think of recording as a single-pole concern; you make notes basically for your own anticipated use. Composing, however, is bipolar. You compose when *you* want to influence a *reader* in predetermined ways. Even when you compose for yourself, you compose for yourself as reader; as one for whom the symbols construct a desired experience.

The point is that these two different kinds of writing have quite different aims and abide by different rules. If we fail to note this, we often assign the wrong kind of writing. Many times we ask students to compose when we would be better served to have them record. Students also get confused, not realizing, for instance, that polishing a set of notes can never produce a composition.

The point of note-making is to serve the notemaker, who wields supreme authority regarding what grammar, syntax, and symbol systems should be employed. As an instructor, you can of course negotiate for a response to your needs. You can point out that, when you have to look at the notes, properly spelled words and abbreviations would help. But it's good to keep in mind that you are asking the notemaker for a translation here, and not asserting a superior authority. It's useful for the notemaker to begin with a sense that he or she has full responsibility for creating notes that will do his or her work. It would be especially unwise to invoke the full panoply of language rules that govern composition. They don't apply, save where the notemaker sees a need for them.

There's a good pedagogical reason for fostering the notetaker's autonomy as just recommended. Much in language and math that appears complicated and arbitrary to the young can be seen differently by the fully enfranchised, all-powerful notemaker. The search for better ways to note things can show us why we use words and numbers the way we do. One task notemakers often have to perform is check frequency; record how often something happens. A row of check marks or slashes resulting from such a chore is a good place to demonstrate what's neat about Roman numerals. Attempting to juggle a collection of Roman numerals is a good time to trot out the power of Arabic ones. Likewise, a series of recordings about some happening is often a good basis for examining the virtue of precise and specific language over that which is general and vague. You can compare, "Some kids were fighting in the cafeteria" with "Sally and Janice were trying to grab each other's lunch bag. Timmy stopped them and made them read the names on the bags. They quit: It turned out they each had their own."

The business of making effective notes is one that the thinking skill instructor picks up early and never lays down. It leads naturally to broader issues about collecting, organizing, and sifting information. Remember that you're exercising generic thinking skills, and that they grow recursively. The more we attend to experience, the more information we glean, the more use we have for better ways to capture, organize, and apply data.

Many of the recording tasks and exercises we suggest in the next chapter are well met with lists of phrases and check marks. But soon, new ways of organizing and noting information will arise. A simple empirical question like, "How much of what network television will your family watch next week?" might produce something like this:

	ABC	NBC	CBS	PBS
Programs:	(1,2,3)	(4,5,6,7)	(8,9,10,11,12)	(13,14,15,16)
Mom	1	4,5	10,12	14,15,16
Dad	1,3	5,6	9,10,11	
Philis	3	6,7	8,9,11,12	
George			8,11	15
Tom	2,3	4,7	8,9	13

Here our recording focus has led us to explore the power of a simple matrix for arraying information, disclosing things we might otherwise not notice (Mom hardly watches anything the kids watch), and stimulating an interest in information that's missing (How many TV sets are there, and who controls them?). And this is just the tip of the iceberg: Note-making leads to the whole world of information managing.

As you proceed toward more mature and extensive forms of recording, other challenging problems surface. It's worth observing, for instance, that there's a difference between "note-taking" and "note-making." Your earliest ventures in getting students to record will probably involve their "taking" notes. Here, *you* set the criteria and purpose for their recording; you tell them what to look for in your lecture, say, or reading, and how they might best get it down. In "note-making," the recorder decides on the specific question and, in light of it, what to look for, what to look at, and how best to capture it. It is obvious that the "notemaker," on her way to picking the right information, has to resolve a series of problems. If you follow recording to its more demanding levels, these problems can be among the most challenging we confront.

In fact, if you cling to note-making tenaciously, it will drag you to and through the heights of science and philosophy. What counts as evidence? What does evidence really establish? What distinguishes strong hypotheses from weak ones, good questions from bad? Making that first little scribble in the margin of a text can lead the unsuspecting student, with your guidance, to generic thinking skill employment of the highest order.

That sets the stage for our final comment on recording. It is easy to look condescendingly on the business of students making notes. It can appear to be an automatic, trivial activity hardly worthy of attention. In some cases it appears that way because the students really are capable notemakers, and their efforts no longer require the instructor's conscious attention and guidance. More often, note-making appears to be trivial because it has been so consigned; it is left a desultory part of student behavior of no interest either to student or instructor. In classes where this is true, you can be fairly certain that the development of thinking skill is either an absent or an ill-considered priority.

A note may seem a meek product, but it carries an imprint of the producing mind that is often clearer, more revealing, and less cosmetized than many more elegant products. If the veteran thinking skill instructor seems to lavish undue attention, interest, even eagerness on notes, that is why. Faced by an instructor who questions, prods, advises, praises, and bemoans his notes, a student can hardly avoid the conclusion that, at least to someone, how he thinks matters.

And the need to know how a student thinks — more precisely, what he is able to notice — feeds the thinking skill instructor's interest in student recording. If she can advance the student's capability at this first point where the mind grasps experience — where it attends — she will be giving all the rest of the student's cognitive processing a significant boost. Without an active, noticing mind, none of the rest will follow.

But please, do not confuse note-making or note-taking — both of which involve an active mind judging and recording salience — with the rushed and spastic activity of trying to copy down everything the teacher says.

THE FILE

THE FILE

CHAPTER 6

PHASE ONE ETSI

Forethought

Get comfortable, lean back, and reflect with us for a moment. We're going to examine a simple recipe for the perfect thinking skills program to suit any learner.

We've seen one ingredient already. We need an elementary program that will spark, sanction, and stimulate our learner's use of those components of good thinking behavior, the generic thinking skills: selective attention, sustained analysis, analoging, suspension of closure, and autocensorship.

The major remaining ingredient for our perfect program is rather easy to sketch. All we have to do is line up a series of master teachers, stretching from the intermediate years through graduate school, who will teach whatever they teach in a way that compels our learner to employ and elaborate these same five generic skills.

That accounts for all ingredients save yeast. What we have so far will accustom our learner to good thinking skill. We need something else to ferment these good habits into conscious, self-directed, skillful thinking.

To ignite our learner's own awareness and control, we will need to supply — at least once in the span from intermediate elementary through graduate school — a set of intense, hard-working class sessions explicitly aimed at introducing the learner to his or her own thinking skills, their use, and their cultivation. We need Explicit Thinking Skill Instruction — ETSI — in our recipe.

ETSI

Properly handled, explicit thinking skill instruction can empower a learner in three important ways, and this three-fold empowerment is otherwise hard to achieve. Remember that the aim of ETSI is to increase the learner's *control* of his or her own thinking processes. With effective ETSI, the thinking skill instructor equips the learner with three kinds of control, and we can think of each of these as a new kind of learner dominance:

1. Dominance over Ability. We normally view ability as dominating our capacity to perform. It seems reasonable to assert, for instance, that we think only as well as we're able. Good ETSI stands this proposition on its head. Explicit thinking skill instruction demonstrates to the learner that it's just the business of thinking to make us more able. Yes, even more able to think.

On one hand, an ability to enlarge ability shouldn't seem too surprising. Athletes are completely at home with the notion that they can improve physical ability. They know that self-control expressed as rigorous training pays off. They also know the price when that control is absent; the cost of being out of condition. But, prior to ETSI, we don't readily see evidence that this is true at the cognitive level.

Even the learner who has come to improve her thinking is not likely to credit a change in her ability. We're too engrossed with the products of thinking—conclusions, propositions, solutions—to sense much shift in the intimate process. Consider a person who has just solved a daunting problem. You'd expect a comment like, "I didn't know I had it in me." It would seem a little odd to hear, "I managed to think pretty well that time." The first exclamation implies a fixed, inaccessible ability; the second hints at a bidable capacity.

But after good ETSI, the learner sees thinking as a composite of manageable behaviors. Moreover, she not only sees herself employing these component behaviors, but she sees her teacher and her peers employing them. In fact, she sees them employed *anytime anyone* resolves an issue thoughtfully. For the first time, managing her own ability to think becomes a clear option.

This is a radical and supremely desirable psychological posture for the learner whose thinking skill we want to improve. Achieving it is one of the thinking skill instructor's prime goals. Once it is achieved, learner and ability change roles. Pawn becomes master and master pawn.

Yes, we know. You hear the whisper of contradiction in all of this. We hear it, too. What we've said boils down to the proposition that thinking can improve thinking ability. Ergo, the ability to think determines the ability to think. Isn't there an empty circularity here?

Not if you recall what we said about the recursive nature of the mind's growth. Thought works on its own product, thought, to produce new modes of thought. The ability to think *is* self-enhancing. It's the whisper that's false. The mind happens to really be a bootstrap operation, building new strength out of its own performance. ETSI not only hands the student a capacity to control that process but initiates two corollary, and equally important, kinds of learner control.

2. Dominance over Task.   The learner's dominance over ability leads to a useful kind of dominance over task. Good ETSI not only introduces the learner to the components of good thinking but shows the learner that those components do different jobs. There is a sense now of a set of mental tools with distinct capabilities.

Without this sense of mental tools with discrete strengths, the thinking task tends to dominate—quite often intimidate and mislead—the thinker. The problem or situation makes its blunt demand: "Deal with me!" We either retreat, or scramble indiscriminately to respond, grasping for anything that might work.

Having no clear sense of options in our thinking—no feel for our tool kit—explains a good deal of our appetite (hunger, often) for recipes, algorithms, and other kinds of "how to" lists. I may have no understanding of what division *is*, but if you can show me the six steps I need to divide, I'll get by. Those steps tell me how to respond. The task here dominates my performance, but at least I can satisfy that task. Wouldn't it be great if you could also give me the three steps to happiness, or the nine to beauty, or the seven to wealth?

But with a sense of discrete mental capabilities there comes a sense of option in responding to task, and that sense of option sponsors what could well be the most critical act of the capable mind: task assessment. "What," asks the capable mind, "does this task really require of me? Will some rote response, some list, some well-rehearsed performance dispense with it, or does it ask more?" These are the first steps on the path to the secret strength of the master mind, which is to carefully diagnose thinking demands before responding to them. Either tacitly or explicitly, the masterful mind will be found making statements like this: "I can't give you a good answer to that question unless you clear up two ambiguities, and even then I'll have to raise three topics you don't mention. One of those three I'm clear about, but I'll have to do some work on the other two." Thinking at its very best *is* exercising control over task. Good ETSI initiates and disposes to that kind of thinking.

3. Dominance over Experience.   At first this may strike you as a peculiar, even trivial, kind of control, but among other things it minimizes what could be a major stumbling block for the thinking skill instructor.

By giving the learner a conscious grasp of component thinking skills, good ETSI supplies the learner with a radical new perspective on her myriad past performances as a thinker. It is helpful to recall that, prior to any thinking skill instruction, the learner has thought successfully. She can now view her best work as the product of a handful of capabilities wielded again and again, rather than as the random "happenings" they once appeared to be. She can understand her worst work in light of mismanaging those same capabilities.

A great deal that is useful follows from this. It is not quite true that the past — what *has* happened — is changeless. The past changes dramatically and powerfully the moment we apply new understanding to it. "Aha! *That's* why!" is usually the result of an adept reshuffling and reinterpretation of something we once set aside as fixed and finished. When we truly "learn from experience," it's because such a re-examined past validates a new insight. We very much tend to underrate the role of this self-induced restructuring in a learner's progress.

The easy, but far too shallow, view of learning holds that it is a process of consuming new input, of *adding* to what we already know. Almost all our efforts as educators minister to this view. Yet much of our most precious and powerful learning involves the old and not the new. It happens when we confront present holdings with new insight.

When the learner comes to see his own thinking history as the play of distinct skills, this new view of past performance can have much of the impact, and do much of the job, of new training. If 6 weeks of problem-solving exercises can tilt us toward a new thinking skill, why not a reconstructed understanding of 5, 10, or 50 years of past thinking experience?

The ability we have to govern experience by reinterpreting it, and to let our own pasts, newly seen, re-educate us, helps unravel an aggravating problem for the thinking skills instructor. The problem rises when we walk into class and discover that part of our students have been exposed to sound, systematic thinking skill instruction, and part have not. How do we bridge this disparity in thinking skill development?

Properly employed, ETSI can quickly narrow the gap. First of all, we should recognize that what we have here is mostly a gap in consciousness about processes that both the initiate and the newcomer employ. The experienced thinkers control these processes; the inexperienced don't. And it is just the point of ETSI to develop the kind of control over process that constitutes skill. The business of mixing students well tutored in thinking skill with those who aren't really isn't the same as mixing students with disparate knowledge of a discipline. The student with no exposure to algebra introduced to Algebra III has not been unconsciously doing algebra all his life.

Second, good ETSI is so constructed that those who can and those who can't deal extensively with, and gain solid benefit from, one another. Clarifying the differences between the versed and unversed thinker is just what ETSI is about.

Third and perhaps most importantly, ETSI awakens and employs the capacity to control experience we've just described. With a new perception of thinking skill, the previously untutored learner gives new voice to his past experience. This new voice—ratifying and strengthening new insight—can vastly speed the process of "catch-up."

Faced with classes of students with mixed experience, the thinking skill instructor will need to adjust some and adapt, but the adjustment is minimal and good ETSI is a great leveler or, more accurately, "raiser." What differences persist are more likely to be pedagogically useful than disruptive.

Apparently, we face another paradox. In teaching thinking skill, as in teaching anything else, it's best if everyone starts at the beginning. Clearly, it helps if we've encouraged good thinking behavior in *all* our students, by stimulating and rooting those habits of mind that underpin effective thought. The early elementary program we've described is so dedicated. But it is important to distinguish *good thinking behavior* from *skillful thinking*. Skillful thinking *begins* when the thinker perceives, favors, and controls good thinking behavior, and that is ETSI's goal. Oddly enough, then, whether the student is well or poorly schooled in good thinking behavior, ETSI *does* start at the beginning in respect to awakening the skill of managing thought. The difference is in the trauma that awakening will cause. Those well schooled in the generic skills will have apt tools to control; the poorly schooled will have deficient ones, with new cause to remedy the deficiencies.

We said earlier that our ideal thinking skills program would expose the learner to ETSI *at least once*. We need to do it at least once to be sure that the learner can achieve dominance over (a) ability, (b) task, and (c) experience. But obviously it would be better to do it more often— periodically, in fact. And there is definite call for ETSI whenever (a) students have had no prior systematic thinking skill instruction or (b) you face a mixture of students who have and students who haven't.

Now that we've seen what good ETSI is supposed to do, let's examine what it is. The sample we've caught here happens to be unfolding in a fifth-grade classroom.

ETSI PART I: EXAMPLE

"Hello, Class. Today we begin to study something we all do. We're going to study how you and I think.

"First, I'm going to show you how *I* can think. *My* teacher has assigned me a problem, and I'm going to solve it in front of you. So that you can follow what I'm doing, I've put the problem on the board, here, behind me. Now, I don't want you to do anything but watch and listen."

(The problem on the board could be practically anything, as long as it's within the skill range of the students, yet requires too many steps to solve at a glance. The one *this* teacher has put on the board is: *Cathy knows French and German, Sandra knows Swedish and Russian, Cindy knows Spanish and French, Paula knows German and Swedish. If French is easier than German, Russian is harder than Swedish, German is easier that Swedish, and Spanish is easier than French, which girl knows the most difficult languages?*[10]

What our teacher does next is pull a copy of *Sports Illustrated* out of his briefcase and toss it on his desk. Then he lifts up a ghetto blaster, slips in a rock cassette, and flicks it on. "I've got to keep this low or Mom'll be all over me," he explains. He lounges in his chair, feet on the desk, and starts to move with the music. He picks up a sheet with the problem on it and gives it a quick silent read. Then he begins aloud.

He puzzles through the first few words straight: "Cathy knows French . . . and German. . . . Oh, brother." He starts again, this time picking up the music's beat: "Kathy knows French, Kathy knows German. Sandra knows Swedish, Sandra knows Russian. Cindy knows Spanish, Cindy knows French. . . ." He tosses down the paper.

"Man, I don't know *any* girls who speak those languages. The ones I know just speak *a lot*. There's that Cindy who never quits. . . . and Mary. Ooo-hoo! She talks with everything she's got!"

The teacher idly soaks up a few more beats and then grabs the *Sports Illustrated*, flipping it open. "Dig that Gretsky. His puck's in the net and he hits the boards. I'd like to make a puck talk like that, but instead I've got girls and girl talk." He picks up the beat again. "Most *dif*-fi-cult, most *dif*-fi-cult. Who . . . knows . . . the most *dif*-fi-cult?"

"OK, let's see. 'Kathy knows French and German. . . .' What's it say about French and German? Ah, so. 'French is easier than German . . .' That don't help. Wait. Here's German again. 'German is easier than Swedish. . . .' A*ha*! So Swedish is harder than German and German is harder than French. Let me check those gals again. Sure E-nough! Ole Paula, here, knows Swedish and German, and that's tougher than German and French. Paula's my *gal*!"

---

[10]The problem items employed in this guide could have simply been concocted. Instead, wherever possible, they have been drawn from Whimbey and Lockhead, *Problem Solving and Comprehension*, and sometimes slightly modified. This first item appears on p. 49 of that work.

The teacher jumps up, punches a hip hard one last time, and snaps off the portable player.

"All right, students. Forget about my answer and whether it's right or wrong. What do you think about the way I think?"

The teacher now stimulates the class to make any and all observations it chooses to about his performance. He does not, however, "lead" the class toward making "right" observations: no question like, "Did I concentrate enough?" He does affirm accurate observations wherever he can, and he prods students who make vague observations to make them more precisely, in greater detail. He's pleased to hear what the students have to say and is earnest and conspicuous about taking notes, occasionally asking the class to hold up a minute while he gets something down. When the class exhausts its comments, he begins again:

"All right. You've seen one way I can think. Now let me show you another."

(In this second demonstration, our teacher will of course model sound use of the generic skills. But wherever possible, his modeling will incorporate what he actually does do when he wants to give a problem his best shot. One thing he wants to convey in this next performance is that some things are optional in good problem solving, and some things aren't. When he does something optional, he spends a few words pointing that out. For instance, if our teacher is a pacer, he might say, "When you solve problems in class, you have to sit still so you don't disturb others. Some people find it works best to sit still even when they're alone. But when I'm alone, I like to walk while I think about a problem." Our teacher this day, however, doesn't like to walk. He perches on the edge of his desk.)

"Sometimes I think best sitting in a chair. But when I first consider a tough problem, I like to get up, flop on a couch, sit on the floor with my back to the couch, or lean on a desk. It makes me feel freer — less boxed in."

The teacher flicks the cassette player back on. "Some people like to turn on music to drown out other distractions while they think. I can't do that." He flicks the player off. "I like good music too much. My mind gets into music when I play it, so I lose concentration and my thinking gets sloppy."

"But I'm right where I want to be, now, leaning against this desk with a copy of the problem in my hand. And the first thing I've got to do is find out just what this problem is, so I read it."

The teacher carefully reads the problem aloud.

"Wow. I'm confused. All I got from that reading is that this is about some girls who know some languages, and some languages are easier than others, and I'm supposed to tell what girl knows the hardest languages. I'd better read it again."

The teacher begins once more, reading aloud slowly:

" 'Cathy knows French and German, Sandra knows Swedish and Rus-

sian, Cindy knows Spanish and French, Paula knows German and Swedish.
. . .' Wait a sec. Let me check that. Cathy . . . Sandra . . . Cindy . . . and
Paula. . . .Yes. Each girl knows two languages. Right?"

(The teacher addresses that question rhetorically to the class. He needs to
make certain they understand his observations as he makes them.)

"Let's check." The teacher turns to the board and points. "Cathy: French
and German. Sandra: Swedish and Russian. Cindy: Spanish and French.
Paula: German and Russian. Each has two. Okay. Let's finish reading:

" 'If French is easier than German, Russian is harder than Swedish,
German is easier than Swedish, and Spanish is easier than French, which
girls knows the most difficult languages?' "

The teacher addresses the class. "Boy, I haven't the foggiest. Too many
words. My head can't keep all that straight. I need to break this into smaller
pieces. This, class, is where I have to sit down with a piece of scrap paper
and make some notes. But so you can see what I'm doing, I'll make my
notes on the blackboard."

"Before I write anything, though, let me think what I know about the
problem so far. I know I've got four girls. . . one, two, three, four (the
teacher points). . . and each girl knows two languages. Then the question
tells me that some languages are harder or easier than others — that's the
part I can't keep straight — and I'm supposed to find out which girl knows
the hardest languages. OK. So let me look at the part that's giving me
trouble — the part about the languages I can't keep straight."

The teacher reads the second sentence of the problem aloud again.

"All right. Let's see. There's French, German, Russian, Swedish, and
Spanish. Five languages. But I can't see which is harder and which is easier
by reading that sentence. It would be nice if I could put them in a row, like
the ABCs, or like numbers. Numbers go from smaller to bigger: one–two–
three. I'd like to see those languages in a row, from easier to harder,
one–two–three. Let's see if I can do that."

The teacher begins the troublesome sentence again, one phrase at a time.
" '. . . French is easier than German . . . ' OK. I'll write down French and
German, but I'll leave space between them, because at this point I don't
know where the other languages fit." On the board he writes:

French   German

"Next, it says, '. . . Russian is harder than Swedish . . . ' That means I
have to write "Swedish" in front of "Russian." But I don't know where to
put those in my row, because I don't know whether either one is harder or
easier than French or German. So I'll just write them *under* my row until I
find out more about them." The board now shows:

French   German

Swedish, Russian

The teacher briefly queries to see if the class is still with him. They are.
"Next it says, '. . . German is easier than Swedish . . . ' Well, that helps.
Now I can put Swedish and Russian in my row." The teacher crosses out his
note on Swedish and Russian and adds the two languages to his row:

French   German   Swedish   Russian
~~Swedish, Russian~~

In an aside to the class, the teacher observes, "I could have just erased the
"Swedish" and "Russian" down here, but instead I crossed it out. That way
it's easier for me to look back and see what I've done.
    "Next, it says, '. . . Spanish is easier than French. . . ,' so I know where
I have to put "Spanish."

Spanish   French   German   Swedish   Russian
~~Swedish, Russian~~

"Now I have all the languages in a row, from easiest to hardest. And if I
write down the girl's names, I can show which languages each girl knows:"

Spanish   French   German   Swedish   Russian
~~Swedish, Russian~~
    Cathy   Sandra   Cindy   Paula

The teacher reads each girl's name with her pair of languages, drawing
lines between the two rows as he goes until he has:

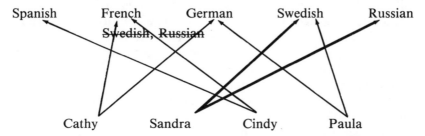

"Well, it's easy to see the answer now. Swedish and Russian are the two
hardest languages, and (here the teacher redraws Sandra's lines for emphasis) *Sandra* is the only girl who knows those two.
    "But now I see I could have done this another way. I said I put those
languages in a row like numbers, from easiest to hardest. I really *could* have
numbered them. The easiest language gets a one, the next easiest a two, and
all the way up, so I'd have a list like this:"

Spanish = 1

French   = 2

German   = 3

Swedish = 4

Russian = 5

"Now all I have to do is add each girl's numbers, and the girl with the highest number knows the most difficult languages. See? Like this:"

Cathy =   2 + 3 = 5

Sandra =   4 + 5 = 9

Cindy =   1 + 2 = 3

Paula =   3 + 4 = 7

"Now I feel pretty good. I've worked the problem two ways, and both times Paula comes out knowing the hardest languages. But let me just make sure I've got it right. I'm going to read from my solution now, and see if it agrees with what the problem says:"

The teacher points here to his row of languages.

"This was the toughest part for me; figuring out which languages were harder than which. So I say Spanish is easier than French. . . ." The teacher now scans the original problem on the board and finds the appropriate phrase. "Yes. It says, '. . . Spanish is easier than French. . . .'" The teacher continues, language by language in his row, to confirm his ordering by the evidence in the problem statement. Next, he checks that the problem statement confirms the languages he's assigned to each girl. "Yep," he concludes, "I haven't made a mistake on which girl knows which languages, so the answer has to be Sandra."

"Now, class, what do you think about the way I solved the problem *this* time?"

The teacher presides over his class's discussion exactly as he did after his first demonstration. He encourages comment, avoids leading questions, and takes careful notes. He tries to keep the student focus on *this last* performance, not on a comparison of the two.

If sufficient class time remained, our teacher would begin the third major part of his demonstration, which is to offer his own analysis of his performance to the class. However, he doesn't have a good 15 minutes left, so he leads the students past their reactions to his last performance into a compare and contrast assessment of his two ways of thinking through a problem, and he takes notes again about what students have to say regarding the differences.

On the next day, with his boardwork either saved or reconstituted, the teacher offers his analysis. Wherever possible, he employs the observations his students made during the prior session to emphasize his points.

"I'd like to talk about my two ways of thinking last class session. Remember what Phyllis said about my first performance? She said I didn't seem to *care* whether I solved the problem or not. She's right. The first time I didn't seem to care, and the second time I did."

Finding a clear spot on the blackboard, our teacher writes:

1. Good problem solvers *want* to solve problems. Bad problem solvers don't.

"The first time I didn't care as much about the problem as I did about my music and my magazine. The second time, I cared enough to set aside, for awhile, everything else I care about.

"Maybe I didn't care the first time because I wasn't interested. The problem didn't catch my fancy. But that just means I'm not a good problem solver. Good problem solvers bring their own interest to the problem; they don't wait for the problem to interest them.

"Have you ever pretended you weren't interested in something because you were afraid you couldn't do it well? Maybe that's why I wasn't interested the first time. Good problem solvers not only *want* to solve problems. They know they *can* solve them."

The teacher writes again:

2. Good problem solvers believe they *can* solve problems. Bad problem solvers aren't sure.

"The second time I wanted to solve the problem, and I was sure I *could* solve it. Why was I sure? I was sure because I knew I could call on the team."

Once more the teacher writes:

3. Good problem solvers call on the team:

"What team? You mean you don't know you have a team? Didn't you see my team when I solved the problem that second time? Of *course* we each have a good thinking team. Maybe I'd better introduce you to the members."

"I called on the first member of my team even before I read the problem. In fact, I called on him the first second I knew I had a problem to solve."

" 'Attention,' I said, 'focus on this.' "

"He said, 'What's up, boss?' "

"I said, 'We've got a problem.' "

" 'Oh, great, boss,' he said. 'I'll scoot around and turn off your other interests, kick out the distractions, and we'll get you ready to look at the sucker.' "

"Now I had my attention focused, and he's hot when he's focused. He becomes a skill, then, and I call him 'Selective Attention.' He turned off the music, got the room quiet, and led me to a comfortable spot where I could lean against the desk."

" 'OK, boss,' he said, 'Let's read the problem, c'mon, let's read the problem!' "

The teacher makes an addition to item 3 on the board:

> 3. Good problem solvers call on the team:
>   A. Selective Attention: The focus manager.

"I didn't call on Selective Attention the first time I handled the problem. I let my attention go where he wanted, and he was into rock music, magazines, and anything that popped into my head. But now I've got him on the job and he's set me up to read the problem. Getting me set up, he woke the rest of the team, and they're starting to peek over my shoulder.

"At this point I called on the team's toughie."

" 'Analysis,' I said, 'you like to take things apart. We've got a problem coming up, and I want that baby totally uncoupled, with every last piece laid bare.' "

" 'Just let me at 'em,' Analysis rumbled."

"I have to be careful with Analysis. On his own, he tends to pry a few pieces off something, then drop the whole mess and go on to something else. But when I talk to him like I just did, he turns into a bulldog and won't let go. He's so determined he becomes a skill, called 'Sustained Analysis.' "

Item 3 on the board now becomes:

> 3. Good problem solvers call on the team:
>   A. Selective Attention: The focus manager.
>   B. Sustained Analysis: The dismantler.

"With Selective Attention holding the focus, Sustained Analysis takes a quick first pass through the problem."

" 'What we've got here,' he says, 'is a problem about some girls who know some languages, and we have to figure out which girl knows the most difficult ones.' "

" 'Fine,' I say. 'Let's take a closer look.' "

"Analysis begins on the problem again, just starting to get a feel for some parts, when Selective Attention tugs on his sleeve."

" 'Hey,' Selective Attention says, 'you've turned up something that caught my eye. Let's just concentrate on this first sentence for a moment.' "

"Selective Attention does this kind of thing all the time. It's his business to look for new patterns, things that don't fit, anything at all that stands out. When he finds something, he puts a spot on that and dims the lights on everything else."

"What caught his eye this time was a *sameness* in the problem. Analysis found that Cathy had two languages, and then that Sandra had two languages. Selective Attention said, " 'Whoa. Let's check this out.' "

"Analysis showed that, in fact, each girl knew two languages. We filed that information away, with no idea yet whether it would be useful. Selective Attention turned down the spot on that issue and raised the lights back on the rest of the problem."

"Analysis starts poking at the second half of the problem, and I begin to feel uneasy. Just then, a new member of my team blows a whistle, and we all stop."

" 'You're confused.' says the new member."

" 'You're right,' I answer."

"Now, this new member is really interesting. She's a little bossy and has a funny name, and maybe the best way to introduce her is tell you what she does."

"She's a kind of quarterback. Whenever I or anyone on my team gets confused, is unsure of themselves, or thinks someone might have made a mistake, she stops the action right in midstride. Then she makes us look at where we've been, what we're planning to do, and whether it's really the best way to go."

"At first, we had trouble working with her. The rest of us want to dig in and get a problem over with. It's annoying to have someone blow the whistle on you. But we soon learned she was playing on our side. Although we all want to get it done, she wants to get it done *well*."

"Remember the first time I tackled this problem? I didn't listen to her then. When I finally got around to the problem, I just held my breath and dove in. I let Analysis kick around a few pieces of the problem till I saw something that looked like an answer, snatched it, and got out as quick as I could."

"But this little gal makes us stop. She puts us back in the huddle, makes us rethink what we've done, correct things if we have to, and then sends us back into play. Some people signal when they're done with something by saying, 'I've got closure,' so we've come to call this lady, 'Suspension of Closure.' "

Now item 3 reads:

3. Good problem solvers call on the team:
   A. Selective Attention: the focus manager.
   B. Sustained Analysis: the dismantler.
   C. Suspension of Closure: the action stopper.

"Well, Suspension of Closure had us stopped now, and after pointing out I was confused, she asked me to reflect on what the trouble was."

" 'I can't get all these 'harder' and 'easier' languages straight,' I said."

" 'What are you going to do about it?' she asked."

" 'I suppose I'll just let Analysis keep banging away at it,' I said."

" 'Good idea,' Selective Attention says."

" 'Just let me at 'em, boss,' Analysis says."

" 'One minute, guys.' Suspension of Closure has this snippy way of butting in. 'Before you get back to it, give me a run-down on what we've got so far.' "

" 'Well,' I say, 'we've got four girls, and each girl knows two languages.' I show the team and they all nod. 'Then we've got this sentence that tells us some languages are harder or easier than others—that's where I get confused. And we're supposed to find out which girl knows the hardest languages.' "

" 'Let's concentrate on that sentence about the languages!' Selective Attention says."

" 'Yeah,' Sustained Analysis says. 'I'll take 'er apart!' "

" 'Hold it,' Suspension of Closure says. 'There are all kinds of ways to take something apart. Just how are you going to handle this, Analysis?' "

" 'Uh, I dunno,' says Analysis. 'I got to see which language is harder than which. Just let me at 'em.' "

" 'We'd better get Analoging in on this,' says Suspension of Closure."

"Just then she was calling in another member of the team. 'Analoging' means pointing out how things are alike. Analoging is in charge of all my files. He has access to everything I know and everything I've done. What he does is check those files to see if he can find anything there that's like what I'm trying to do now."

The teacher adds the new member:

3. Good problem solvers call on the team:
   A. Selective Attention: the focus manager.
   B. Sustained Analysis: the distmantler.
   C. Suspension of Closure: the action stopper.
   D. Analoging: the comparer.

" 'Well,' says Analoging, 'if you want to see which language is easier and which harder, it looks like a job of putting things in order, lining things up.

You've all done a lot of lining up before: Halloween candy in piles from favorite to less favorite, shoes from newest to oldest, books alphabetically, by the first letter of the author's last name, and numbers from smallest to largest. It would be nice if these languages lined up like numbers, but from easiest to hardest. Number one would be the easiest language, number two would be the second easiest, and so on.' "

" 'What do you think?' asks Suspension of Closure."

" 'Sounds good,' Selective Attention says."

" 'Let me at 'em,' Sustained Analysis adds."

" 'It's worth a try,' say I."

"Analysis now gets to serious work and puts the languages in a row for me. All we have to do is connect the right pairs up with the girls and we've got our answer. Then, just as I spot that Sandra is my answer and I'm about to wrap things up, the whistle blows again."

" 'Very good,' says Suspension of Closure. 'Looks like you've got an answer.' "

" 'Yep,' I say. 'I think we did it.' "

" 'Well, before you send us to the showers, let me mention that we might be able to do this another way. Selective Attention and Analoging have been whispering to each other, and I think we should hear what they have to say.' "

" 'Well,' Selective Attention says, 'when Analysis was picking out two languages for each girl, the ones further to the right counted for more—they were harder. It reminded me of something.' "

" 'It should,' Analoging chips in. 'It's very much like adding. In fact, you *could* solve the problem by adding. Just number your languages from left to right. It's like giving each language a point every time it's harder than another language. Now you just add the numbers for each girl's pair of languages, and the girl with the highest number knows the toughest languages.' "

" 'Sounds reasonable,' I say. 'Let's try it.' "

"We do try it. And the answer we get, again, is 'Sandra.' "

" 'That's great, team,' I say. 'We worked it two ways and got the same answer. We've nailed this one. Well, till next time, I. . . .' "

"The whistle blows again. I look at Suspension of Closure and she's pointing a finger at the last member of the team, who so far hasn't said a thing."

"This fellow steps forward with a pained expression on his face. He's used to my almost forgetting him. 'You think you have the answer?' he quietly asks."

" 'Well . . . sure. We did it two different ways, and. . . .' "

" 'What if you made the same mistake twice?' he asks calmly."

" 'But we . . . oh, all right. I guess we'd better check.' "

" 'Take every element of your solution and make sure it fits the information in the problem,' he instructs."

"We do that, and when we're finished I say, maybe a little uppity, 'It all checks out.' "

" 'So you've got an answer.' he says, 'What are you going to do with it?' "

"Now I really get a little huffy. 'I'm going to write it on my exercise sheet and hand it to my teacher.' "

" 'Does he just want the answer, or does he want to see the steps?' "

" 'He wants the steps. I'm going to write the steps.' "

" 'What about your notes?' "

" 'He said we could add our notes if we want to.' "

" 'Better add the notes.' "

" 'OK. I'll clip on the notes. Satisfied?' "

" 'No. What problems were you assigned?' "

" 'Oh, for cryin' out loud! I was assigned 1, 3, and 4. This is problem 4.' "

" 'Remember 2 weeks ago?' "

" 'I knew you just had to bring *that* up.' "

" 'You handed in problem 7. Right answer, wrong problem.' "

" 'I know, I know. It pays to check. Here's my assignment sheet. "Do 1, 3, and 4.' "

" 'I don't like waste,' he says, and steps back with the rest of the team."

"This guy is harder to get to like than Suspension of Closure. He's called Autocensorship, and he keeps wanting me to check everything I do just when I think I'm finished. And not just whether I see the right *answer*, but whether I see the right *problem*. I have to say, though, whether I like him or not, I'm glad he's on my team."

The teacher completes item 3:

3. Good problem solvers call on the team:
   A. Selective Attention: the focus manager.
   B. Sustained Analysis: the dismantler.
   C. Suspension of Closure: the action stopper.
   D. Analoging: the comparer.
   E. Autocensorship: the checker.

"It isn't just that Autocensorship has kept me from handing the wrong assignment into class. He makes me check the problems I handle elsewhere. Once I was trying to solve the problem of how to keep my mother from finding out I'd busted the sugar bowl. He helped me see that wasn't the right problem. My real problem was finding the guts to tell her."

"So that's it, class. I've introduced you to my five team members, but that's all I've done. Just barely introduced you."

"You have the same members on your good thinking team. We're going to introduce you to your own teams next, and more. You'll find out just what each member can do for you."

ETSI PART I: EXAMPLE REVIEW

The first thing we should affirm about our example to this point is that it is neither the best nor the worst we might have chosen. It is a passable opening for an explicit thinking skill instruction segment. We can't call it excellent, because that quality depends heavily on how perceptively the instructor has read the students in his class, and how well he's tailored his instruction to fit that reading. Because we don't know the class, it's hard for us to judge.

We can call it passable, however, because it addresses and emphasizes those things that an introductory ETSI session should address and emphasize.

First of all, notice the radically new role of the specific problem in this ETSI introduction. It is simply a stage we erect on which the various thinking skills can visibly perform. In most other classroom appearances, the problem and its solution dominate. Conquering the problem usually represents the peak of student performance. Here, and throughout ETSI, the problem is context for the real work. The peak of student performance in ETSI is new discrimination about, and new capacity to direct, one's own thinking behavior.

Second, the teacher introduces the unusual idea of exposing one's thinking—of making it public—by *doing* it. Explanations of why such exposure is useful and observations on how important and uncommon it is would simply make the prospect more awesome for the student.

Third, the teacher models two approaches to the problem, one unsound and one sound. This tactic offers the students the clear purchase of comparison, always a nice thing to have when confronted with the unfamiliar. But beyond that, it establishes important premises without laboring them. The teacher has made it quite clear that there are different ways to think, and that some ways are better than others.

Fourth, the teacher has very quickly sanctioned a new kind of dialogue for students; talk about thinking. He gets them to comment on his thinking performance right after he models it. He rewards that discourse immediately in the little, but oh-so-powerful, ways a teacher has: by being attentive, supportive, and taking good comment seriously enough to note. He distributes greater reward later, by using student insights wherever he can to bolster his own observations.

Fifth, and very admirably, the dialogue our teacher has sanctioned thus far has an important quality. It neither theorizes nor psychologizes.

Students aren't struggling with thinking skill models, nor are they rapping about how it feels to think. They are trying to *make clear* specific examples of problem solving. Throughout ETSI, the thinking skill instructor wants to sharpen this student appetite to *make clear*. He does not want to dull it with premature theory or dissolve it in self-exploration. When that appetite grows insistent about theory, he gives just as little as he can.

Sixth, he's neatly managed to emphasize his good thinking model by using it twice: first to solve the problem, and second to introduce the generic skills.

Seventh, our teacher has avoided formal introduction of the generic skills. He says as little as possible about them, preferring rather that the students get to know them at work. It's a bit like meeting the proprietor of a local garage. "Glad to meet you. I'm Butch," he says. "That's Joe under the Chevy's hood. Tom's swinging the transmission over there, and Bob's out at the pump." You haven't really been introduced, but you're already forming a sense of what the men do. What the generic skills do, and how they do it, are the themes our teacher chooses to emphasize from the beginning.

Eighth, our teacher has made it clear, through comment, through his listing on the board, and most importantly through his modeling, that disposition and confidence are key to successful thinking.

Our teacher has also made some questionable calls, and he's done this consciously. There's no escaping risk in teaching. He's decided to name the generic skills by using their arcane, unfamiliar, and somewhat clumsy "learning theory" labels: Selective Attention, Sustained Analysis, Analoging, Suspension of Closure, and Autocensorship. If this had been a third-grade class, he'd probably have stuck with something like our elementary labels: Point Out, Take Apart, It's Like, Another Way, and What If. But he chose to use the clumsy terms, adding simple if not entirely accurate translations, for two reasons.

He judged that the unfamiliarity of the terms would help prevent the students assuming a too-ready familiarity with the skills. Comfy or kid-like labels, he feared, would promote a premature condescension, a feeling that, "Oh, yeah, anyone knows what *that* is." Also, although he had no intention of spouting theory to impress with his superior knowledge, he felt that an easy deployment of these strange labels might usefully project a sense of his having a store of expertise. Events in class could change his mind about either or both of these calls.

He also decided to personify the generic skills—pretend they were a team of individuals—rather than just straightforwardly point out their function in his problem modeling. This little act certainly isn't essential to an ETSI introduction. But he felt a touch of drama might stimulate some useful first impressions and discourage some unproductive ones.

He wanted to distance himself and his class from the notion that the generic skills are a problem solving "how to" list. "Here are the five things you must do to solve a problem: one, two, three, four, five." He did want to convey that the skills are somewhat idiosyncratic, and that they do cooperate, but not in predetermined or necessarily predictable ways. Each generic skill expresses an appetite and an agency of its own, and they work together best much as a team works best—when the members understand and enlist one another's distinctive capabilities. The team caricature also nicely foreshadows the student's forthcoming challenge, which is to captain such a set of capabilities.

There are numberless other ways to achieve all these goals. The only thing our example teacher did that anyone who wants to introduce ETSI must do is clearly line up the objectives of an ETSI introduction and carefully pick what seem to be the best means of achieving them. Here is the core of the lesson plan our example teacher worked from:

I. Explicit Thinking Skill Segment.
  A. Introduction.
    1. Objectives:
      a. Cause students to contrast unsuccessful and successful thinking performance so as to. . . .
      b. Highlight the following qualities of effective thinking:
        (1) Motivation
        (2) Confidence
        (3) Component skills:
          (a) Selective Attention
          (b) Sustained Analysis
          (c) Analoging
          (d) Suspension of Closure
          (e) Autocensorship
      c. Note factors that aid and inhibit good thinking, especially:
        (1) Choosing and controlling work setting
        (2) Handling distractions
    2. Method:
      a. Present and explore "good" and "bad" examples of problem solving. (I'll do this by modeling each for class. Can incorporate goal c. here.)
      b. Elicit student comments on examples.
      c. By comparing "good" and "bad" examples, highlight qualities of effective thinking. (Can model confidence and motivation. By running through "good" example again, I'll point to component skills. Note where missing in "bad" example.)

3. Evaluation:
   No required student performance or product in this phase. But
   need to assess student comments and feedback following modeling
   to see how effectively I've suggested:
   a. Thinking is variable and can be controlled.
   b. We can talk about and examine thinking.
   c. Thinking involves distinct, explorable skills.

As a lesson plan outline for the introductory phase of ETSI, something
like the preceding would prove adequate as a guide for *any* level of
instruction, from third grade through graduate school. It will flesh out
differently at various grade levels, but surprisingly, the differences will not
be as great as you might at first imagine.

At third grade, for example, one would pick a simpler problem on which
to base the problem-solving examples and, as already suggested, use simpler
terms for the component skills. But our fifth-grade example could "play"
almost in its present form at the high school level. Introductions very much
like it have been used effectively at the Masters degree level.

The ETSI example we're inspecting is applicable across such a broad
range because it does a job that is unprecedented in most students'
experience, regardless of age. Taking a close look at how one thinks
effectively does not have to be complex or highly embellished to be "new."
More mature students find it provides a unique vantage, rich enough for
fresh insight, even when couched in simple terms.

The primary adjustment we could make for older students in our sample
introduction would be to lean more on verbal example and a bit less on
demonstration. We might, for instance, list the five generic skills and
discuss each in terms of instances of its use, rather than "discover" them in
a modeled problem solution. We *could* make this shift because the more
mature language skills of older students let them more easily draw example
from discourse. However, we don't necessarily counsel this shift. It's really
a question of your teaching style. But whether acted out, or verbally
described, examples are critical. They vastly reduce the load exposition has
to bear.

The point is that our sample introduction, with relatively minor alter-
ations, is easily and broadly generalizable. That will continue to be the case
throughout ETSI. Why this is so becomes clearer as we inspect Phase II.

THE FILE

THE FILE

CHAPTER 7

PHASE TWO ETSI

Forethought

We need to place a warning label on our upcoming example of explicit thinking skill instruction. There is a serious danger that the more obvious features of our example will lead to its being misconstrued. The example, for instance, will heavily employ problems of the kind used in our ETSI introduction and commonly found in IQ tests: verbal reasoning, analogy, trend and pattern analysis, and math story problems. A cursory glance at all this problem-solving activity could convince you that the purpose of ETSI is to develop intelligence test problem-solving skills. It is not.

The purpose of ETSI is to establish and maintain a thinking-intensive environment that will prompt the use and exposure of operant thinking skills. This is ETSI's unwavering, dominant goal, and it governs all its permutations. It happens that at the beginning of ETSI this purpose is best served by working with single-answer, relatively unambiguous, IQ test-type problems. The initial ETSI unit we are now exploring concentrates on these. But as ETSI matures, it will raise many other cognitive challenges in its thinking-intensive environment: anomaly detection and analysis, purpose assessment and action planning, to name just a few task-oriented activities.

If we were looking for an archetypal task for cognition — something that was meant to represent the mind's higher order skills facing their toughest challenge — solving short, carefully phrased written problems would be a very poor choice. We would want an archetype that submerged the mind in confusion, emotion, conflicting special inter-est, flawed and erroneous information, contradiction, insufficient time, and inadequate resource. Solving verbal reasoning problems is a very narrow, very artificial, and in many ways inadequate paradigm of the work life sets before the mind.

But IQ-type items serve as an excellent test tube from which to precipitate and examine the skills that cognition will take to its real work. This kind of problem solving offers a superior way to launch our explicit thinking skill venture. The launching, however, should not be seen as the total voyage. Some workbook-bound thinking skills packages seem to suggest it is.

There are a few other things we should realize about problems and how the thinking skill instructor uses them.

We often tend to use the word "problem" in a very loose way. We assign a sheet of exercises and say, "Here are your problems for tomorrow." Careful inspection of that sheet will often fail to reveal a single real problem. Most likely, the sheet contains questions and instructions designed to elicit what a student knows or can do, and if the student knows it or can do it, there is no real problem.

Among those items he can't answer, the student usually finds clear indications of what it is he has to know or be able to do. Now he must go to the text or notes and recover the knack or the knowledge. These aren't problems either. They are chores, useful chores, one hopes, but not strictly problems.

A real problem will cause puzzlement no matter how trivial it is or how much one knows, because it comes in the guise of being intractable, unmanageable. A problem for you is a difficulty that hides its mode of resolution from you. The first thing a mind must do with a real problem is to penetrate that guise, tear away the unmana-geable facade, and reveal the mechanics of the difficulty. That, preeminently, is a task that requires managing the operant skills. So the thinking skill instructor spends considerable time shopping for such camouflaged difficulties. She mulls puzzles, conundrums, un-usual tasks, games, and confusing story problems to see what kinds of mental operations they will trigger on the way to resolution.

Thinking skill instructors seem always to be doing this, and it's worth asking why. You can easily buy workbooks full of "problems" such as, for instance, the one we employed in Phase I. Or, if you're parsimonious, you can sit down after you've taken that problem apart and write 20 just like it yourself, right?

Wrong, sad to say. Suppose you've fashioned 20 items like the one in our example. Do you have 20 real problems? Not necessarily. Their "problemhood," excuse the expression, lies solely in the eye of the beholder. Put an inexperienced student to work on those 20 items. The first one really is a problem, but with much labor she solves it. The second is less opaque. More easily, but still not sure of herself, she solves that. The third is even less opaque. By the fourth or fifth item, she is no longer solving problems. She's doing exercises.

For the thinking skill instructor, shopping for problems is a complex business. It needs to be done with a fine assessment of the students you're teaching, a feel for what will still be opaque and yet permeable for them. And you make your choices knowing that the true "problem" quality doesn't keep. It evaporates as student perception grows. Once students are skillfully penetrating one kind of facade, you need to find another.

The thinking skill instructor does not disparage exercises. They are useful and she employs them. But only real *problems enable her to fully spark the operant skills and bring them to the open alive and kicking. That's why workbooks and worksheets can't teach thinking skills. They have their place, but it isn't as the cornerstone of the thinking skill venture. We need a wise teacher in that spot.*

ETSI PHASE II: EXAMPLE

Day 2, Continued. We are about to pick up our fifth-grade example where we left off. Recall that midway through his second day of class, our instructor concluded his introductory analysis of his own problem-solving performance. With his introduction now finished, he moves immediately into the real work of ETSI. He picks up a stack of papers and hands one sheet to each student in the class.

Each sheet in the stack has a single problem typed on it. There are really three distinct problems; each sheet bears either "problem #1," "problem #2," or "problem #3," and they are collated in that repeating sequence throughout the stack. A given student will, consequently, receive any one of the following:[11]

Problem #1:
Three pails weigh 6 pounds. Each pail, when full, can carry 12 pounds of Mars bars. How much will 2 full pails of Mars bars weigh?

a. 14 lbs. b.18 lbs. c. 24 lbs. d. 26 lbs. e. 28 lbs. f. 30 lbs.

[11]The following three problem statements are close copies of items found in the WASI pretest that appears on pages 4 through 10 of Whimbey and Lockhead, *op. cit.*

Problem #2:
Circle the letter before the letter in the word violent that appears in the same place in the word as it does in the alphabet.

Problem #3:
You are facing west. You turn right, make an about face and turn left, then make an about face again. Which way are you facing?

  a. East   b. Northwest   c. South   d. West   e. North   f. Can't tell.

"Class, we have, ah, . . . 14 minutes left in today's period. I want you to solve the problem you've received. If you are unclear about anything, puzzle it through on your own. Don't seek help. Do any work or figuring you might need right on the problem sheet and hand your sheets in when the bell rings. If you finish early, treat the remaining time like study period. Keep yourself quietly busy. Next session we'll examine what you've done."

At home that evening, our instructor sorts the turned-in problems. He has 11 each of Problems # 1 and # 2; and ten # 3's. The annotations and scriblings on the problem sheets vary from none to quite a bit, and from relevant to mere doodling. He finds 7 correct answers in stack one, 9 in stack two, and 7 in stack three. He thinks a bit about how he will organize things around his single goal for next class period, which is to get students to tease out the problem-solving approaches they actually employed.

Day 3.   Next period, the instructor begins, "You did quite well, class, but I think I should get the credit for giving you such easy problems, right?"

The class expresses robust disagreement.

"Well, then I have to give you credit for superior problem-solving technique. Before I can do that, however, I need a much better view of your technique, and we're going to take that look today.

"Here's what we'll do. There are three groups in this class: those who did Problem 1, those who did Problem 2, and those who did Problem 3. I'm going to call on several of you to tell us how you solved your problem. If I call on someone, for example, who solved Problem 2, then I want the rest of you Problem 2 solvers to take *careful* notes on how that person solved the problem. Your notes need to be so good that you can repeat to me, step by step, just what the problem solver did. They should also be good enough to let you see whether and where you approached the problem differently. Those of you who aren't a member of the group whose problem we're discussing also have a task. Keep an eye on us and form an opinion of how well we're doing. Ready?"

Our instructor has decided to bite the bullet and call on Tom first. Tom is a very bright loner who participates only to the minimum he can in class, and never with an ounce of warmth. He handed in a Problem #3 sheet with not a mark on it save a short slash under the correct answer.

"Tom, you handed in a correct Problem 3. Tell us how you solved the problem."

Without in the least altering his slouch, Tom says, "The two turns cancel out. So do the about-faces. So you're still facing West."

There's a low murmur with a distinct touch of awe from the class. Even those who don't understand recognize a rapier-like thrust. As he suspected, our instructor has to watch his step here.

"You've described your solution, Tom. What I want to know is how you arrived at it. Let's take it one step at a time. What did you do first?"

"I saw there were two about-faces and two turns, one each way."

"Class, what did Tom do first?. . . What was the first thing he had to do?"

A moment, and then three hands shoot up. The instructor acknowledges one.

"He read the problem."

"Correct. Tom, you had to read the problem. How many times did you read it?"

"A couple."

"All right. Did you read it the same way each time?"

". . . No."

"What was different?"

"I read it first to see what it was. Then I read it to solve it."

"When you read it the second time, what did you do? There are three sentences in that problem. When you read the first one, did you stop and think about it?"

"No. That just said which way you're facing. I went to the second sentence. That's the one that tells you what you do."

"So you concentrated on the second sentence. Tell me what you saw when you did that."

"I saw you did two kinds of things. You turned twice and you did an about-face twice."

"What did you make of that?"

"I told you. They cancel out."

" 'about-face' and 'turn' are just words on paper. They don't cancel anything out."

"They do if you know what they mean."

"Oh! So you recognized what they meant?"

"Sure. About-face means turn to the opposite direction. You do 180°. Turn means change direction. Like 90°."

"OK, so what then?"

"Well, if you do 180° twice, you're back where you started, and if you turn right and then turn left, you're facing the same way too."

"Do you follow, class?" There are several nods and "yeses" from the class. "Well, I see what Tom did, too, but now I think he got the wrong answer. Watch. First I turn right." Our instructor turns a slight 10° to the right. "Now I turn left." He spins a broad 120° to his left.

Tom has his hand up. "I thought of that, but then I figured it wasn't right. It's like when you're driving a car and someone says, 'turn right' and then 'turn left.' They don't tell you 90°, but that's what you do and you end up going in the same direction."

"I see. So to get your answer you have to add something that wasn't in the problem statement. You have to assume that 'turn' means "turn 90°.' "

"Not really. You can turn any degrees one way as long as you turn the same number back."

"Very good, Tom. But the problem doesn't say you turn the same number of degrees both ways. So you have to assume that, right?"

"Right."

"Well, I thought the assumption was reasonable, so when you underlined 'west' in your problem, I marked it correct. No one in the class picked 'can't tell' as an answer to Problem 3, but if they had, I might have marked that correct too. Just as an aside, let me point out that I could only be sure an answer to number 3 was absolutely correct if you wrote something along with your choice. For instance, if you picked 'West,' you might have added, 'Assuming both turns are the same degree,' and if you picked 'Can't tell,' you might have added, 'because the problem doesn't specify how far you turn.' But I didn't ask you to justify your answer, so you have the benefit of the doubt.

"Lisha, you did Problem #3 also. Did you solve it Tom's way?"

"I don't think so," Lisha says.

"Tell us how you went about it."

"I read it a few times just to get the sense of it. But then I started working on it from the beginning. . . ."

"Was that when you did something funny with your hand?"

"You mean like this?" Lisha made a fist, extending her index and middle finger and placing the tips on her desk. Her hand was a miniature standing person. "Yes. I picked what I thought was West and made my hand face it. Then I did each thing the problem told me to and I ended up facing the same way. I did that two more times to make sure I hadn't made a mistake."

"Did you wonder how you should make your turns?"

"No. I didn't think about it." Lisha gave Tom a quick glance. "I just went right angles. Ninety degrees, I guess."

"Excellent, Lisha. It got you a good answer."

Our instructor next called on Joe, another Problem 3 student. His solution closely paralleled Lisha's, though he had just imagined himself facing west and making the moves in turn.

"All right. I'd say you three used your problem-solving teams very well. Remember those odd names? Selective Attention, Sustained Analysis, Analoging, Suspension of Closure, and Autocensorship? Now, the rest of the Problem 3 group has been taking notes, and I want to ask them some questions about how those team members were used.

"From your notes on what our three problem solvers did, can anyone tell me where someone used Selective Attention?"

Hesitation, then finally a hand.

"Tom? When he picked the second sentence to work on?"

"Very good. Tom was drawn to the second sentence because it seemed to hold the heart of the problem. He focused his attention on that and for a time ignored the rest. But did anyone use it earlier?"

Our instructor acknowledges another hand.

"When they read the problem to see what it was about?"

"Exactly right. You use Selective Attention when you push everything else aside and concentrate on the problem to see what it's about. But wait a minute. Is that really using a skill? What else can you do? The teacher hands you a problem and you're going to read it, right?"

There is a nod or two from the class, but no other response.

"Suppose," continues the instructor, "that I'm sitting in the row next to Joan, there, one seat behind her. Teacher hands me Problem #3. I've got sharp eyes and I'm checking to see who gets what. Joan also gets Problem #3. I glance through the problem quickly, but I keep checking Joan. I know she's a good student. I can't quite see her paper, but I can see her working on it. She seems to be making notes or something near the bottom. Then she stops. Looks like she's reading the problem again, kind of following along with her pen. Then I see the pen stop, and its top makes a quick little arc. Seems she's made a mark a bit past the middle of the page; maybe item 'd' or 'e.' I get a brief glimpse as she shifts her page. Yep, there's a mark under the fourth choice in from the right of the page. Has to be item 'd.'

"Would you say I'd been using Selective Attention?"

Laughter from the class.

"Yes, I was attentive all right. I was concentrating. But on getting Joan's answer, not on mastering the problem. You always have an option about what you attend to. Getting yourself to concentrate on the problem is a skill. Were there other places someone used Selective Attention?"

"Didn't they use it all through the problem?" someone asks.

"Well, Selective Attention keeps you working on the problem, yes. But you use it again when something new comes up in the problem you hadn't noticed before. Let me ask something else right now, and I'll come back to

Selective Attention in a minute. Remember I had a team member that was especially good at uncovering new things about a problem. He was called Sustained Analysis. Did any of our #3 problem solvers use him?"

Our instructor acknowledges another hand. "Didn't they use it when they read the problem to see what it was about?"

"Good. Whenever you try by yourself to answer the question, 'What is this?,' you're analyzing—taking apart. Sustained analysis told Joe and Lisha that the problem was a set of directions—a list of things to do: about-face here, turn this way, and so forth. It told Tom the same thing, and also that the heart of the problem was in the second sentence. But remember the 'sustained' part of Sustained Analysis. This is analysis that keeps on ticking—trying to make sense of what it is working on.

"For Lisha and Joe, analysis showed that the problem asked for the result of doing a handful of things. This is where Selective Attention went to work again, narrowing the focus to each thing that had to be done in turn. Analysis showed what each thing was; 'First I face West, next I do an about-face,' and so forth. Selective Attention let them concentrate on each step and Analysis told them what each step was. They took each step, and doing so brought them to an answer.

"It was a little different for Tom. Just as for Joe and Lisha, Analysis showed Tom that the problem required doing a set of things. But Selective Attention did not immediately lead him to concentrate on doing each thing in turn. Instead, it lead him to a question: 'What *kinds* of things does the problem want me to do?' Because he focused on that question, his way of solving the problem was very different from Lisha's and Joe's.

"To see how it was different, we have to call on another team member. Remember Analoging? A moment ago, I said 'What is this?' is the question Analysis always asks. 'What is this *like*?' is always Analoging's question. OK, Problem #3 group, did Joe and Lisha use Analoging?"

There was considerable mumbling in the class, but no one ventured a hand.

"Of course they did. Early on, Lisha saw that the problem was *like* a set of directions. She had followed directions before, so she acted out following them again. Joe did the same thing.

"But Tom asked what *kind* of directions they were. They were directions about making turns and about-faces. Analoging got him thinking about what an about-face was *like*. It was like turning 180°. If you did it twice, you turned 360°—full circle—and were back where you started. Two about-faces sort of cancel each other out. There were right turns and left turns as well, which, like subtracting degrees, could also cancel each other out. Tom found he didn't have to follow the directions. He could solve the problem just by using his knowledge of what turns and about-faces are *like*.

"I want to say more about the difference between Lisha and Joe's approach and the one Tom used, but let's look at how our three problem solvers used the last two members of their problem-solving teams.

"I'm going to show you two different approaches to working the problem the way Lisha and Joe did. Lisha, Joe, I want you to tell us which approach you used."

The instructor physically performs each instruction phrase in Problem 3 as he reads it: "I'm facing west. I turn right. I do an about-face. I turn left. I do an about-face again." The instructor is once more facing west. "So west is my answer. Now, watch what I do differently this time.

"I'm facing West. I turn right. Then I do an about-face. Now I seem to be facing south. Let me do that again. I'm facing west, then I turn right, and then I do an about-face and I'm facing south. OK. Next I turn left. Now I'm facing East. Let me do that again. I'm facing south and I turn left. That puts me facing East. Now I do an about-face and I'm facing where I started from. Let's see. I was facing East, did an about-face, and that puts me back facing west.

"You'll all notice I did a lot more shuffling around that second time. Which way was most like the way you went through the problem the first time, Lisha?"

"Most like your second way. I wanted to make sure I went from one step to the next without any mistake."

"Joe?"

"I did the last two steps again that way. My first time, I mean."

"Then you both used Suspension of Closure. You stopped your run to the answer to make sure you weren't making mistakes on the way. While you were doing that, do you recall if you had any thoughts about doing the problem another way?"

Joe shakes his head. Lisha says, "I started to draw the points of the compass. I was going to trace the moves with my pencil, but then I decided I didn't need to do that."

"Suspension of Closure again, Lisha. At least you conjured up another way you could go about it. How about you, Tom?"

"After I worked it out, I did imagine the moves the way Joe did."

"Suspension of Closure asks two questions. The first is, 'Am I doing it right?' Am I moving through the steps of my solution correctly? The second is, 'Is the *way* I'm doing it right?' Is there another way to go about it? It appears, among the three of you, Suspension of Closure was at work both ways."

"We know you used Autocensorship. Lisha and Joe both went through the directions a few times after they got the answer, just to check. Let me give you a tip, though. You didn't do one thing that would have been a stronger check. You could have worked the problem backwards from your answer to see if it took you to the start. You're not as likely to repeat a mistake that way.

"And Tom took Autocensorship a step further. It got him questioning the problem's assumptions about turns. He saw that those assumptions could lead to trouble but decided to accept a set that supported his answer as reasonable.

"So you good problem solvers did use the members of your problem-solving teams. What I want from the Problem #3 group next is a list of steps each of our three problem solvers took. Let's begin with Lisha."

Relying on Group #3's notes, his own prompting questions and feedback from the three problem solvers, our instructor produces the following three lists on the board (ignore the numbers in parenthesis; they'll be explained in a moment):

LISHA:

1. Reads problem first time. (1) Sees the problem is about which way you're facing after making a set of moves. (2)

2. Reads problem again. (1) Sees that you start facing one direction, then make some turns and about-faces. Must decide which way you're facing or whether you can tell which way you're facing. (2)

3. Decides to follow the problem like a set of directions. (3)

4. Begins to draw a compass star. (3) Stops and decides to make a pretend-person with her hand. (3)

5. Starting at the beginning of the problem, she models each position and move. (1, 2) When she adds a new move, she remakes the earlier ones to be sure she hasn't made a mistake. (4)

6. Arrives at an Answer: She's facing west. (2)

7. Checks to see if that is one of the choices. It is. (2)

8. Goes through the moves with her hand while reading the problem two more times to make sure she hasn't made a mistake. Underlines choice "d."(5)

JOE:

1. Like Lisha's.

2. Like Lisha's.

3. Like Lisha's.

4. Imagines a compass star. (3) Imagines himself at the center (3).

5. Starting from the beginning, imagines each position and move. (1,2) Rethinks the moves when he adds move 3 and move 4. (4)

6.   Imagines going through all the moves four or five times. (2) He does this more quickly each time, until he's making them automatically, like a member of a drill team, and it "feels right." (4) He always comes out facing west.

7.   Same as Lisha.

8.   Goes through the moves while reading the problem one more time. Underlines choice "d." (5)

TOM:

1.   Like Lisha's.

2.   Reads problem second time. Sees that the second sentence contains the heart of the problem. (2)

3.   Concentrates on second sentence. (1) Sees that it contains two opposite turns and two about-faces. (2)

4.   Thinks of about-faces and turns in terms of degrees. (3) Concentrates on about-faces. (1) An about-face is 180°. Two of them is 360°, or full-circle. (2) The problem makes two about-faces. (2) In effect, these cancel out. (3)

5.   Checks on turns. (1) There is a right turn and a left turn. (2) In effect, these cancel out. (3)

6.   If all the moves cancel out, then you face the way you started. (2) In the problem, you start by facing west. (1)

7.   Checks. "West" is one of the possible answers. (1)

8.   Reads problem again, imagining himself making the turns. Comes out facing west. (4)

9.   Notices he imagined himself making 90° turns. (4) Checks, and problem doesn't specify degree of turn. (2) Imagines small turn right and large turn left. (3) Checks and sees that "Can't tell" is an answer option. (2)

10.   Debates whether answer is "west" or "can't tell." (5) Thinks of cases (i.e., when driving a car) where people just say "turn" when they mean "turn 90°." (3) Also sees that answer is "west" no matter how many degrees you turn one way, as long as you turn the same number back. (2) Decides that if the answer really is "can't tell," the problem is misleading or poorly written. It should have said something like: ". . . turn right *slightly* . . ." and "make a *large* left turn. . . ." (3) He decides the answer *could* be "can't tell," but the better choice is "west." (2, 5)

In addition to these three lists, the instructor has placed the following key on the board:

1. Selective Attention
2. Sustained Analysis

3. Analoging
4. Suspension of Closure
5. Autocensorship

He explains that the parenthetical numbers in the lists indicate where one or more of the generic thinking skills has played a decisive, but not necessarily exclusive, role. After all, they are a *team* of skills, and they work closely together. Next our instructor leads the class in examining the lists:

"It doesn't take more than a glance, class, to see that Tom seems to have done a good deal more work than Lisha and Joe. You can see he kept his problem-solving team much busier, and he called on a lot more information than Lisha or Joe did. And yet, after all that work, he came up with the same answer. Think of Lisha and Joe's solutions as one approach, and Tom's as another. Which do you think is better?"

The instructor's monitoring of the class discussion at this point proceeds oddly. As positions evolve, he opposes the stronger and supports the weaker, switching sides several times. Not surprisingly, the class discussion dissolves into something of a draw.

"In this case, class, there is no winner. Both approaches solved the problem at hand. There could be dozens of other approaches that would get the job done, and if getting that job done is the goal, any of them are fine."

"But for getting this job done, Joe and Lisha clearly did less work—close to just what this job needed and no more. Tom worked with a lot more information, and on top of that, if you look at step 8 on his list there, he did just what Joe and Lisha did to solve the problem—he imagined himself following the directions. So what does Tom's approach have going for it? To see that, we have to ask a different kind of question: not which solution is better for this problem, but which solution is more powerful."

"Imagine my giving you a problem that's the same kind as Problem #3, but much more complicated. If I wrote it out, it would be two pages long. The problem would ask you which way you were facing after you had made 47 about-turns, 33 right turns, 14 left turns, 8 half-turns to the right, 6 half-turns to the left, 17 quarter-turns to the right, and 21 quarter-turns to the left. And all these turns and about-faces would be mixed up.

"Now try solving that Lisha and Joe's way. How long do you think it would take? How would you repeat your moves if you thought you'd made a mistake? What are your chances of getting a right answer?"

"But look what you can do with Tom's approach. First you sort out how many of each move you need to make, and you come up with the list I just gave you. Then start with the quarter-turns. There are 16 of those in a circle. Subtract that from 17 and you have one quarter-turn to the right. Subtract it from 21 and you have 5 quarter-turns to the left. Subtract 1 from

5, and you have 4 left quarter-turns remaining. That's the same as one 90° left turn.

"Next, take the half-turns. 8 half-turns to the right is the same as 4 turns to the right, and that's the same as a circle, so it cancels out. Six half-turns to the left is the same as 3 turns to the left. Add that to the 1 left turn we have from the quarter-turns and it makes 4 left turns, which again cancel out. Now we only have full turns remaining.

"Four goes into 33 eight times, with 1 left over, so we have 1 right turn. Four goes into 14 three times, with 2 left over. Our 1 right turn cancels out a left turn, so we have 1 left turn remaining. All our turns reduce to 1 left turn. Now we go to the about-faces.

"Two goes into 47 thirteen times, with 1 left over. So all those numbers reduce to 1 about-face and a left turn. That means if we were facing west and made all the moves, we would be facing north."

"Using Lisha and Joe's method, it would take all day to solve that problem. Using Tom's, it took 3 minutes. Tom's approach can handle many much tougher problems more easily than Lisha and Joe's can. His way of solving the problem is more powerful.

"What makes it more powerful? Look at Tom's list. He pushed his analysis farther and brought more of his own knowledge to the problem. Lisha and Joe used their experience. They looked at the problem and asked what it was like. They saw it was like a set of directions and they followed those directions. Tom saw it was like a set of directions, too, but then he asked what the *directions* were like. He pushed analoging harder, made it do more work. It uncovered a likeness between making turns and his knowledge of circles and degrees. Now he could apply what he understood about circles and degrees to the problem."

"There are two important lessons for us problem solvers here. The first is that the most powerful problem solvers are the ones who best use what they already know. They know that any solution they shape has to come from their own knowledge and experience, so they poke that knowledge and experience hard. Second, they prize knowledge. They want to know about things and they are receptive learners, because they realize that anything they understand might be an important tool in their problem solving. Lisha and Joe didn't need to know much about circles to solve Problem #3. But if they had no knowledge of circles to apply to the more complicated version we just looked at, they would probably have given up."

"This, by the way, is one reason all of you are spending so much of your lives in school, a lot of it learning things that seem far from your own interests. We're trying to give you the knowledge you'll need to solve your own problems. People with no interest in learning are people who depend on others to solve their problems for them."

Comment

We lay out the rest of our ETSI example before we begin a review, but there is something we need to note right here. This class session is not going the way our instructor had anticipated.

He realized that the period would have to shape itself around the problem solutions students actually employed, and these are not totally predictable. But he had not expected a solution quite as elegant as Tom's. He expected the solutions to Problem #3 to be in the range of Lisha's and Joe's. He would have explored these, as in fact he did, and then turned to at least one wrong-answer Problem #3. One of the students had picked "a. East" as an answer. That student had sketched a compass star on his page, and it seemed probable that he had made the mistake of not placing himself in its center for his second turn. Making his left turn from the outside converted it into a second right turn. If this were so, the instructor would have an opportunity to generate a "list" of that student's approach and show the class how a little Suspension of Closure and Autocensorship could have saved him. In like manner, he intended to go on with right and wrong examples of Problem 1 and 2.

The comparative power of different solutions was not a topic he had planed to raise in this session. His goal was simply to get students familiar and at ease with examining their own solutions. Also, by initiating an informal note-taking, he wanted to give them an idea of what it was they should "notice" about their own problem-solving approaches — particularly the presence and employment of the generic skills.

But Tom's unusual and only vaguely suspected solution, once out, had to be placed in perspective for the class. The instructor responded to it as thinking skill instructors should generally respond to the unusual in class: directly and analytically, the way a problem solver rather than a problem avoider would.

On the whole, the instructor is pleased with the detour. Problems 1 and 2 haven't been touched, nor have any wrong-answer examples, but the class discussion and student participation exhibit the right stuff. He will have plenty of time to address all his deferred topics when he gets the class into paired problem-solving teams.

Right now, the period is nearly over and he is winding down his comments on the power of Tom's solution. It occurs to him that this might be a place to raise an example from his introduction that he had decided not to pursue. Well, in for a penny, in for a pound. . . .

ETSI PHASE II: EXAMPLE CONTINUED

"We have time for one more example of how different ways of solving a problem — all successful — can have different power. I think it will help you see why good problem solvers, even when they know of one way to solve a problem, look for other ways."

The instructor erases a section of board."Remember our problem about the girls and the languages? We had . . . " Here the instructor writes as he speaks:

Spanish   French   German   Swedish   Russian

Cathy   Sandra   Cindy   Paula

"We drew lines between the girls and their languages, and we found that Sandra knew Swedish and Russian, which were the two hardest languages. But let me change our original problem just a little. Let's say — just like the original problem — that Cathy knows French and German, Paula knows German and Swedish, and Cindy knows Spanish and French. But we'll make one change with Sandra. This time she knows French and Russian. OK, lets connect our lines:"

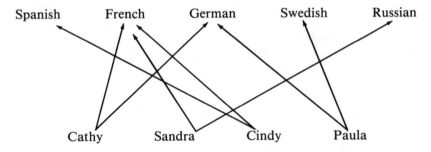

"Now, which girl knows the hardest languages? Sandra knows Russian — which is harder than Paula's German and Swedish — and French, which is easier than both. It turns out that many people still pick Sandra, because she's the only one that knows the hardest language. But is that correct? In any case, the answer doesn't seem clear.

"Think of our other way of solving the problem, which was to assign a value to each language":

1. Spanish = 1
2. French = 2

2. German = 3
3. Swedish = 4
4. Russian = 5

"We add those for our girls, and we have":

1. Cathy   = 5
2. Sandra = 7
3. Cindy   = 3
4. Paula   = 7

"Sandra and Paula share the same high value. It's a little clearer from this approach that there is no right answer to our altered problem. And again, suppose our problem had 14 girls, each of whom knew 3 of 17 languages. Would we be better off drawing lines or assigning values?"

"Once again, our second and more powerful way of solving the problem required us to put more of our knowledge to work. It made us use the notions of assigning ordered numbers to things and adding, which matching by line did not require."

"Now let me emphasize something. We will not be concentrating in this class on getting the most powerful possible solutions to problems. There is nothing wrong with solving a problem the simplest way you can. In fact, there's a lot to be said for it. Problem solving is work, and there is some value in not doing more of it than you have to. But keep this in mind. The simplest way to solve a problem may not take you very far. Just as we've seen, when problems grow more complex, the simple way can quickly become too hard to use. That's why good problem solvers are restless when they see only one way to proceed. They take the time to stop — suspend closure — and search their knowledge for another way. Once they find it, they may not use it, but now at least they have a choice."

"That's it for today, class. See you next period."

Day 4. "Last time, class, we were only able to look at what some of you did with Problem #3. We didn't even get to Problems 1 and 2. One reason is that it took so much time to put together those three lists that showed the steps that Tom, Lisha, and Joe used in solving their problems. By the way, there is a word often used to name lists that show the steps you take to do something. The word is 'protocol,' and we'll use it to describe the steps someone takes to solve a problem."

"To come up with Tom, Lisha, and Joe's protocols, we had to keep questioning them to get them to remember what they had done. You'll recall that sometimes they didn't remember very well, and we had to correct steps as they thought about them some more. In fact, we're still not sure those protocols are accurate; they are just the best our problem solvers could remember.

"What we need is a quicker way to come up with protocols, and I have one. Greg, would you step up here, please?"

As Greg arrives, the instructor hands him a sheet with problems typed on both sides.

"Pick any problem you'd like on that sheet, Greg, and write it on the board for me, would you?"

As Greg makes his choice and begins to write, our instructor continues to address the class.

"I'm going to try to solve whatever problem Greg puts on the board *out loud*. This takes a little practice, but it isn't really very hard. I simply have to put everything into words as I'm doing it. Once you get the hang of it, it's easier than putting things into words *after* you've done them.

"What you have to do, class, is simply take notes on what I'm doing. If I read the question aloud, you put down, "Reads question," and so on. When I'm finished, my problem-solving protocol should be right there in your notes."

"One other thing, class. If I get in trouble, I might ask for help. If I do, the rule is you can't give me an answer, or even a part of one. But you *can* tell me what to think about, or concentrate on. You're finished, Greg?"

Greg nods on his way back to his seat.

The instructor glances at the board. The odds were Greg would pick a short problem, and he did.

"Here I go, class. First I read the problem." The instructor reads the following:

"Write the three letters that should come next in this series:

B A A C E E D I I E M M F _ _ _ ."[12]

"Let me read that again." He does. "There's something about that set of letters that should tell me how to add three more. Let's see. I don't see any words in there. CEED sounds like a word. BAA could be a sheep call. IIE sounds like a scream, and MMF like talking with your mouth full. That doesn't seem to go anywhere. If I look at it backwards, it's even worse. This is embarrassing, class. It's just a string of nonsense. Help! What can I do?"

There are chuckles from the class at this obvious ploy. But one voice finally commands, "Look for patterns."

"Patterns? You mean in the string of letters? OK. There *is* a pattern. There are single letters followed by double letters, BAA, CEE, DII, and

---

[12]This is a direct steal of problem 25 on page 8, Whimbey and Lockhead, *op. cit*. Thinking skill instructors lift items shamelessly.

EMM, ending with a single letter, F, and three blanks. Let me look at that more carefully."

"BAA. A is the letter before B. CEE. Let's see: 'C, D, E.' " The instructor ticks his alphabet counts off on his fingers. "E is the second letter after C. Next is DII. 'D, E, F, G, H, I.' So I is the fifth letter after D. This doesn't seem to be getting anywhere. Let me just check with EMM." The instructor counts his alphabet again. "M is the eighth letter after E. No, this doesn't help. I'll look for some other pattern."

"What do I have if I just look at the single letters? 'B–C–D–E–F.' Well, those go just the way the alphabet does if you start with B. So the next single letter after F should be G. Great! I'm making progress. Now let me look at the double letters. They go A–E–I–M. Let me count through the alphabet. '*A*–B–C–D–*E*–F–G–H–*I*–J–K–L–*M*' That means each of the double letters is the fourth letter in the alphabet after the one before it. OK. The series ends with a single letter, F, so I need to follow that with a double letter. And that has to be the fourth letter after M. '*M*–N–O–P–*Q*. So I put two Q's in the first two blanks. Now I go back to the single letters. The last one was F, so the next one has to be G. So my answer is *Q, Q, G*."

"Before I check this, though, let me think a minute. I got this answer because the person who wrote the problem did one thing consistently with the single letters and another thing consistently with the double letters. To solve it, I had to uncover what that was. If I can express what he or she did, I should be able to generate the whole series. Let's make the first rule about the single letters. Starting with B, simply add the next letter in the alphabet. For the double letters, starting with A, add the fourth next letter in the alphabet. All right. Now I'll do those two things and see what I get: B A A (add one to B) C (add the fourth to A) E E (add one to C) D (add the fourth to E) I I (add one to D) E (add the fourth to I) M M (add one to E) F (add the fourth to M) Q Q (add one to F) G. Now I have 'B A A C E E D I I E M M F Q Q G. That gives me the original series plus my answer. It checks out. I'm finished."

"Now, class, from your notes, what was my protocol?"

With considerable prompting, the class replays the instructor's steps, which he places on the board in the following abbreviated form:

1. Reads problem.
2. Reads 2nd time. Tries to see words. Doesn't work.
3. Flounders. Asks help. Told look for pattern.
4. Sees single letter followed by double letter. Looks for relationship. Doesn't see one.
5. Looks single letters. Sees follows alphabet.
6. Looks double letters. Sees every fourth letter in alphabet.

7. Adds fourth letter from M twice and next letter from F once for answer.

8. Stops before check. Thinks rules for single and double letters. Applies to B and AA. Generates series plus answer. Considers problem solved and checked. End.

"Very good. Now we have my protocol, which we could use to examine how I employed my generic skills, or to compare my approach with someone else's. And it was much easier for you to see what I was doing — also to help me when I dropped the ball — because I worked the problem out loud."

"This time I was the problem solver and all of you were my monitors — watching my moves and helping when I got in trouble. You helped me not by giving the answer, but by prompting me to use my skills. You got me to attend selectively to the letters and analyze them for patterns."

"Now I'm going to divide you into two-person problem-solving teams. I will give the teams a problem to solve. One team member will solve it the way I solved this one. Out loud. The other member will be the monitor, who keeps track of the protocol and helps nudge the problem solver if he or she gets in a bind. When the team has finished working one problem and gets a new one, you will change roles; the problem solver becomes the monitor and the monitor becomes the problem solver."

The instructor next divides the class into two-person teams. He doesn't intend this pairing to be permanent, so he simply counts them off in a way that minimizes movement in the classroom. Later on, when he wants more permanent problem-solving teams, he will tend to pick pairs whose ability differs rather than matches — perhaps good problem solvers with average, and average with poor. Difference in ability will tend to advantage both partners. The poorer problem solver will see close up what the better one does. The better problem solver will need to become more discriminating about her moves in helping the poorer.

"Now we have our teams. Your first task is to decide who is to be the problem solver and who the monitor in your team for the first problem. Flip a coin or volunteer, it doesn't matter how you do it. You have 30 seconds."

The instructor calms the hubbub at the appointed time. "Jessica. Carter. Hand out these sheets, two to a team, while I pick a problem."

The sheets have two words in the upper left corner: Problem Solver and Monitor.

"All the teams have two sheets? Good. Now listen to what I want you to do. While I put the problem on the board, I want each team member to sign his or her name after his or her role on both sheets. After both names are on both sheets, you each take one sheet. All you problem solvers, put a check mark in front of Problem Solver. All you monitors, put a check mark in front of Monitor."

"You problem solvers may use your sheets any way you choose—sketch, make notes, whatever you might find useful in solving the problem. That is your worksheet. If you use it for nothing else, at least write your answer on it. I'll be picking them up."

"You monitors will use your sheet to take notes on the problem solver's protocol—everything the problem solver does to solve the problem. Keep your notes brief, but complete enough so that you can recount everything your problem solver did.

"Now, you monitors really have four jobs. First, you have to make sure your problem solver describes everything he or she is doing out loud while he or she is doing it. If the problem solver does something that isn't clear to you, ask that he or she make it clear. Second, you have to make notes to capture the problem solver's protocol. Third, if the problem solver gets stuck, you can suggest what he or she might try next, but you can't solve the problem. And fourth, after the problem solver is finished, you need to go over your notes together to make sure you have the protocol down correctly."

"Problem solvers, you have two concerns: solving the problem and doing it out loud. I want you teams to talk quietly so all of you can hear yourselves think. If any team has a problem, just wave me over. Ready? Here's the problem." On the board, the instructor writes:

> Willard is shorter than Paul but taller than Sam. One of them is a car salesman, another a banker, and the third a plumber. The banker is tallest, the car salesman shortest, and the plumber in between. What is Willard's occupation?

The buzz begins. The instructor quietly circulates through the classroom, listening and adjudicating. If any team has a real difficulty, he takes them along a step or two. When the teams have finished their work, he asks a team that seems to have worked well to replay its problem solution in front of the class. The instructor turns as much of the analysis and commentary over to the class as he can. Alternate protocols and note-taking techniques are discussed, and any wrong-answer teams are carefully debriefed.

The instructor calls a halt on the first team problem. New team sheets are handed out, team members switch roles, a new problem is placed on the board, and the process repeats.

That night at home, with the team worksheets spread before him, the instructor begins to acquaint himself with the idiosyncracies of his problem solvers.

Day 5 and Beyond.   In the ETSI example we are here considering, the instructor introduces his students to the paired problem-solving technique on the fourth day. Once he has done that, he has established the core ETSI theme. Everything else that happens within this 4 to 6 weeks—about the minimum time needed for an initial ETSI unit—is a variation on that theme.

After the first day or so of paired-team work, once procedures are understood and working fairly smoothly, the instructor reassigns students to more permanent teams. At the beginning, he poses problems of about the same complexity to these new teams, but from an increasing range of types—math story problems, figurial problems, new kinds of verbal analogy, and pattern discernment problems. When the teams are responding well to variety, he steps up complexity. The problem-solving teams are handling the same kinds of variables, but increasing numbers and varying mixtures of them.

The instructor also assigns homework problems, which require the student to provide a written protocol with the solution. He does this in two ways. First, he uses problems in conjunction with his continuing diagnosis of individual student progress, selectively assigning problems that will tend to confront and help remedy individual weaknesses in deploying the generic skills. He specifically assigns problems in such cases wherever he feels tailoring the challenge will be helpful.

Second, the instructor has developed a system for leaving the homework choice to students. He calls it his "Problem Bank." The Bank has six problem accounts. All accounts carry problems of similar kinds, but each account represents a step up in problem difficulty. Account #1 has the easiest problems; Account #6 the hardest. Some Account #6 problems can take 3 or 4 hours to solve. Students are usually required to withdraw a homework problem from the Bank, but from any Account of their choice. Very occasionally, the instructor will levy a prescription: "You have to pick from Account #2 or up." But usually the choice is the student's, and it's surprising how often a student will be found, of his or her choice, wrestling with a #6.

The instructor regularly reviews the protocols students turn in as homework. He comments on these and returns them. He does not seek flawless grammar in these protocol notes, but he does press for clarity and comprehensiveness. What the student leaves unclear or unnoted in his protocol is often unclear and unnoted in his grasp of his own problem-solving performance. The instructor wants his students clearly conscious of what they are and are not doing. Quite often, the instructor's question mark next to an ambiguous step in a student protocol, followed by a note to "See me," will bring forth an account of missing steps. To this the instructor responds, "That makes good sense, but it doesn't appear in your protocol."

At other times the gap is a gap in consciousness or skill, which the instructor can now mediate.

As the students' homework protocols grow more adept, the instructor may tag on assignments that require, perhaps, a brief expository paragraph. For instance, "When you've solved your homework problem, outline an alternate approach you could have taken." Every two or three class periods, the instructor might run a "protocol clinic" in class. Students raise protocol problems during this time, and the instructor uses it to explore difficulties, trends, and unusual protocol examples that the homework brings to him.

Meanwhile, in class, the paired-team theme prevails, and the instructor embellishes it in various ways as the students gain power. He begins to slip in problems with ambiguous or incomplete data—problems that require thoughtfully qualified answers. Toward the end of the ETSI segment he may move briefly to "sham" problems, problems that sound real but harbor missing or incoherent criteria. For instance, he might try, "Billy set the all-state record in highjump and Sam is .14 seconds shy in the 440. Who's the better athlete?" He leads a brief exploration of the pitfalls in resolving who is the better President or human being; what is the better country or profession. But even for such "impossible" problems, he does not accept the tempting rejection: "That's dumb!" "That's stupid!" Stupid questions that do not resolve into coherent problems can yet have examined, considered answers, and building such answers enlists the operant skills.

As the distinctive characteristics and qualities of the paired teams emerge, he may give some of them special assignments. He asks some teams to devise problems for the class to solve. He may "centerpiece" a team with a particular strength or weakness, asking them to solve a problem before the class while he stops action and analyzes or guides discussion. He might permit "challenges" of various kinds in class, where teams argue the virtues of different protocols or conduct a problem-solving "tournament." One tournament model would divide the class into two sets of paired problem-solving teams—say seven teams on each side. The same six problems are given to six teams on each side. The answers from those six problems provide the data for the seventh problem, which is handled by each side's last team. The side whose last team finishes first wins.

But the point of all such embellishment is to sustain the press for operant thinking on the part of the individual student within the paired team. That student should arrive at the end of the 4-to-6 week ETSI with a new and intense awareness of his or her generic thinking skills—Selective Attention, Sustained Analysis, Analoging, Suspension of Closure, and Autocensorship—together with a rich and conscious history of their employment.

Our instructor chooses to end this introductory ETSI segment in conformity with a hallowed tradition. He gives a 45-minute exam. He could have framed his own exam, but he chooses instead to use a version of the WASI

(Whimbey Analytical Skills Inventory) Test.[13] There are pre and posttest versions, each containing problems of the type we've used as patterns in our examples. He administers the exam on the day before the class's final ETSI meeting, and he does so not so much to measure the students as to give them occasion to celebrate their skill. A well-taught ETSI segment usually produces students slightly bewildered by what they are now able to do. On the last day, he goes over the results. indicates how they roughly correlate with standard IQ tests, and then, finally, he indulges himself. He talks to his students about what they can do, and what he hopes they will do, with their sharpened thinking skills.

ETSI PHASE II: EXAMPLE ANALYZED

Well aware that we are risking tedium, we presented a good deal of our ETSI example — all of Phase I and the first 4 days of Phase II — in a highly literal way. We showed you what the instructor was doing sentence by sentence, blow by blow. We did this to display as emphatically as we could the intensity of effort the thinking skill instructor expends, first on exposing the thinking processes of students, and second on channeling those processes toward the growth of generic skills. There are times when *explaining* what it takes simply falls short of *seeing* what it takes.

The weakness of such literal examples is, of course, that thousands of quite different — but equally good or better — ones could be used. And no matter which one is presented, it would be a serious mistake for the aspiring thinking skill instructor to try to teach thinking skills by re-enacting the example. The example is not a blueprint.

Fortunately, though, there *is* a blueprint of sorts, and a fairly simple one at that. Our example shows how one instructor translated the blueprint into the architecture of instruction. We present the blueprint and then reflect on this instructor's translation. You, of course, will make your own translation. You will use from our example whatever materials and techniques please you or promise to suit your instructional style, but you will immediately begin tinkering, adding this and deleting that, heightening here and diminishing there. No matter how much of the example you incorporate, it will — it must — be your translation. Here's the blueprint:

1. Prepare Yourself. Solve at least a dozen problems of various kinds out loud and note your protocols. Examine each protocol as you complete it and think of all the variations in specific moves you might have made without changing your basic solution. Note these. Identify the dominant

---

[13]Note 11 will lead you to the WASI.

generic skill associated with each move. Keep doing this so that spotting the skill employed comes smoothly. Finally, go back to each problem and think not of one, but of three or four substantially different — not necessarily better, just different — ways it might be approached and solved. Employ some of these out loud and again generate protocols. Contrast these different approaches. How do they compare in ease or simplicity, in power or range of utility?

You want to achieve three things by doing this. First, you seek an ease with thinking out loud, an adeptness at expressing the steps you actually take while solving a problem. Second, you require a handiness in spotting and calling out your employment of the generic skills. The third thing is perhaps a consequence of the first two, but very important in its own right. You want to create and inhabit a thinking-intensive environment yourself for awhile, so you know how it feels. The sense of what it takes to achieve and sustain that environment will serve you well in building one within a classroom.

2. Stake out your Space.   A properly taught ETSI segment needs room of its own. It does not blend well with other instructional agendas or objectives. You need to give it a solid, uninterrupted 4-to-6 weeks unmixed with other curricular goals.

3. Consciously Adjust your Teaching Style.   Amplify the coach in you and submerge the lecturer. While exploring and illuminating thinking behavior with your students, show and tell where you must but show rather than tell wherever possible and avoid simply telling. Model the behaviors you want students to comprehend. Describing is seldom, if ever, enough.

4. Move Students to Paired Problem-Solving Team Work as Soon as You Can.   Keep the following rationale in mind for doing so. A minute or two of operant thinking per student per period in a usual class would be solidly above average. The instructor in such a class is seriously pushing for active student thought. Alternating as a problem solver and monitor in a properly run ETSI period, a student can total between 25–35 minutes of operant thinking per class period. ETSI works to the degree that you sustain this geometrical increase in the students' operant thinking experience. There are other benefits as well. In the paired team, the student is systematically switching roles in this business of thinking well — player here, coach there, employing skills here, assessing employment there. Few other pedagogies are as good at fostering this action-reflection dynamic, and that *is* the dynamic of the capable thinker.

5. Center on your Role.   In proposing to teach thinking, you assume a demanding persona. During any ETSI session, you *are* Selective Attention,

Sustained Analysis, Analoging, Suspension of Closure, and Autocensorship. Your overriding role is to represent these skills in action. The students' sense of your commitment to these skills will mark the limit of theirs. If such skills seem to be native to your best thought, they will strive to make them so in their own. Reach for them grudgingly and so will they. This means you represent the skills beyond the occasional modeling of a problem solution, or an unraveling of student difficulties with an assignment. Your explicit coaching and instruction are important, but from another perspective the spaces *in between* explicit instruction are just as important. Students who see their instructor's mind gracefully focusing, considering, probing, and assessing when not constrained to do so by the syllabus will form the truer sense of their goal.

6. Share your Role.   Transplant it as thoroughly and rapidly as you can. Your real gauge of success with ETSI will be students acting just as you are—not mimicking you but deploying the generic skills as situations warrant. When students monitor a problem solution or debrief a protocol as well as you, when you can productively turn a segment of class business over to them, when they can try a new approach out loud, falter and recover unabashed, you have real progress. Remember that you are not just getting students to solve story problems. They can do that and still remain essentially passive. You are coaching coaches, and the more they are able to do your work, the more certainly they're wielding the skills you are.

Example Review

There are ample signs that our example instructor's translation projects this blueprint well. Let's note a few.

1. He has Prepared Himself.   He is adept at vocalizing his own problem performance—adept enough to realize that something very like his own component steps must lie at the heart of any thoughtful problem solution. This little bit of confidence is critical in two ways. First, it enables him to avoid a novice thinking skill instructor's disease called "protocol paralysis." This comes from trying to embrace a total problem protocol at-a-glance. As we've seen, even a simple problem can spark a complex protocol—all those little bits and pieces and shiftings back and forth. Trying to embrace all that at once can cause vertigo. But one move at a time, the protocol is profoundly simple. And it is at the level of one move at a time that the protocol is useful and productive to the newly self-conscious thinker. Our instructor moves calmly and carefully through his initial protocols. He is not awed by the whole nor does he allow the whole to awe his students.

Also, he is conscious enough of his own problem-solving performance to reject overly slick representations of how the mind works. Recall his initially characterizing Lisha's approach as following directions, one, two, three. He could have let that stand, but he suspected the process wasn't so linear, that in fact Lisha was doing some backing and filling and replaying of her moves enroute. The insight made his and Lisha's grasp of what was going on more credible.

2. He has Staked out his Space.   He is exclusively engaged in ETSI and not complicating his mission by trying to pursue an English or History or Math curriculum as well. There are times when he is sorely tempted to bridge ETSI and his discipline, but he resists. He consoles himself with the thought that he will be bringing more skilled and conscious thinkers to his discipline later.

3. He Consistently Models Rather than Lectures.   Take the instance with Lisha again. He could simply have said that one often doesn't just follow directions but checks back on them in progress. Had he done so, the point would have slid past 90% of the class. Instead, he demonstrates.

4. He Initiates Paired Problem-Solving Teams.   After providing the class with several thorough examples of what they are supposed to do therein, he moves the class into paired problem-solving teams, even demonstrating part of his rationale for the move.

5. He is a Coach-Demonstrator.   He has clearly centered on his role, so much so that the students quickly recognize this as a new experience. This teacher is not primarily a dispenser of knowledge or a hurdle-producer. He is a coach-demonstrator and he wants conscious participant action. When someone acts, he *notices*. He is happiest when the student notices, too, and acts in light of it.

6. He Gets Them to do it.   He transfers his role of attending, analyzing, noting likenesses, reconsidering, and evaluating to his students with gusto, taking far more pleasure in their performance than his own. Getting them to *do* it seems his all-consuming concern. Getting them to accept and reflect his explanations of how it is done doesn't appear to count much at all.

THE IMPORTANCE OF INITIAL ETSI: "DO NOT PASS GO"

Now that we have examined an initial ETSI sequence, a few words will help us place it in perspective regarding the thinking skill instructor's overall repertoire and mission.

This initial explicit thinking skill instruction sequence marks the most radical phase of thinking skill pedagogy. This is less like traditional instruction than anything else the thinking skill instructor is liable to do. The student's processes of thought, and control over those processes, nowhere constitute the thinking skill instructor's focus quite so exclusively.

To state it another way, once you have reached this point in our guide, you have encountered all the thinking skill instructor's major pedagogical techniques. From here on, you see these techniques mixed and modified. The initial ETSI sequence has the unique objective of *insuring* that students achieve a consciousness of and control over their own generic thinking skills. We explore other desirable and productive ETSI sequences, but all of them will depend heavily on the degree of self-directed skill in thinking that was the aim of this first one.

There is, consequently, a rule of thumb that the thinking skill instructor can apply when considering options on how best to employ her resources.

She can, first of all, do very good work while avoiding any explicit thinking skill instruction at all. She can, at any level of instruction, foster good thinking behaviors as we saw them fostered in early elementary. She can, as we soon examine, so teach a discipline as to draw a maximum of operant thinking behavior from her students. She can do wonders with well-disposed minds this way and occasionally spark a miracle with an ill-disposed one. But if she wants to do her best to confront each mind with its capabilities, she would do well to consider Explicit Thinking Skill Instruction.

The option now resolves around what kind of ETSI segment to pursue. Remember that ETSI basically involves the creation of a thinking-intensive environment. Many such environments are imaginable. They can be built within, around, and across disciplines. You could build one, for example, around argumentation or debate within the context of a language skills program. Traditional or symbolic logic, math, computer programming, any of the sciences or processes common to them could provide a nucleus. They would all have in common the goal of exercising the generic skills effectively on issues important to the chosen domain. And they would share an added appeal in their clear relevance to the disciplines as traditionally taught. Which option should our thinking skill instructor choose?

Here comes our rule of thumb. If you are going to do ETSI at all, first make sure your students are exposed to an initial ETSI sequence like the one in this chapter. It provides a context in which many students will learn for the first time how to say "go" to their own thinking capabilities. Even when teaching at the college level, if you pass this "go" and simply intensify intellectual demands on your students, many will drop by the way, bemused and unable to perform. So, unless you are content to preach to the elect, avoid passing "go." No matter what age your students or what level you instruct, if you are going to explicitly teach thinking skill, concentrate on introducing students to their own best capabilities before eliciting them.

THE FILE

THE FILE

THE FILE

CHAPTER 8

ELEMENTARY PIE

Forethought

At this point we turn from a new to an old teaching priority, from explicit thinking skill instruction to subject matter instruction. We make this turn, however, with the aims of the thinking skill instructor still in mind. We want to examine ways to teach subject matter that will specially enlist, exercise, and mature thinking skills.

The ways we explore should advantage the thinking ability of any student, whether or not exposed to ETSI. But we think they will have their fullest impact on ETSI-exposed students. The methods we examine challenge the conscious control and application of thought, and we argue that those challenges are more familiar and more readily addressed by those—all else being equal—whose thinking skills have been explicitly cultivated.

Another way to describe our switch in focus is to say that we are shifting our concern from establishing a Thinking-Intensive Environment (TIE) to establishing a Problem-Intensive Environment (PIE). We've dressed our students for the feast (TIE) and now we want them to dig into the disciplinary banquet (PIE).

Groaners aside, the notion of presenting subject matter so that the process constitutes a problem-intensive environment begs a good deal of clarification. It can easily be misconstrued, and a few words now on how it might be misconstrued will help our effort to clarify in the following pages.

An image that could come to mind when someone suggests you teach your subject matter by emphasizing the problematic is that of the Socratic teacher. This able sage confronts students with questions—whys and wherefores—in an effort to have them pry out the roots of assertions rather than simply memorize them. You've already gathered that we are much in favor of questioning, and the Socratic method represents an undoubtedly noble instructional model. Trouble is, the model is astonishingly more complex than it appears, and it is far easier to parody than to execute well.

Part of the Socratic art involves cultivating or uncovering issues of burning significance to the student, of heightening the student's commitment to them, and then, in this charged atmosphere, launching just the right dart to prick the sensitized skin. For every such master in the classroom, there are a hundred others for whom questioning is the constant stimulus they use for recall, and still others in whose hands it becomes an aggravating repetitive style that students try their best to ignore. Even more limiting, the teacher has a valid task of imparting large quantities of information to the student that the Socratic model does not address.

The Socratic method can teach us a thing or two, but adapting the instructor's role to that model is not what we mean by establishing a problem-intensive environment.

Another interpretation and defense of teaching problematically stems from noting the kinship between any discipline and the business of solving problems. The kinship is real, even profoundly so. History is our attempt to solve the problem, "What happened?" In similar fashion, we could go through the whole roster. Grammar: "How do I express myself efficiently?" Physics: "What is motion and matter?" Literature: "Can we convey experience, and how much?" And so on. You do little damage to any discipline by seeing it as a prolonged struggle to resolve some aspect of humanity confronting its condition.

But, however penetrating and insightful this view, it doesn't much smooth the student's encounter with a discipline. In fact, it underlines what makes that encounter difficult. To the student, the discipline is not a series of problems but an awesome rank and file of affirmations. Even if we point out that these are the answers to problems, they usually don't happen to be answers to any of his. And, thanks to the un-simple processes that shape understanding, he will usually have to digest and master a great deal of the discipline's information before he gains much sense of its salient problems, let alone the urge or capacity to embrace them.

Sketching an enlightened philosophy of the disciplines will not take us very far in making sense of a problem-intensive environment for students.

Perhaps we've chosen the wrong goal. Most current efforts to improve student mastery of subject matter, we must admit, are aimed in quite the opposite direction—at devising a problem-free environment for learning. The tendency is to look at what makes a subject difficult to learn and, step by step, diminish that difficulty. If it is hard for a student to retain what is "important" in a reading, for instance, there are several things you can do. First, delete difficult language and pare away as much of the "unimportant" parts of the reading as possible. Reduce your copy to the bare, simply stated essentials. Introduce the reading with a "study skills" paragraph that preps the student—tells her what to look for and how to spot it. Conclude the reading with a "lesson review" section that shows new ways to mark and retain priority information. Add a "thinking skills" component that prompts her to trace cause and effect, evidence and conclusion.

What we have here are textbook authors and teachers diminishing what is problematic in the learning process. They are doing it quite successfully. The student achieves, say, her grasp of the Civil War much more easily, and tests will prove it. But other assessment hints at a limpness in the achievement, a lack of utility, significance, long-term retention. The knowledge comes easy, and it stays or goes indifferently. The products of such diminished-difficulty learning are a few generations thick about us, and there is not too much pointing with pride.

Yet it is in this approach that we see a sound impulse. It makes sense to concentrate on diminishing the difficulties of subject matter learning. The effort to do that should be encouraged, and encouraging it is the point of our desire for a problem-intensive environment. Building that environment is, however, the result of one important change. Don't give the problem of smoothing out learning to the teacher or the textbook writer. Put it in the lap of the student.

The idea is to shape a classroom context in which learning is the consequence of students resolving a series of problems they identify and come to want to resolve. Wherever possible, so structure it that our educational rewards—new comprehension, new insight—are no longer dispensed but won through the exercise of operant skill. You will see as you examine it that this is not a popular approach. It is no more fashionable in education than in the realm of social welfare. Yet it still seems to be the case that what we earn means more to us than what we receive on the dole.

In this chapter we examine techniques for establishing PIEs in a variety of subject matter fields. We try to avoid repetition so keep in mind that a technique raised in one context may, with some tailoring, serve you very well in another. And there is one topic — an essential dimension of PIEs — that we do not discuss, just because it is so important and its utility so general. It's the form of writing called composition. We give that our full attention in the next chapter.

CULTIVATING THINKING SKILL IN SOCIAL STUDIES

Consider a fifth-grade social studies teacher equipped with a modern, newly assigned social studies textbook. She is going to teach American History with it this term but wants to do so with an emphasis on developing her students' thinking skills as well.

As you flip with her through the text — glancing at the study units and occasionally reading the instructional suggestions, hints, and activity ideas in this Teacher's Edition — you can hardly help but be impressed. The modern textbook, especially if designed for the earlier grades, is a marvel. Look here, for instance. There's a paragraph on how to sharpen student awareness of likenesses and differences by getting them to make charts. There is thinking skill insight here, and this is only one instance of a strong concern, expressed in text and teaching comments alike, for developing student thinking ability.

Moreover, the text clearly and consciously raises these concerns with the students. A brief paragraph outlines the unit readings, previewing what the student will encounter. Review questions follow reading segments, as do highlighted study help units that show students how to trace cause and effect and otherwise analyze the material. A larger review segment concludes the study unit by rehearsing vocabulary, checking main ideas, and once again exercising study and thinking skills.

Logically, step by step, the text unfolds not only American History in pleasant, digestible chunks, but actively calls on and marshals the skills required to make the most of them. We could easily forgive our Social Studies teacher should she conclude that careful employment of this comprehensive text will do both jobs for her: teach history and develop thinking skills. In fact, the need for care seems minimal. It almost looks as if the text might do these jobs by itself.

Perhaps what saves her is the suspicion that every silver lining has its cloud. In any case, she begins to examine the text in a different light. The shifting mountain of complexity that is American History is here a series of — this sounds disparaging but it isn't meant to be — easily negotiable mole hills. Well, that's not too bothersome. One expects considerable boiling down and simplifying for young minds. What you want fifth graders to grasp is history in outline — the major events and forces with a sense of the overall scale and pattern, right? Then the thinking and study skills are systematically called on and stimulated by the text. Repeatedly, in fact. To master the mole hills? That's putting it unkindly, and yet the skills seem to be called forth primarily to enhance retention of the book's careful, grade-level-conscious version of American History. Is that teaching thinking skill, or is it co-opting thinking skill for an enterprise already made too anemic by extensive pre-editing and sifting?

At this point our teacher, who is experienced, recalls a past uneasiness she has felt in using texts of this kind. There is a danger, in calling on thinking skill, of "Crying Wolf" — of beckoning skill when skill isn't needed. You ask for an analysis of cause and effect where cause and effect have been clearly spelled out. Students easily perform, but the performance seems trivial and quickly becomes boring. If this is all you beckon the skill for, analysis itself comes to carry the taint of seeming trivial and boring.

Well, textbook writers don't have it easy, either. They work awfully hard and use awesome skill to reach a difficult balance that can't please everyone. Our teacher decides she will use the text, thinking skill cues and all. But she intends to use it in ways that will take her students' thinking skills on a wilder ride than the text proposes.

First, she makes her students take the same initial step a historian would either implicitly or explicitly take when approaching some segment of the past. She has them take stock. The historian would rehearse what she already knows about the topic. What she does know, or thinks she knows, defines and sharpens her interest in what she doesn't. Her inventory focuses what needs to be resolved.

Our social studies teacher spends the first few days taking an inventory of what the class knows about American History. Her syllabus defines this term, *American History*, in a rather rambling way. It concentrates on United States History from the beginning to the present but places it in the context of the development of the New World, past and present. So it begins with Columbus' voyages and includes major events in South America and Canada from that time till this.

Keeping these parameters in mind, she asks her students what they know about the topics her syllabus will raise. She might simply ask questions, or she could pose as a foreigner or alien able to speak only to the "experts" in this room for an understanding of the American past. She keeps track of the information. She could do it in a number of ways but decides on a time-line chart, which she fills in on the board.

What unfolds is a very peculiar time-line chart, with many gaps, few dates, and serious doubts about some of the sequences. Columbus, a Spaniard or maybe an Italian, discovered America in 1492. No one is sure what part. Then come the Pilgrims to Plymouth Rock somewhere along the coast of Main around 1788, or maybe 16 something. Then Cortez was doing something in Mexico. There was a War of Independence, a Civil War,

World Wars I and II, Korea, Vietnam. They raise cattle in Argentina. There is quite a bit of detail under the Civil War about Stonewall Jackson and the Shenandoah Valley Campaign from a student whose parents trace back to Jackson's relatives. Another student had a lot to say about the dates and times and significance of Martin Luther King. Seven names of U.S. Presidents appear. Washington was the Father of our Country and brought democracy to the 13 original states. Castro is the only head of state named for another American country. Nothing besides the Northwest Mounted Police seemed to be happening in Canada. And so forth.

A little time is spent on the second day by students adding to the chart and making revisions. When everyone agrees they have a fair picture of what the class knows, the teacher uses it to stimulate some questions. Did nothing really happen here for 300 years? Someone thought the French had owned some of America. If so, when? How did they get it? What did they do with it? How did a handful of pilgrims create such a powerful nation? When we started adding states, why didn't we continue through Canada and all of South America? Because there were nations there? Who were they and how did they get there? The question-posing possibilities of the student-generated chart are limitless, but the teacher concentrates on raising those that her syllabus can help clarify. After setting the question-generating pace, she turns the process over to the students. With the chart as a reference, they begin to express what they don't understand and what confuses them.

The point of this brief exercise is to demonstrate to the class, individually and collectively, that its knowledge of American History is highly problematic. (In the unlikely event that a class should display a satisfactory grasp of a syllabus, the teacher has strong evidence for not teaching it that course.) Each student sees that what he and others know does not satisfy. Here and there, individual students begin to identify issues about which their ignorance is personally troublesome — things they'd like to know about. The few students who have a well-formed understanding of some part of the subject matter expose it in a context that clearly underlines its value.

The completion of this inventory does not mark a pleasant moment for the class, nor, perhaps, for the teacher. There is a sense of chaos, confusion, frustration. The ambience is quite different from that of a typical class at the end of its second day.

The average class neither seeks nor wants an exposure of the student's relevant state of knowledge. The demeanor of the text and the teacher suggest that it would be convenient if students behaved as though they knew next to nothing. What they know or don't know doesn't matter. All they need do is follow the text and the teacher and exhibit performance when it's requested. This is an orderly, systematic procedure in which the initial state of the student's skills and insights plays no role.

But our inventory-taking teacher wants her students to actively express their starting condition, and to see the class's goal in light of that condition. She wants the unease they experience to be part of the motive for their trip. As much as feasible, the class becomes the students' effort to resolve that unease. In the typical class, the reason for the trip is that it is required, and the proper deportment is passive cooperation.

Next, our social studies teacher transcribes and mimeographs the students' inventory of American History. She distributes it to the class. The class is aware of its starting point. Altering, editing, and reshaping the inventory will mark its progress. Each individual and collective gain will be apparent to everyone.

It is time now to turn to the text, but our teacher postpones handing copies out. Instead, she duplicates the first unit readings with all vocabulary, study, and skill aids deleted. She hands out just the readings themselves.

She has a few students read several paragraphs aloud, then stops. She asks whether, with an eye toward understanding the material, there are any problems. The class volunteers little, but her probing reveals that a few words turn out to be obscure for some students. Names, dates, and places have occurred in the reading — places like Lisbon, Genoa, Asia — and few have more than a vague idea where some of them are, how close or how far apart. She inquires what good it does to read place names without knowing where they are. Offhandedly, she asks the following: "When Queen Isabella finally convinced Columbus to sail, was she sending him to Asia or to India?" "Asia!" assert some students who recall the word from the reading. "She convinced him to go to Asia?" the teacher asks. After a bit more badgering, one student observes that Queen Isabella didn't convince Columbus; it was the other way around.

The teacher notes the problem with vocabulary, the need for map skills, and the importance of trying to keep cause and effect clear (no point to history otherwise). She points out that these problems will constantly recur and asks whether the class has any suggestions about handling them. It's decided each student should make a vocabulary list following each reading. Each student, of course, checks meanings for his or her own list, but is there anything else you could do with the list? Well, any student might be asked to quiz the rest of the class about his or her words. The class would like a map of the world, and maybe other maps later, in the classroom. There will be a rotating "map assignment," where a student is responsible for locating sites in class following a reading. The teacher discusses two kinds of questions — "Why did?" and "What happened when?;" cause and effect questions — and part of each reading assignment will be to prepare three of each kind that could be posed to the class.

All these and several other learning problem issues are, of course, beautifully handled by the textbook. But our teacher wants the act of raising them, and the process and responsibility for dealing with them, to rest with the students. After the class handles a few more "clean" readings (devoid of skill, vocabulary, and study support materials), she hands out the text. Time is spent in class looking at the study helps for the readings already completed. Some class pride is expressed in having already spotted and resolved issues that the 'helps' are raising. The teacher praises the text for its considerate helps and encourages their use, but makes it clear that it's still each student's responsibility to spot and chase their own learning problems and bring them up in class. Students accept the helpful text, but not passively. In fact, there grows — and the teacher encourages — a covert competition in class to raise questions, spot problems, and try learning techniques that the help sections in the book don't address.

Occasionally the teacher assigns short readings from other sources. These enable her to check that students are still maintaining their study skill responsibility. They also demonstrate that those skills are useful quite apart from the class textbook. Her selections also give her a good basis for compare-and-contrast discussions and exercises in the class. Students view alternate expositions and learn that textbooks aren't gospel. But the teacher doesn't do this often because she's found a better source for alternate readings. One of the added benefits of her initial class inventory was a sense of her students' personal interests. When she feels class curiosity heighten about some topic, she will, as often as not, come out with something like this: "Clare, you are our resident expert on early Central America. Find us a few good paragraphs on Cortez for the class period after next."

Periodically, the class updates its time-line inventory. This gives them a sharp sense of how much they've gained and learned, but our teacher takes the update quite a bit further. The teacher points out how the new information, in contrast with the remainder of their inventory, raises new issues and questions that liven the work remaining. There is a constant adjusting of aim, a sharpening of involvement with the subject matter. The teacher is not pursuing answers here; she's cultivating questioning minds. The students are engaged in forming hypotheses, projecting consequences. The teacher encourages "what if's." They fuel and mature continuing student inquiry.

There is another technique our teacher employs when she wants her students to develop an especially firm and rich grasp of some idea. She usually picks cornerstone, "taken-for-granted" ideas that everyone is sure they understand and treats them like this:

"It's Question the Answer time, students. Our answer for today is 'Farming.' You all have 5 minutes. Samantha, Betsy, and Philip will be our lucky jury for today. Remember, they'll pick the five best questions that earn their authors an extra point each. And I will add as many of my five questions as haven't been asked. You know what happens if you get all five of mine. No homework!"

The last remark generates a good-natured hoot. The class has yet to catch all five of her questions, and she's had to defend herself against the charge of using ringers. But pencils begin scratching heads and making notes. Some hands go up before the 5 minutes and the teacher begins to write on the board. Eventually, she has:

1. What was the main occupation in the thirteen colonies?

2. What work did 82% of the people do for 14 hours a day in the Southern Colonies?

3. What business created the major market for the fancy goods that made Philadelphia famous?

4. What did they do mostly to survive in the Northern Colonies and to make money in the Southern?

5. What did people want to do in Pennsylvania that made them cut down so much wood?

6. If you weren't building ships or trading or trapping or hunting or fishing, you were probably _____ .

7. What job would the whole family most likely have a hand in?

8. What did people mostly want slaves for?

9. People left settled places to find more land for _____ .

10. Most people didn't go to school much. You could learn all you needed to know from your parents about _____ .

11. What did you need about 50 acres for to support your family in the Middle Colonies?

12. A large part of early industry was geared to make tools for _____ .

13. Owning and protecting your own land was very important if you were _____ .

14. At first, most of the goods we traded with England did not come from _____ .

15. Wherever people found climate, soil, and water that would grow something well that others wanted, there would be a large growth in _____ .

16. One way to change earth and hard work into money is by _____ .

17. Because colonists couldn't go to a Supermarket, they *had* to take up _____ .

18. If any profession tied people to the land, it was _____ .

19. If _____ didn't earn money, there wouldn't have been any slaves.

20. Some men in England started communities in America because they thought _____ was the best and most honest way of life.

21. All the towns and cities depended on people who did _____ .

The class is hushed while the teacher compares her list of five questions with those on the board. "No . . . I can't ask this one. Hmm. You've got this one, too. And this. Uh oh, you caught this one, too. Now I'm worried. Aha!" There is a groan as the teacher writes: What occupation produced most of the taxes collected by local colonial governments and benefited most from the taxes spent?

"Sorry, students. But you did get four of my five, so skip your reading assignment for tonight and just do the cause and effect questions on today's reading. As I've told you before, you'll *never* get all five of my questions. I'm just too smart. All right, jury. What's your verdict on the five best questions?"

The process our teacher has cultivated here is very much like the one minds must follow to establish a sound *concept*. One has to trace and define a whole network of relationships between the idea and its context.

As the teacher leads the examination of the students' questions, she strives for two things. First, she wants to stimulate a deeper and more mature conception of farming and its role in this phase of history. Second, she wants her students to sharpen their questioning skills which, after all, are expressions of their generic ones. She points out that questions reveal a great deal about what the questioner knows. She favors question 2 over question 1 because it is more knowledgeable, more precise, less general. Someone ignorant of colonial culture couldn't ask question 3. There is good compare-and-contrast in question 4. Question 15 expresses an important, repeating dynamic in colonial growth. There is interesting imagery in 16 and a significant grasp of motive in 20. As she leads students to expose the thoughts behind their questions, they sometimes improve both. Question 19, for instance, becomes, "If farmers couldn't have increased profit more by using slaves, there wouldn't have been any."

There is a subtle boon to this approach that tends to be overshadowed by the obvious gains in exercising operant skill. Students come to be connoisseurs of questions. Questions themselves are things to be compared and contrasted, rather than simply feared and avoided. Nuances can be noted, strengths and weaknesses assessed. It is an important step forward.

In selecting these and other techniques she employs in class, the teacher is expressing two constant impulses. The first is her love of her subject matter, which poses the following problem: "How do I get the students out of themselves and into the subject matter, just as I'm drawn out of *myself* into the subject matter?" The second impulse is her desire to share the rewards of dwelling in her discipline, and those rewards do not come from stockpiling information. They come from the stimulating performance of an active mind in a challenging arena, and that poses the following problem: "When they're in the discipline, how do I get them to notice, to examine, to liken, to consider and reconsider, to play out the consequences as I do?" Sound familiar? Yes, the generic skills coupled with the age-old quest of the teacher. But it is sharpened here by the teacher's clearer sense of her own reward. It is how she *thinks* in her subject field that matters. She wants that to be what matters for her students.

If her students had come to her fresh from ETSI, she could perhaps worry less about stimulating them to think actively in the discipline and draw them productively into less usual, more demanding ways to do so. Paired problem-solving teams might become paired project teams who would understand the commission to proceed by way of employing the generic skills. One team, for instance, could be the "Isabella" team; another the "Columbus" team. The project would be to present to the class the issues implicit in their historic encounter. Each team would strive to capture their namesake's position. What might Isabella's point of view have been, and what were her reservations about Columbus' venture? How come she was a better approach for Columbus than King Ferdinand? What would Columbus have to plead to overcome resistance? The "Isabella" team would role-play Isabella's position and the "Columbus" team his in an effort to win her support. The class could then debrief and examine the dynamics.

This is only one of numberless approaches our teacher might use. ETSI exposed students have been accustomed to taking on and building a case of their own. The teacher's tactic is to set those tasks for operant skill that will best illuminate her subject matter. She has, with students explicitly instructed in thinking skills, the added advantage of being able to openly examine their use of the generic skills in any instance of analysis or problem solving.

We revisit the strategies of our social studies teacher later and probe them a bit more deeply. But now let's turn to how a math instructor might teach to strengthen thinking skill.

CULTIVATING THINKING SKILL IN MATH

With justification, we all presume that thinking is central to the mastery of mathematics. One reason for our presumption is the plain fact that the products of mathematical operation are so obviously countless; we can't commit them all to memory. True, the products of some basic operations — times tables and such — can be committed to memory, but that alone does not take us very far. We quickly reach a point where we have to command method. Despite pocket calculators, we need to process numeric quantities; to divide, multiply, subtract, add. Strictly speaking, these processes could in turn be memorized, but strict memorization here is poor policy for a number of reasons. The most telling reason is simply that it is harder to command them by memory than by understanding them. Among other things, understanding what division is makes retaining a cluster of division techniques or algorythms easier.

All in all, the modern math text is highly accomplished in addressing the development of numeric skills, and even in showing how those skills apply in practical contexts. A good text might present students who've covered the basic arithmetic skills with an exploded, dimensioned plan of a dog house, and elicit all those skills by having them prepare to build 20 of them. Parts have to be economically layed out in purchasing materials, pounds of nails and screws determined, costs established — perhaps including wages — and so on. Some very important skills in applied mathematics that were once ignored are now usefully stressed: estimation, for instance. So what, beyond skillfully assisting students through the text, is left for the math instructor to do?

What is left may seem like, but is far from, more of the same. The math instructor can vastly enhance the generic thinking skills by accustoming them to critical new ways of grasping experience. This can be stated simply, but the doing is complex. He gets students to *attend* to quantity (more than/less than), shape (likeness, difference), frequency, and motion. He gets them to *analyze* these properties of their experience, to consider, assess, and evaluate in their terms. He heightens the students' perception of these basic dimensions of experience as well as their ability to treat them with appropriate precision. To the degree that he does this, he advances his students' capacity for useful abstraction and precise generalization. He gives them not just number-crunching skills, but the seed perceptions of the scientist or engineer, and the savor for precision required by mature thought. The numbers are merely his grammar; he is teaching a powerful language about experience, and he wants them to "talk" that language effectively.

The first thing our fifth-grade math instructor needs to do is realize that in adding thinking skill to his concern he has subtly altered his goal. His aim is no longer simply getting students to "do" arithmetic in the sense of mastering computation skills. It is rather to get students to "arithmatize" experience; embellish, enhance, and reform it with mathematical insight. This latter aim includes the former but goes considerably beyond it.

He might start by showing students that all the arithmetic impulses — to add, to subtract, to multiply, to divide — are already vigorously alive in them. What he is going to teach will show them how to more skillfully and powerfully do what they already do. Long before they come to understand how to do it well, arithmetic has invaded their language, their imagery, and their mode of thinking.

The teacher gets his students to *notice* the math they already presume and employ. "Tell me what you divided yesterday," he requests. The list can be extensive, beginning with the day itself that falls into sleep, breakfast, chores, school, lunch, more school, recess, school again, dinner, chores again, play, study, TV. There are subdivisions. School into interesting and boring classes, homework hard and homework easy, lunch shared with a friend, a candy bar split in three pieces, playtime between baseball and model-building. When we take anything apart, anything at all — a bicycle by hand or a day in our minds — we seem to be dividing things into pieces or kinds.

He asks if there are other places they might suspect they are doing math. Oh, sure, when they count their change. But what about comparing things? Can you name a time when you compare things that didn't involve some kind of adding, subtracting, multiplying, or dividing? Maybe not with numbers and maybe not clearly, but you're doing some or all of those things. You have a story you like and a story you don't like. Compare them. Does one have more or less of something than the other? If it doesn't, they aren't different; they're exactly the same. You don't think they have anything in common? Then you can't compare them. A ten-speed will go three or four times as fast as a tricycle, and we can measure that. Does it mean anything to say one story is twice as exciting as another, or that you don't like this one half as much? Sure, at least by analogy. By analogy with what? With the only things that let you add, subtract, multiply, and divide perfectly: with numbers.

And if our language and thought leans on number, how much more so does the world around us? Number hides everywhere. The students' experience of the world is redolent with implied math that the instructor can make explicit. Mom divides at the dinner table when she'll only have half a piece because of her diet. Dad is at the table because of math; his watch told him when to drop his tools in the garage and wash up. Nothing in the house, nor the house itself, would be there without it. No, really. We mean nothing. Behind that bowl of peas on the table stands all the math of commerce, real estate, plant biology, weed control, and fertilizer ratios, to name a pittance. The people are there because the family has somehow managed to stay on the upside of the income/expense ratio. Everything the student does, wants to do, and has to do involves juggling quantities. To please himself he wants more play, less study. To succeed in school, he needs more study, less play. To understand any change he has to grasp increases and decreases: less heat, winter; more, summer. Higher wages, a better car; lower wages, the bus. To make any or all of this clear, and especially to control it, we have to turn to math.

The pure mathematician might rebel here and point out that our instructor is far from developing the skills of computation in all this, and he is right. But our instructor *is* developing the student's sense of the kinship between arithmetic and his own affairs. The teacher wants to show students that they already strive to do weakly what a mastery of arithmetic would empower them to do well.

We look at just one instance of this approach, because it is easily generalizable. During a class session just prior to seriously broaching division and multiplication, our instructor sketches a rectangle on the board, sprinkles it liberally with dots, and poses this problem:

"This is the situation, class. I've got a bunch of rabbits in my pen here. I want to build hutches for them and I'm going to put three rabbits in each hutch. The problem is I don't know how to divide, and I have to decide how many hutches to build. I need to know so I can buy material to make them. If I had plenty of material, I might not need to know. I could just keep building hutches and putting rabbits in them until I ran out of rabbits. But I don't have any material, so how do I do it?"

A student suggests that first he ought to count how many rabbits he has.

"What good would that do? I don't know how many I've got, but suppose I had 109? Remember, I can't divide."

Eventually, one student suggests he could take three rabbits out at a time and . . . By the way, do you have stakes you can pound in the ground? Yes? . . . tie the three rabbits to a stake. Then get another three and keep doing that until you don't have any more. Then count the stakes and you know how many hutches you need.

Another student says there's an easier way. Do you have some fence, like chicken wire? OK, then herd the rabbits to one side and put the fence down the middle of the pen. Now you've got an empty part of the pen. Pick up three rabbits, put them in the empty part, and make a mark on the ground. Keep doing this until all the rabbits are on one side of the fence and then count your marks.

"Sounds good," the teacher says. "I'll do that. But I don't like to scare the rabbits too much, so I'll just add a temporary pen next to this one. . . " He adds an empty pen to the one on the board. ". . . and start moving the rabbits." He erases three dots at a time from the original pen, adds three to the new one, and makes a mark on the board each time he does so. His last move only involves switching two dots. Finally, he counts his marks. "Eighteen. I've got to build 18 hutches. That's great, class. You got me the answer and I didn't need to know division. But hold on. You were so good at that maybe you can help me with my next problem. I've gone through sketching out this hutch I want to build and I figure I need 47 nails to make one. I can't multiply, either, so how do I figure out how many nails I'll need?

The class shows him how to add 47 nails for each hutch he wants to build. With a little guidance, it isn't hard for them to conclude that dividing is finding out how many times to take something away and multiplying how many times to add something.

Our example isn't remarkable and everything in it might appear in a good math text, with one exception. Here students make the discovery. They are not handed it. It comes to them as the product of operant skill. From the point of view of developing thinking skills, this exception takes on momentous proportions. No other subject matter succumbs as cleanly and neatly to employment of the generic skills as does math. Nowhere else does an insight, a distinction, a mental operation so clearly crack things apart or so precisely fit them into place. Students led to unravel math as a result of their own active thought discover this early and often develop a distinct taste for this distinctive flavor. A person could become an addict.

CULTIVATING THINKING SKILL IN SCIENCE

To many unacquainted young minds, science can be very much like broccoli: at best an acquired taste, and not easily acquired at that. Someone will surely object to this observation and counter it by noting that it seems easier to introduce students to science than to math. Students do seem to have fun with early science curricula and their often fascinating introduction to the world around them. The problem emerges when one carefully considers what counts as science.

The path most students take to the gates of science is the path of taxonomy. They are introduced to phenomena in all their types; kinds of plants, animals and terrain, natural and man-made structures, the things that constitute all our systems, from micro to macro. Coming to grips with this rich array and attending to increasingly detailed segments of it comprises the bulk of introductory science for most students, at least up to middle school.

This constitutes an extensive introduction to science's various subject matters, but it barely nods at the whys and hows of doing science. The introduction is engrossing and it will carry most students along for several years until the time is reached for the Great Shift — the shift from touring to doing. This shift is unexpectedly demanding, and the shock of it dislodges many students from the path to science.

From the point of view of the thinking skill instructor, this is doubly unfortunate. First, while in the introductory, taxonomic phase of science education, there is small occasion for the students' operant skills. Second, just at the threshold of "doing" science — when the operant skills are more likely to be called from the bench — most students abandon the enterprise.

An obvious strategy recommends itself to the science teacher who wants to develop thinking skills, and that is to get students "doing" science much sooner; to blend the doing with the early taxonomic tour. Happily, some science texts and pedagogies have already moved in this direction. Of course, in the strict sense we cannot get intermediate students to "do" science. We can't expect unprecedented proofs of scientific theories or unprecedented inferences from data. But we can expect the behaviors that underlie both of these kinds of outcomes. We can expect young minds to deduce from theory, infer from data, and govern both processes in light of evidence.

We can expect this kind of performance because intermediate students are already, though unconsciously, experienced in it. Doing science is doing what we already do in a more intensive, systematic, and purposeful way. That is just the point a science teacher is trying to make to her sixth graders in the following example:

"I'd like to begin this science unit with a question. How many of you students believe in fortune tellers?"

There is a brief silence, then some giggling. A few hands shoot up in mock affirmatives.

"No, seriously. How many of you believe you can tell the future?"

The class isn't quite sure of itself, but there are negative sounds and some shaking of heads.

"I'm astounded. I'm shocked. How can none of you believe in telling the future when you do it all the time? I have a classroom full of fortune tellers who don't believe in fortune telling! Let me ask some questions and I'll prove it to you."

"Kenneth, what will it be like outside in 4 months?"

"Cold. Maybe snowy," Kenneth says.

"Judy, what will you be doing around 6 this evening?"

"Eating supper, probably," Judy says.

"Jerry, what will happen after school when Mr. Simonson holds up his sign at the corner crossing on Walnut?"

"The cars'll stop," Jerry says.

"Shirley, what grade will you be in 5 years from now?"

Shirley counts to herself quietly. "11th," she says.

"Four students I picked at random, and all of them predicted something about the future. Think of all the other things we can tell about the future. For instance. . . " The teacher takes the room calendar off the wall and hands it to a boy in her class. ". . . what day in the week will it be 143 days from now, Sam? While Sam checks on that, class, tell me some other things we either can be certain or pretty sure of about the future."

The list grows extensive, from sun rises and seasons through vacations and fights with siblings, to the hunger before meals and who you're likely to eat them with. Sam informs everyone that 143 days from now it will be a Thursday.

"You see? By far the greatest part of what will happen to you tomorrow, each of you can tell me today. Seems to me that's pretty good fortune telling. But we don't think of it that way. We just take what we expect of the future for granted.

"So all of you can tell a good deal about the future. Since you are fortune tellers, I wonder if you are also wizards. In addition to telling the future, can you change it?"

In discussion, the class decides it can. Jeff, who's planning to shoot baskets on the outdoor court after school, could go home instead. Cindy, who expects another spat with her pesky younger brother when she gets home, could keep things mellow by helping him play with his Robotrons.

"So two things are true about all of us. We know a lot about the future and we know we can change things in it. A good part of the time we try to make the future better for us and those we care about. But there are important connections between these two truths, between predicting the future and making changes in it. Anyone have ideas about what they are?"

In her guidance of the discussion, the teacher leads her class to several important insights. Lots of times our personal future changes in ways we don't intend. We put 5 dollars in a jean pocket that has a hole. In line at the show we discover the money's gone and we have to go home. Accidents and things we aren't aware we've done change things for us, often in ways that aren't pleasant.

But when things go our way, when what we plan to do works, it's because our predictions about the future were sound. What we know *now* about how something works tells us what it will probably do *later*. If we know *now* how something reacts to changes, we can make changes and get it to react that way in the future. The more we know about things, the more we can predict and control.

"Cindy, you know Gregy will have just finished his nap when you get home. He'll be rested, rejuvinated, and bored, just aching for excitement. If you ignore him, or tell him to leave you alone, there *will* be trouble. If you play with him—blue skys.

"Jeff, you know a half-hour of baseline shots after school will keep you in the grove. You also know you could beat your mom home from work. You know she's had a full day and will come in tired. You also know that walking into a house where the garbage is stashed and the clothes out of the drier and folded would put a smile on her face.

"In your two cases—and in everyone's case—what we know now is our only handle on the future. The more we understand about how things work, the better our grip. People who really get serious about this—about advancing what we know so we can better predict and control our tomorrows — are called scientists. And everything we have that can't just be picked out of the fields and woods and waters is a product of that scientific effort — the effort to know more so we can predict more and control more."

Our science teacher has anchored a theme, and she'll play variations on it throughout her class. She's anchored it in the student's own behavior — more intensely and with greater care, scientists do what students do. Becoming a scientist is doing what you now do better.

True, her position seems at odds with that of some real scientists who claim a disdain for utility, who say that insight is their only concern, and that they could care less about consequences. Science is a large enterprise with ample room for people of such persuasion, but *as* an enterprise it outstrips all others just in its consequences. Subtract its consequences and science would be unintelligible.

The strategy our teacher uses to underline her theme is to demonstrate that scientific insights and perceptions make a real difference. Wherever she can, she enlists her students' operant thinking skills in uncovering that difference, even at the level of introductory science.

She knows, for instance, that the taxonomies she is supposed to introduce her students to are the products of a great deal of projection and problem solving. They are not simple a priori listings meant to tidy up a messy biosphere. So rather than introduce students to taxonomies, she makes taxonomists of them.

"What," she asks as she draws a hoof on the board, "can you tell me about an animal that has a foot like this?"

"It's a horse," someone says.

"That doesn't tell me anything about the animal. It just names him. Suppose someone brought you a hoof and asked you what kind of a creature it must have come from. What could you conclude just from the hoof?"

Guesses trickle out painfully until the class gets the hang of it. But eventually the hoof says — unless its owner had arms as well — that the owner wasn't a flesh eater. You couldn't catch anything very well with a hoof, or hold it to feed once you caught it. Seems great for running, though, so you could get away from flesh eaters. Wouldn't be bad for defense, either; make a great club. Given the round shape of the hoof, its lack of length, and the angle of the connecting bone, or wrist (can't deduce it's a fetlock), it looks like the owner would have four of them rather than just two. The class spends a little time exploring why they don't think the owner would have five, or maybe six, or eight. They consider how much weight four such feet with bones that size might carry, and so on.

A few more sessions of deduction from this kind of evidence and the teacher assigns her class field work. They are to bring in specimens from two sites they are familiar with and quite happy to visit. The first site is the after-school deluge of superhero shows on TV. The second is anyone's collection of sci–fi adventure comic books. Their task is to bring in pictures and sketches of specimen monsters, a minimum of four each.

When the monsters are all in, the job is to analyze and organize them, to form a monster taxonomy. The students will know each monster's astounding capabilities, but the teacher lays a ground rule. They have to treat the monsters like they treated the hoof and make their judgment on the basis of what it looks like. They discover that, stripped of their atomic and death ray and antigravity capabilities, many monsters would have trouble getting a square meal. *With* those abilities, a 6-month human infant would be invincible.

In keeping with the ground rule, each monster is assessed. There is some comparison between monsters designed to look awful and monsters that would really work. Then comes the question of how to organize this formidable group. Oblivious of the phrase, students begin debating taxonomic criteria. How should we order and classify them? By size? Shape? Whether robot, cyborg, or living thing? Capacity for havoc? Degree of nightmarishness? Degree of functional design? The issue of the *purpose* for the classification is raised, and with it the realization that taxonomies aren't absolute. Different taxonomies are good for different things. If you need to ship monsters, taxonomies based on size or diet might be helpful. If you have to fight them, a taxonomy based on the kinds of damage they can do, or their weaknesses, could be the thing. The teacher aids the class in building several alternate taxonomies and guides them in comparison, contrast, and some deliberation on how these classifying systems might be used.

Now, when she turns her class's attention to the established taxonomies of real sciences, she has on her side some student empathy for the accomplishment. She can point out, for instance, that biology employs criteria in its taxonomies that they could not have used in theirs. Biology is interested in things insofar as they live, and it classifies according to the infrastructures that sustain life and enable it to flourish. Students would have had to get their hands on monsters to really analyze and compare such infrastructures.

The approach our teacher has used in introducing her students to taxonomy can, with a little ingenuity, be applied to any other subject in her field. She does, in fact, use it several times because it paves the way for, and stimulates, operant thinking. It is worth considering a bit more carefully how it does this.

First, the teacher tries to begin her approach to any scientific subject, process, or technique from some point well within the students' experience. It's important to be clear about why, as a thinking skill instructor, she does this. Notice that she could, and probably does, reference student experience fruitfully just as a science teacher. She can draw all kinds of useful analogies between scientific phenomena and events familiar to students. The path of a baseball, for instance, lends itself admirably to illustrations of acceleration, velocity, resistance, and gravity. But this is the science teacher's — not the thinking skill instructor's — reason for accessing student experience.

The thinking skill instructor wants to base new learning on ground familiar to the student for quite other reasons. When it comes to employing operant skill, most students have done their best thinking outside of classrooms. It is in dealing with the inescapable, everyday, personal affairs of life that people tend to do whatever unguided assessing, analyzing, and reflecting they do. Perhaps not much of this goes on, and there is precious little awareness of self-consciousness about it when it does, but whatever play the operant skills are given does tend to arise in situations that are familiar and personally relevant. It is in the student's fund of personal experience that the thinking skill instructor will likely find operant skills, undoubtedly disguised, but nonetheless alive and to some degree kicking.

So the thinking skill instructor searches for a tie with student experience in order to connect with the student's most effective thinking. She can then reveal to its author what *is* effective about such thinking, and lead, coach, and encourage such thought elsewhere. Captured scrawny in the wild, she wants to bring those skills to full potential in her discipline. In a phrase, she's making the most of transference.

Consequently, when the time arises in her science class to introduce a fairly typical model of the scientific method (1. state the problem; 2. make a prediction; 3. experiment; 4. check the data; 5. draw a conclusion), our teacher makes the extra effort to erect a familiar situation like many that could have sparked students to behave in those ways:

"Jack, suppose you've been invited to a Friday night rock concert 2 weeks from now by a couple of buddies from a neighboring town. It's a very "in" rock group and you really want to go. The concert is 25 miles away, but one of the friends has a brother who's a senior, and he'll drive over, pick you up, and take all of you there. Trouble is, there's a standing rule at your house that you don't ride in any car without your parent's permission. They've never even *thought* of your going on the road with an unknown student driver. Besides, they've been drawing the reigns on you for spending too much time out of the house as it is. What would you do?"

Jack allows he'd try to get around it.

"Try to get around what?"

"The driving ban. I'd try to get that lifted."

"You think that's the real problem?"

"Well, I could maybe get my folks to take me, but even that would be tough and it would ruin everything. Yeah, I guess the main problem would be getting them to let me ride with a high school driver. If I could get them to buy that, I could probably get permission to go."

"So what do you think you'd do?"

The teacher encourages him to build his plan in open class discussion. Other students make suggestions, some of which Jack adopts. In outline, his strategy unfolds like this:

Jack will tell his parents about the invitation that very night. "It would be great," he plans to say, and then casually add, "but I didn't think I could go because of the driving and because I really have been out a lot lately." He expects that his parents will agree with this, perhaps with a twinge of admiration for their son's common sense. He's raised the issue, scuttled any confrontation, and just maybe planted a seed.

The next week, he will be dutiful and conspicuously around at home. Meanwhile, he will contact the buddy whose brother plans to drive. He wants to see if the brother, or better still, one of his parents, would call his folks on signal and extend the invitation, with special assurances about the brother's character and driving record. Jack plans to give that signal when his sterling behavior and special chores have raised his stature to the necessary point.

"Fine, Jack," the teacher says. "Now, in summary, tell us why you think your plan will work."

In effect, Jack says that what would trouble his parents is a vision of their irresponsible son with three other irresponsible youths careening on a wild, 50-mile race through the night. He has to dissolve that vision. As the date nears, he wants his folks to look at him and see a dependable, responsible son. He also wants his buddies to be seen in that light. The call from his friend's folks will show that they are the kind of people who understand, sympathize with, and respect a parent's concerns. If his parents come to view this as a healthy, reasonable outing, and himself as someone who *deserves* such an outing, he'd probably get permission to go.

"OK. Suppose you run things just as you plan. And still your parents say "No." You end up staying home that Friday night. Any idea where things might have broken down?"

Jack and the others kick this around for awhile. Several things could have happened, but Jack thinks the real danger in the plan is overdoing it. "If I'm really *not* dependable, it would be tough changing my parents' minds. I might push too hard, and they might decide I don't ring true."

"So you don't think your plan would work as a scam, but only as a way of presenting your best side, assuming you have one."

"Right."

Via Jack, the teacher has led the class through all the major behaviors involved in the scientific method. She's had them identify a problem, predict a feasible resolution, segregate the data that's especially important and needs to be monitored, run through possible consequences of executing it, and draw various conclusions from various possible outcomes. True, they haven't actually *done* the experiment, but they've used their minds in all the ways they would if they *had* done it. That is one of the virtues of the *gedankenexperimente,* or thought experiment. To a degree, we are all employers of this approach. It is the incipient scientist in each of us trying to foster and manage a reasonable future.

The teacher's next task is of course to make this clear. She picks a favorite from the boundless instances of applied scientific method. Perhaps she picks one from Galileo, the very father of experimental method — say his encounter with gravity off the leaning Tower of Pisa. She then draws, step by step, the parallels between Galileo's approach and Jack's.

The science teacher who seeks to instruct thinking skill has, by the nature of her trade, a conspicuous advantage. The larder in her field contains more of the overt fruit of effective thinking than does any other discipline's. But it isn't enough to put those fruits on display. She has to track student thinking to its hidden den, coax it out, and demonstrate that when revealed the student's best personal efforts, and the scientist's lofty professional ones, are kin.

What remains of her strategy we've seen in earlier examples. Wherever she can, she resists just dispensing scientific insights. She arranges instruction so that students gain them as a consequence of operant thought.

STEPS TO THINKING SKILL IN ANY DISCIPLINE

Our treatment so far implies a set of considerations that could be useful to any teacher of any discipline who wants to enlist and advance thinking skill. We'll try to pinpoint those considerations and apply them to one final example.

Determine the Skill/Content Mix.   Whatever the subject matter you wish to teach, it involves a mix of two things. First there are the relevant facts, the assertions and "givens" — often a seemingly bottomless quantity of them. In history, for instance, who could ever exhaust the dates, names, places, and events? Second, there are the relevant operations: the things one must learn to do with skill if the goals of the discipline are to be achieved. If you teach Auto Shop, the nomenclature of a gasoline engine would fall into the first category. Safe tool and shop procedure, diagnostic skills and repair strategies would fall into the second. Back to history, the operations would be those acts of analysis, comparison, inference, and deduction that resolve the "Whats" and "Whys" and "Hows" that discipline pursues.

As a teacher, you need to reflect carefully on this mix in two ways. Do it the easy and fairly automatic way first. Imagine a successful graduate of your class, someone who's achieved the goals you set and to whom you would gladly hand a healthy grade. How much of what that student has gained are relevant facts, and how much are skills of operation? Try to segregate your successful student's attributes into those two categories.

Once you've done this, you need to reflect on the outcome in the second way. The question you ask this time is, "Is the mix appropriate? Is it the mix I want?" This, too, is a fairly simple question, but the reason for asking it is a bit complex.

Basically, the problem is that much of what we put in our category of "relevant facts" is arbitrary. There are no facts that aren't themselves products of operations. In some cases, the operations may seem trivial, like naming and dating an event: the Battle of Cannae, 216 B. C. Actually, this is only trivial *after* someone has invented a language that can label, a calendar that can date, and a set of criteria that determines what the label does and doesn't reference. But jammed next to these seemingly trivial kinds of facts are many others that are products of obviously extensive and laborious operations on our part, such as the fact of a heliocentric solar system.

So the "givens" in the class you teach are the conclusions of prior operations. We make them "givens" because we couldn't possibly review all the operations that produce them. Besides, we expect — frequently incorrectly — that students have encountered those operations in prior classes. Sometimes we try to insure that they do, as when we insist that you must have Algebra I before taking Algebra II. But the point of reflecting on this is to see clearly that the mix of facts and required skills that constitutes the aim of any class is an artifact very much at the discretion of the teacher. You have all types of options, and you should ask yourself if you want or need to invoke some to change the mix.

Maybe you need to convert some of your "givens" to "problems;" to take something that in the past you expected students to simply accept as an assertion and convert it to a conclusion students reach by exercising operant skill. On the other hand, maybe you have been calling on some skills past the point of diminished return (it can be frustrating to operate trivially) and would do better to convert some "problems" into "givens." Tinkering with such questions refines the art of teaching.

At this point you are considering changes in light of the aims and content of the course, and you might very well decide not to make any. But if you began your consideration with a novel desire to improve thinking skill, you will likely find you've shifted to a new "mix" of course objectives, with a greater emphasis on operations and a trimmer set of "givens." Even if you make no change in the mix, you will have a clearer sense, to put it roughly, of what you want your students to "know" as distinct from what you want them to be able to "do."

Set Skill Strategies.   Once you've reflected on, and possibly adjusted, the "mix" in your course objectives, it is time to concentrate on that part of the mix comprised of skills you want to develop. On inspection, these will tend to fall in two categories. One is the category of skills students have probably used before, but perhaps not in the context of this subject matter. The other is a category of skills, important in handling the subject matter, which seem unprecedented, or whose ties to prior student performance appear tenuous and unclear.

The issue you now face is pedagogical: How do you teach to best develop these skills? We've already explored the strategy for that category of skills students have probably used before: Expose students to their prior use of the skill—demonstrate their own skill to them by getting them to use it as they did before—then demonstrate its application to your subject matter, and finally constrain them to use it there.

You take a slightly different path for skills of the second category: skills that seem unprecedented. First, keep two things in mind. All real skills are learnable. If it isn't learnable, it's a natural attribute, not a skill. If it is a natural attribute, you should not be trying to teach it: No amount of arm flapping will bring your students to flight. If it is a skill, then exercise of the generic skills—selective attention, sustained analysis, analoging, suspension of closure, and autocensorship—can achieve sufficient grasp of it to initiate employment, practice, and increase in proficiency. That, in fact, is what we mean by saying skills are learnable. They are adjustments of behavior amenable to the generic skills.

The other thing to note is that those skills that seem unprecedented in student experience seem so because the intervening steps—the steps between what a student *can* do and what you want him to do—either aren't apparent or haven't been taken. You want your students to be skilled at scansion. A number of them may never have read a poem, let alone analyzed one for its meter. Well, you can have them memorize the classic meters and try to fit those patterns to poems. Or, you can harness their sense of beat and rhythm—a sense widespread in this Age of Rock—to their skills of analysis and let *them* discover the models, classic and otherwise, with all the fun and insight that attends arguing the exceptions.

When it comes to the seemingly unprecedented skill, *you* have to divine the intervening steps. And, although it is easy to take those steps yourself and beckon students to follow, it is better from the thinking skill perspective to make those steps "problems" rather than instructions. The paradigm we tend to follow is, "Here we are at point A, students, and here's how we get to point B." In developing thinking skill, the paradigm we want is, "Here we are at point A, students. That is point B. How do we get there?"

There are times when the distance between skills students have employed and the performance you want is really extensive. This occurs when your target performance is especially rich and sophisticated. Usually, this is a kind of performance not well characterized as the product of a skill; it is rather the product of a medley of integrated and harmonized skills. Written composition could be an instance of this kind of performance; a topic we've reserved for the next chapter. But so could be the preparation or analysis of a case study of some real event. All kinds of assessments, judgments, qualifications, and choices go into such a performance.

There is a useful strategy for bridging broad gaps between past and desired student performance. It is called *modeling* or *gaming*. As a strategy, it stems from something all teachers do. Every time you raise a "What if?" question with a student, you stimulate the impulse to game or model.

A model, setting aside the fashion mag sense of the term, is invariably some simplification of the thing it represents. It is like the thing it represents in important ways. In fact, its whole purpose is to represent important aspects of its referent. But the model simplifies, leaving out a great deal that isn't relevant to its function. If it didn't leave anything out, it would be a duplicate. Because they are relatively simple, models are very effective "staging points" for accustoming student skills to complex performances.

Suppose you have a dual objective. You want your sixth graders to have a sound grasp of political dynamics and you want them to savor some of the major skills of political behavior. Role modeling could be a good first step, with initial emphasis on understanding the priorities and concerns of people in various walks of life. What are the hopes, problems, needs, wants, wishes of a fireman, banker, meat packer, policeman, department store manager, or retired widow? Let students find out, and model each role for the class. Next, model those who represent such individuals, who give them the voice of a constituency. What are the concerns of a labor union rep, a club chairwoman, a Chamber of Commerce board member, and so on. Then there are the people who seek constituency support to gain a position, for which they promise to serve the constituency's interests. Students can role model a city council member, department head, or mayor. Finally, you bring students to model the political interactions themselves: a city council meeting, a ward election, what have you.

You begin with a relatively simple modeling task. Insight gleaned from that prepares students for a more complex modeling task, and you repeat the process until you arrive at your target level of performance. Failures in classroom modeling and gaming usually stem from disregard of this recursive process. If you start by modeling a city council meeting, students will wallow in poorly understood roles and dimly grasped generalities. Modeling can be powerful. It is a means of condensing and giving to students experience they have not had, thereby developing, with remarkable speed, an experiential base for complex insights and performances otherwise beyond their scope. But modeling has to begin by calling on experience students *have* had, and it has to follow a reasonable gradient toward the target performance. Leave too many gaps—fail to provide critical experience—and things fall apart.

At this point in your course planning, you should have a pretty good sense, not only of your target skills, but of how you might bring students to exhibit them.

Blend Skill and Content Strategies. But you don't have a teaching plan yet. Now you need to integrate your skill and your content aspirations, and here there is another strategy we would like to commend. *Where possible—* and sometimes it isn't—get students to "operate" before you hit them with the "givens." Alert them to, and get them to unlimber, the relevant skills before you introduce the required knowledge base.

At first, putting it this way sounds contradictory. How could you, for instance, get students to analyze the causes of WW II without enumerating them? You can't. But you *can* get them to analyze causes of something they are familiar with, say the loss of a homecoming game. Many of the *kinds* of assessment of the latter could be a beginning in assessing the former: identifying the opponents, their strengths, weaknesses, past performance, game plans.

We are back to the strategy of reaching into students' experience base to get them in a performance mode, but this time our aim is different. We aren't doing it to develop skills, but to develop a content appetite. Learners have a limited capacity for just plain information. They have a much larger capacity for information they have a *job* for. Reading a required, eye-glazing text on WW II is one thing. Searching that text operantly—to build an understanding of the opponents, strengths, weaknesses, and game plan—is another.

Wherever large quantities of information have to be dispensed to and mastered by students, try to establish a foretaste of its utility. A good way is to get them to *do* something similar to what you want them to *do* when they get the information. Again we are modeling, and again we are modeling to provide students with experience, but this time it is modeling a forthcoming experience they can only fully achieve by mastering a body of information. First, whenever you can, cultivate a reason and a taste for the data, not by lecturing its importance, but by making it the means to a capability students realize they don't have and want to achieve. You can sometimes build an appetite for information in students by modeling failure. You assign a deceptively simple group exercise or game that, by lack of insight and knowledge, the students bring to a shambles. Debriefing the failure—like debriefing a blown football play—can be a good way to awaken students to their needs.

Keep in mind your overall aim as a thinking skill instructor at this point in planning your teaching strategy. You want to maximize the gain of information through employment of operant skill and minimize the gain by sheer rote. Where rote is called for, make it rote fed by a view toward performance.

Make the Course Thinker Friendly. You are now in a position to sketch lesson plans — and you do need those to set your day-by-day aspirations. But be careful not to cram them too full. Allow, in both the mechanical and literal sense, for a little play. Novel expressions of student insight, intelligence, and inquiry will occasionally burst forth in class. Similar impulses will occur in you, with the temptation to parade them a bit. For reasons we suggested in the section on early elementary, you should give reign on such occasions. Our task constrains us to emphasize the power and effectiveness of good thinking, but good thinking loses none of these attributes when it is spontaneous or nimble or delightful. So modestly encourage mental play. It doesn't hurt for intelligence to appear pleasing, and these little gaps in the regimen can act like slits in a pie crust. They let off pent steam.

It's wise to be prepared to modify your pace, with all that implies about altering your lesson plans, and even your skill/content "mix." For no immediately apparent reason, one group of students will respond slowly and cautiously to your demands for operant performance, whereas another group will tug *you* along.

Suppose your course plan contains four fairly major challenges to operant learning. You may be forced, with a slow response group, to reduce it to one. It would be far better for them to respond operantly once—to truly resolve the learning challenge by themselves—than to be dragged past or boosted over the hurdles four times. Conversely, don't let a fast group twiddle its thumbs. The mechanics of this balancing act are obvious. For the fast class, you convert more "givens" to "problems." For the hesitant class, you do the opposite, but you insist that the operant performance you do call for is real.

For the thinking skill instructor, this balancing act is inescapable, because he must adjust instruction to the student thinking that actually occurs. Careful course preparation is even more important to the thinking skill instructor than to the pure subject matter advocate, but that greater care will not produce a full term's final set of lesson plans. The thinking skill instructor must adapt this day's plan to yesterday's performance. By embracing the thinking skill goal, the teaching task changes markedly. It is no longer simply to cover the material, but to make room for, encourage, and then guide productive thought toward coverage.

Consciously abetting thought in the classroom does require more work. Posing information as a product of operation rather than as a fixed lore to be absorbed will have you swimming against the pedagogical tide, but your stroke is in keeping with the deeper currents that form and reform the disciplines you teach. The disciplines with all the information they array *are* products of operant thought. Demonstrating this is simply demonstrating what's there.

ONE LAST EXAMPLE

Considerations like those just outlined produced the teaching examples we explored earlier in this chapter, but let us see how they might influence course conduct in one last and more limited situation. We won't deal here with approaching a whole discipline, but with a specific problem that arises while teaching in one. Let's take a seventh-grade Spanish teacher who is having difficulty with some of her content. She isn't doing as well as she would like in getting students to master Spanish verb conjugations. Many students seem confused and are, in forming simple Spanish answers to simple Spanish questions, tacking on whatever verb ending comes to mind. So next time, the teacher designs a game to play prior to introducing Spanish conjugations.

"We are going to invent a language, class. When I raise my hand I'm going to say a word. When you hear the word, I want the first row to clap. Follow me? OK." The teacher raises her hand. "RAPO," she says. The first row claps.

"Very good. The next time I raise my hand I'm going to say another word. When you hear it, I want the second row to clap. Ready? RAPAM." The second row claps.

"Good again. Now, this time when I say my word, everybody claps. RAPAMO." Everybody claps.

"It looks to me like you are all quick learners. Now let me give you a test. RAPAM!"

The teacher gets a firm response from much of the second row, but there are a scattering of claps elsewhere in the room. She continues the drill until the right groups participate and remain silent at each call.

"Not bad. Now let's look at these words." She writes the three in column on the board. "As you can see, the words are partly the same and partly different. What part do you think means 'Clap?'" RAP is quickly nominated. When asked what "O", "AM" and "AMO" mean, it doesn't take long for the class to couple them, respectively, with "first row," "second row," and "everybody."

"Cryptanalysts are people who crack secret codes. I think you could all get jobs as cryptanalysts. Now, in our new language, 'SIMP' means 'Pull your right ear.' What would I have to say to get the second row people to pull their right ear?"

The class coins SIMPO, SIMPAM, and SIMPAMO this way, and the teacher gives them some practice with all six words. Next, she calls three students to the front. She joins them in four chairs facing the class, one student on one side of her and two on the other.

"Now, students, you have to imagine that Frank, Paul, and Maxine are each something else. Frank is 'first row,' Paul is 'second row,' and Maxine is 'everybody.' They are going to do some things, and you have to tell me, in the order they do it, what they are doing. But you have to use our new language. You have a minute to make a note of anything you want on the board, and then I'll erase it."

After erasing the board, the teacher whispers for a moment with her three students. They straighten up, and Maxine pulls her right ear. "SIMPAMO" can be heard among the things the class yells out.

But the class gets better. Soon it is responding accurately with strings from the new language: "RAPO, SIMPAM, RAPAMO." The teacher seems suddenly to discover that some of the quicker students have made charts. One of the better charts, with rows for Frank, Paul, and Maxine, and columns for "Ear Pull" and "Clap," is placed on the board and discussed. Performance gets even better.

At the end of this class session, or perhaps the next, the teacher makes the inevitable transition to Spanish regular verb endings in the present tense. There are *ar* conjugations, *er* conjugations, and *ir* conjugations, but we won't go into those.

Instead, we will observe that the teacher has (1) adjusted her mix of "givens" and "operations." She could have taught verb endings by rote, but she sees that might not be best. Students need to make unfamiliar distinctions and decisions with these peculiar structural components even if they've memorized them. She wants students to actively pattern their skills for this task. She then (2) carefully identifies some of the sensibilities and capabilities her inexperienced students will need to wield and designs a game to model them. This (3) gives students a basis *in experience* from which they can both relate to the new data they are about to receive and apply alerted skill to the new performance that will be required of them. She has done all this (4) in a manner that is at least partly appealing to students, welcomes their operant thinking, and is not completely devoid of fun.

THE FILE

THE FILE

THE FILE

CHAPTER 9

COMPOSITION: C = A + d

Forethought

Two observations will help pave the way for this chapter. First, although it is the last chapter in our treatment of the elementary period, it is not simply of that period. More than any other chapter, this one applies — just as it stands — to all points of the educational continuum, from K through graduate school. Wherever and whenever you want to enlist the act and art of composition in ways that will advantage thinking skill, this chapter will serve you.

We quickly get to the second observation by imagining the plausible reaction of a good number of readers upon turning to this chapter: How dare we? A single short chapter on composition? Few topics can boast a more monumental literature — a literature of great sensitivity and complexity. What kind of boiling down could we do that's of any use?

Rather than boil down, we set our cap for a more specific goal. We want a simple, but not simplistic, model of composition that will put any teacher of any subject matter in control of its capacity to exercise and enlarge thinking ability. We believe we have it.

There are many powerful models of composition — real bulldozers. What we are offering is a hoe. It will fit any pair of hands, and with it you can carefully cultivate any student's capacity to write thoughtfully.

There are three ways the model can serve. First, if you believe that students write badly and you want to do something about it, this model will help. Aiding that labor of love may be justification enough.

Second, the model is attuned to the deep parallels and shared dynamics of writing and thinking. It insists that writing well demands and amplifies thinking well. The model reveals that interdependence, so that you can gauge and guide thought by its compositional fruit. It will also help you set writing tasks that specially exercise target thinking skills.

Third, the model prompts us to harness a simple truth. Writing offers a most natural and immediate arena for the expression of thinking skill. The student who masters thinking skill needs occasion to employ it. A better one than writing offers would be hard to imagine. As a matter of course, the student would exercise her mastery in writing paragraphs, themes, answers to essay tests, and, perhaps ultimately, theses, dissertations, and books. An educational program without a strong, integral call to write denies the thinking student her most effective modality; she is Cinderella—sans gown, sans coach, sans fairy godmother.

ASSERTION

Fortunately, we are seldom fully awake to a permeating fact of our social condition. We are aswim in a sea of assertions.

"He's a louse." "She's a beaut." "The kid's a brat." "Sun City for a fabulous vacation." "He's a capitalist war-monger." "Damn Commie." "Nothing like Cadillac Style. . . ." All you need for an assertion is to actually or implicitly plug some subject to a predicate. Any subject to almost any predicate: "Angel Dust's cool." "I'll stomp you." "Work sucks." In our world, subjects get plugged to predicates millions of times a second. But why imply, as we did, that it's good we aren't fully conscious of these ceaseless couplings?

Our lack of consciousness is a tribute to our survival instinct. It suggests we realize something we don't put into words, namely that assertions, in and of themselves, are worthless. They aren't worth even a penny a million, and we do well to ignore the vast bulk of them.

Assertions convey meaning, but there is nothing in the assertion itself that guarantees its meaning isn't misapplied, misleading, trivial, distorted, or false. Whether intentionally or not, a great bulk of them *are* misapplied, misleading, trivial, distorted, or false. A prime key to our sanity is the ability to let the great wash of assertions pass us by, to catch and attend only to a very, very few.

Which ones are worth a second's thought? The ones that claim evidence—

that offer credentials for the wedding of subject and predicate. There is a reflex action on our part for any assertion we truly entertain. We reach for the evidence. Much of the time, the evidence is ostensive. "It's raining," and we note the droplets hitting the windshield. "She's a beaut," a friend says, pointing. Or we accept on grounds of past performance by the assertor. "You'll love this book," Sam says, and Sam has never steered you wrong. Or we attend because we're disposed to trust some kinds of people, or accept their authority. Those assertions we entertain are assertions that respond to whatever we count as evidence. Even so, we're often dismayed to discover that our standards were too low.

There is a basic caution in this for the teacher in the give and take with students. Teachers, never simply give assertions, unless you're challenging students for the evidence. Always make your evidential basis clear. And never take a student assertion as an act of understanding without sign that the student commands evidence. Above all, take this last imperative to heart when you engage students in the task of composing.

THE COMPOSITION MODEL

It will help if we recall that the basic goal of any composition is to convey a designed experience to a reader. The experience is one intended by the writer, hence it is "by design," and it is successfully conveyed only to the degree that the reader gleans it from the composition itself, apart from any other intrusion by the writer. The writer cannot count on being at the reader's elbow. He cannot write, "She's a beaut," and then point a finger. Whatever *evidential* basis the reader requires to achieve the experience must be triggered by the composition itself. That is why simple assertions can never a composition make.

Yet we know compositions are made of sentences; subjects plugged to predicates — assertions. The trick of a successful composition is its sense that there are roughly two kinds of assertions from the reader's point of view: assertions on which the jury is out and assertions on which it is in.

We share a whole stock of assertions on which the jury is in: assertions whose evidence we've examined and accepted, assertions that we've used and that work well for us. We've heard, "76°. What a pleasant day." We've experienced such a temperate day. We concur. We count the assertion as well evidenced.

There is a whole other set of assertions on which the jury is necessarily out, because we're in no position to validate them. The assertion, "Despite the good weather, it was the worst day in my life," leaves us mute and waiting for the evidence. The good composition will provide it, approaching the assertion whose jury is "out" via assertions whose jury is "in." A simple word for the process is demonstration, which means to make evident.

In expository writing, argument, and most description, composition is *assertion demonstrated* (C = A + d).[14] Every good composition harbors a key assertion, around which it marshals an array of acceptable assertions whose images, details, illustrations, and examples "bring the jury in" by giving the key assertion its evidential basis. The reader may be several removes away from any direct experience of that to which the key assertion refers. There may *be* no possible direct experience of the key assertion's referent. Try actually experiencing a day in my past, or $E = MC^2$. But in the sense that he has been made to call out his own experience as evidence, the reader now "lives" the assertion. He has had a designed experience.

"It's a pleasant day" is assertion. "The temperature is 72"; "A gentle breeze blows from the south"; "Fleecy clouds drift by the young sun and ride slowly across the bright blue sky" are demonstrations.

"I'm really cold" is assertion. "My nose feels like an ice cube. My face looks like a frozen cherry. There are goosebumps over my whole body. I think my left little toe just fell off" are demonstrations.

When assertion is subtle, the composition may be sophisticated. ("It's a pleasant enough day." "Evil is the absence of the appropriate good.")

When demonstrations are specific and image-giving, the composition may be effective. In her song "Chelsea Morning," Joni Mitchell *asserts* that the day begins beautifully. She demonstrates by providing sensuous details — milk, toast, honey, a bowl of oranges — and saying, "the sun poured in like butterscotch and stuck to all my senses."

A theme (essay, paper, term paper, etc.) is a composition (C = A + d) with complex assertion: "For several reasons I love summer." "Although Shakespeare's Sonnet 73 may be read as a traditional 'September Song,' some suspect that the puzzling final couplet turns the lovely verses into grim 'black comedy'."

Some teachers refer to this assertion as the *thesis* of the essay. If they are using the term to refer only to the body of the essay and to mean "that which

---

[14]We must emphasize that our composition model — C = A + d — is in no sense intended as a *descriptive* model of the composition process. It cannot approach the work of theorists and investigators like L. S. Flower and J. R. Hayes in illuminating composition underway and exposing the give and take, subtle shifts, complexities, and restarts that typically occur in the actual process. (See *Cognitive Processes in Writing*, L. W. Gregg & E. R. Steinberg, Eds., for examples of such work by Flower, Hayes, and others).

Ours is a heuristic model, which is a fancy way of saying it serves the learner. It does this by constraining and prioritizing the learner's focus, so that the process of composition for the less-than-professional writer — and the process of evaluation for the less accustomed assessor of writings — can proceed with much less confusion, complexity, and wasted effort.

is to be demonstrated," a proposition to be proved, then the term may be satisfactory.

However, confusion arises and teachers get into trouble because many use *thesis* as a synonym for *subject matter*. "Your thesis," someone says, "is Democracy during the French Revolution." Being merely a subject with no predicate, this is not an assertion, simple or complex, and cannot be demonstrated, however carefully one writes. Having been assigned such "theses," numberless students throughout history have scratched their heads, wondering futilely why they have nothing to say.

As a term, "thesis" is sometimes reserved only for argumentative essays. And traditionally, the term signifies the paper submitted by a master's candidate. Thesis can be a slippery and misleading term and should be used, if at all, with care.

The important thing here, though, is that because the composing process for themes is exactly the same as the process for simple compositions, there is no need to speak of the assertion as anything other than the assertion. A good deal of student confusion might be eliminated if the term were universally applied.

One further distinction should be made. Whether the central idea is called *assertion* or *thesis* or *central idea*, the term refers only to the body of the essay, not to its introductory or concluding sections. Introductions and conclusions have their own work to do. It is a travesty of that work to insist, as some do, that introductions are paragraphs meant to present "the thesis sentence," and that conclusions "summarize" the essay's effort. Such things occur per instruction in much student work but are seldom encountered in mature literature.

It is the introduction's business not to state the key assertion, but simply to initiate the reader's encounter with it, hopefully in an interesting or captivating way. The conclusion does not summarize the key assertion or its demonstration. More usefully, it points the reader toward some noteworthy consequence of the demonstrated theme.

Thinking (making and assessing assertions) and composing (expressing and demonstrating them to a reader) are obviously close-coupled, and it helps to trace this commonality back a bit. The composition process begins well before facility at writing. Early in life the child learns that "I want" is an unsatisfactory route to "I get." He discovers the road is smoothed by reasons."I have to go to the store. I'm going to get some candy and bubble gum. And I'm going to buy Jerry's birthday present." Thus the child has made an assertion and has demonstrated it. And although his demonstrated argument is not especially a winning one, it is greatly superior to the bare assertion.

Through first job application and young love, the youth polishes the technique. ("Why do you want this job?" "Do you really like me?") And as the prizes grow, so does the youth's composing repertoire.

With this marvelous head start, composition teachers and instigators of composition in whatever discipline should have an easy time. It hardly seems necessary to say that such is not the case.

UNRAVELING COMPOSITION

The ability to compose well seems to emerge as grudgingly as the ability to think well, and for many of the same reasons. Composing, like thinking, is hard work. Slipshod responses often satisfy demands for both. Life seldom constrains us to give the very best of either. We have many handy surrogates for either kind of performance. We can mimic and copy rather than think, and we can do the same rather than compose. Perhaps that is why, under the skin, the challenge of the composition teacher and the thinking skill instructor are so alike. Both must penetrate the oblivion of the student, must reach and stimulate nascent skills that are unrecognized and hence seldom valued.

But in teaching composition, we often compound the difficulty. In Chapter 5 we distinguished composition from recording. We noted that composition was a complex, bipolar enterprise. Many things must occur before the writer's incipient idea becomes the reader's informed and tailored vision. The heart of this process, we've just affirmed, involves demonstrating assertions. But the process has anatomic structure as well as heart. Sometimes, by projecting this structure poorly, we can befuddle students, who get lost and lose heart.

We've already intimated one serious confusion, which is the presumption that all writing is composition. We've suggested (Chapter 5) that writings can be usefully distinguished, and taught, as either recording or composition. But before it can become either of these to the student, writing is first of all mechanics.

Initially, the student learns to print, to script, and to spell; the normative training method is repetition. The mode of writing is usually the less demanding of the two; recording rather than composing.

When it comes time to teach composition, however, the student is seldom given warning that he will now ply his new tools in a distinctively new trade. Perhaps the teacher has not clearly grasped what is distinctive about composition, but even if she has, the transition from mechanics and recording to composition is hard. The student's attempts at composing are so much more private and personal—hence so much less accessible—than his recording efforts. The real "stuff" of composing—the student's demonstration—is so often flawed by the student's limited experience. And none of this is half so striking, apparent, and accessible as how he handles the overt machinery.

It isn't surprising, then, that misspellings are grievous; run-ons and fragments lethal. Usage, grammar — even penmanship — are vital (and often exclusive) concerns of the composition teacher in the early grades.

Little credit accrues for satisfactory assertions or effective demonstrations.

And the irony is that the skills of managing writing's machinery remain major criteria for evaluation as long as the student uses composition in his schooling.

The elementary teacher "taking off points" from a composition in which *cat* is spelled with a *k* has a soulmate in the august professor of literary criticism who "knocks off a grade" because a doctoral candidate has spelled *primitive* p-r-i-m-a-t-i-v-e.

Clearly, if a student is ever to learn to compose, he must have knowledgeable and accurate counsel at every level. He must be shown that writing (i.e., "composing") entails three stages [15]: precomposition, composition, and postcomposition; and that errors of use, grammar, and spelling such as those indicated accrue to — and point out a flaw in — part of the postcomposition stage. They *are* critical errors, and teaching to resolve them is important, but teaching to resolve them is not teaching composition.

In precomposition, the writer's first responsibility is to determine — tentatively — his topic and to make an assertion for himself about it. Here he could profitably exchange ideas with his peers or his teacher, especially as regards his audience and/or tone and more especially limiting his topic.

At this point, again for himself, he might restate his assertion and "brainstorm" it, realizing clearly that he is searching his consciousness for experience to *demonstrate* his assertion.

Once he begins his rough draft — begins, in fact, composing — he must focus all his effort on assertion and demonstration.

If he is writing something large — say an essay — he needs to remind himself to attend to the smaller composition units, the paragraphs, in a manner that fully utilizes the composing process. What does the *paragraph* assert, and how is that demonstrated?

In postcomposing, the writer first of all should be alert to possible revisions. In "For several reasons I love summer," for example, should he eliminate one of the areas of enjoyment and concentrate more fully on the remaining? Has he demonstrated enough each of the areas? Does he need

---

[15]We use "stages" here because the notion is immensely convenient, even though in some ways misleading. The most serious distortion involves the suggestion that a writer cycles once through three sequential stages and is finished. Writers often generate quite a volume of traffic back and forth and across stages before they finally let go.

more details? A vivid example? Are the demonstration units in their best order and is that order underscored by transitional words and phrases?

Generally, has he communicated his assertion satisfactorily to his audience by demonstrating it fully in the tone he had chosen in precomposition?

In the second phase of postcomposition the writer edits his work carefully. He does everything in his power to make certain his writing is correct, the vehicle of conveyance near perfect. He understands that others, rightly or wrongly, will view his handling of these mechanics as a gauge not only of his writing ability but of his intelligence—and even his character!

So, a great deal goes on in composition, and all of it requires the composition teacher's nurture and modulation. But you are merely arranging dead limbs unless the student has first been prompted to assert and demonstrate. To do that, of course the student has to think. This is what awakens the composition teacher's interest in thinking skill. And this is why any teacher concerned about thinking skill is well advised to call forth composition.

COMPOSING INTELLIGENCE

Regardless of whether you do or do not teach composition, you can employ it powerfully in developing thinking skill. There are several things you need to do.

First of all, don't scruple to *use* composition. There are understandable reasons why you might. Here you are, about to use at least the Prince if not the King of all the arts, as a means to some other end. Shouldn't you teach composition solely for composition's sake, so that someone can write the nonpareil essay, the perfect theme? Yes, if you put it that way, as long as you fully understand composition's sake, which is—even when it produces the perfect essay—to be a *means* for successful communication. Keep in mind that composition's real goal is not achieved by the word in print; it is achieved by *composing the intelligence* of the reader in accord with the writer's intent. To do this, the writer has first to compose her own intelligence by asserting and demonstrating *her* intent. In your concern to develop thinking skill, you will use composition to perfect that process. As you succeed, as you develop more adept self-composers of intelligence, you unavoidably strengthen the root capacity for composition. Deja vu? Do you sense recursion at work again?

You may also hesitate to use composition because it isn't your bag and the prospect leaves you ill-at-ease. You don't teach writing and you've never considered yourself a writer. Furthermore, you may be teaching in a field with a long and stolid tradition of avoiding composition; math, perhaps, or machine shop, or one of the sciences. Who needs a new headache?

A headache maybe, but not a new one. Whatever you teach and however you pursue it, you are not as far from composition as you might suppose. To see this, first examine a bit of composition closely.

Listen to its simple heart beat; $C = A + d$. You can detect it in any expository work of any size from a few lines to several volumes. Even the Harvard Classics arrayed on their shelves are a collective exposition of sorts. "Here is the best of Western literature," they assert. "Got a couple of years? We'll demonstrate."

Now listen for that same heart beat in the subject matter you teach. Do you detect assertions and demonstrations in your field? If you teach in any kind of field at all, it will be wall to wall with such products of composed intelligence. In fact, you will likely count yourself successful precisely where you get students to compose their intelligence accordingly.

You are inspecting four lines of algebraic notation from a student, and because they constitute a valid proof, you are pleased. If you're lucky, what you have before you is a successful student composition. Though you have placed immense limitations on the permissible vocabulary and draconian constraints on what can count as evidence, there lies a demonstrated assertion. The luck enters in because it's hard to know if the proof is really the student's. The stringent rules governing notation and evidence make it difficult to tell whether it is the product of composed intelligence or simply a copy. For this very reason, concerned science and math teachers experiment with having students write their problem-solving "protocols" in the vernacular. Here lies the strength of composition as we commonly understand it. While it is not science or math at its most elegant or powerful, the written composition does open a clearer window on the student's intellection. Looking through that window, teachers can more easily diagnose and correct unproductive uses of the mind.

Nor is composition far away in the machine shop. Here, composed intelligence becomes composed manipulation. A product is elected—asserted. The instructor's hand and eye perform in precise sequences—the demonstration—and the product results. The shop instructor who wants to be *sure* his students understand has been known to turn to composition. "Write me up the steps in turning an Acme thread. You pick the size, but I want full specs for a production carbide cutter. That means *all* the clearances."

So composition is implicit in your teaching, whatever you teach, and you should make her explicit when you want operant student thinking in your discipline stimulated, examined, assessed, or any combination thereof. With a consciousness of how to tailor the two key variables in our model of composition—assertion and demonstration—you can trick operant thinking out of your students in innumerable ways.

1. Assertion.   Keep in mind that 60% of the battle of getting students to compose well, or getting them to compose what you will count useful, is fought right here. Whether you are determining the assertion, or getting students to determine one, take the process seriously and perform it carefully. All of us have the wrong-headed tendency to think that assigning a topic is a piece of cake; the tough part is doing the writing.

The moment you make your assertion, you have *uniquely* split the universe. Where before there was chaos, now there exist two things: everything relevant to your assertion's demonstration, and everything irrelevant. Remember that we nominated predication as one of the Ur-acts of the mind; one of the irreducible capabilities of intelligence. You've just done it—joined subject and predicate—and once you've done it in earnest, nothing is quite the same.

A few little words can make all the difference. Consider the wildly differing domains of relevance established by these two assertions:

"It was a pleasant day." What's relevant here are all the day's winning attributes.

"It was a pleasant enough day." Suddenly all the day's attributes, pleasant and unpleasant, are allowed, and that's not all. A complex relationship between these two vast categories is implied. On some delicate scale, says the assertion, the day reveals more pleasantness than unpleasantness.

Whether made by student or teacher, the assertion requires *very* selective attention. Be clear about its domain of relevance and make certain that is the domain you actually want to traverse. Edit the assertion most carefully; modify and qualify until the ground it covers is just what you intend.

A composition is mostly demonstration, yet we suggest that care with the assertion is more than half the work. This is because the assertion goes far toward *defining* the allowable demonstration. It sets the demonstration's scope, and if it does this cogently enough, untold difficulties with demonstration are avoided.

From the perspective of the thinking skill instructor, this phase of the composition process alone is rife with possibilities. Getting students to make assertions and then trace the consequences for demonstration, perhaps outlining a few, then *modifying* the assertion and identifying the consequences of that, can quickly harness all five generic skills, even before a line of composition is written. And by highlighting the importance of shaping an assertion—by establishing a sense of this in students' minds—it should earn the composition teacher's nod.

Concentrating on assertion and its consequences will serve these good ends for the subject matter teacher also, but here, within a discipline, it has an added utility. It is a useful trick to explore an assertion from your discipline with students in a certain way. Take the assertion and deliberately suspend your discipline's demonstration of it. Find out what the assertion means to *them*. How would the students go about demonstrating it? Where would they turn?

Doing this can be a valuable check on your instructional progress. It can save you and your students from the Box Canyon syndrome. The Box Canyon syndrome occurs when students follow you into the strange territory of your subject matter and discover less and less along the way that ties them to their experience. Finally there is so little that they can only follow you, rote step by rote step, with nary a glimmer where they are or where they're going. If they can't give you a clue as to how they would demonstrate the assertion, you're in Box Canyon. If they can, perhaps even using subject matter lore in novel ways, you know they're mastering the territory.

In all this, be clear about the overweaning power you have in governing assertions. By picking an assertion carefully in assigning a composition, you are asking a student's operant skills to excavate a specific range of demonstrations. If you want to explore or develop mastery of a certain kind of demonstration , all you have to do is tailor the right assertion. You are, in fact, channeling operant skills with every composition assignment, be it a paragraph or a term paper. You might as well make the most of it.

And your control is subtle as well as powerful. You can even shape your assertions so that composition will emphasize and specially exercise specific generic thinking skills. Here, off hand, are some examples:

Selective Attention — assertions that concentrate on a factor or quality as distinct from others: "It was my Dad's *tone of voice* that made all the difference." "Of these three principles of systems theory, the second is most critical."

Sustained Analysis — assertions that compel taking apart: "Driving a car is more complicated than it seems." "It isn't true that No Man is an Island."

Analoging — assertions that pose unexpected similarities or differences: "Peace is war resting." "Debugging software programs is like walking beans in Iowa."

Suspension of Closure — assertions that entertain an alternative or contrary: "You can't buy happiness. . . can you?" "Never vote a split ticket — unless you favor democracy."

Autocensorship" — assertions that explore potential consequences: "I'd be poorer but happier as a Life Guard." "The West would be stronger if Eisenhower had aimed at political rather than military goals on the Second Front."

2. Demonstration.   A little laboring of the obvious may be helpful here. It is in the substantive demonstration of the assertion that you will find the student's thinking skill most readily revealed. Your concern for shaping the assertion was aimed at giving those skills clear and manageable scope. You can do several things to increase the odds that you will find what you hope to in the demonstration.

First, and so simple that we tend to overlook it, be clear yourself about what you want to see. What will you count, or allow, as demonstration? The possible range is vast, from anything the student cares to bring to the task — feelings, recollections, hunches — through close argument in a specific subject matter area, to the axioms and lemmas of logical or mathematical induction.

Once you have a good grip on what will satisfy you, make your preferences very clear to the students, both by explanation and example. They must be able to recognize a satisfactory demonstration to create one.

Realize also that what you desire by way of demonstration must be suitably tailored to the intended exercise; don't ask more of a competent paragraph than it can capably deliver. Then again, don't ask less. If the paragraphs you receive are simple recasts of one in the book, you aren't asking enough. A good self-test before you give a composition assignment is to ask what you want the students *themselves* to demonstrate. If all you want is assurance that they've read the text or remember the material, don't ask them to compose. Have them record or take a multiple-choice test. Ask students to compose only when you want students to *make* something — to behave operantly.

Once the composition is completed and in your hands, be very clear that this is the point where your task as thinking skill instructor (for that matter, also composition or subject matter teacher) begins, not ends. Producing the composition has exercised student skill, but not necessarily improved or amplified it. It is not putting it too strongly to suggest that having students crank out unevaluated compositions is worthless in expanding thinking capability. And a paper with an unexplicated grade on it, whether good or bad, is for our purposes an unevaluated composition.

True, the lonely writer can improve, but only if she engages in the often slow-to-master, difficult process of self-criticism. To advance the student's thinking skill, you must assess the student's composition with all the care lavished earlier on his problem-solving protocols (see Chap. 7). Only when he sees where he used his skill well and where poorly can the student improve his wield of it. But how do you evaluate compositions if you're not a composition teacher?

Let's assume the worst case. You've never been moved to assign or grade a composition. If someone asked you how, you'd say you didn't know.

Again, just listen for the heartbeat: $C = A + d$. Concentrate on the assertion–demonstration distinction, and for the moment set all else aside. Is the assertion feasible? Does it make sense given the scope of the assignment and does it allow for plausible demonstration? Is it in fact demonstrated? How well or how poorly in your mind, and by what communicable standards? Where it does well, why? Where poorly, why? How might the demonstration have been salvaged, or strengthened? If you requested that the demonstration exhibit special characteristics or spotlight special skills — of comparison, perhaps, or analysis or analogy — does it do so? Once you've made and settled these assessments, see that they are effectively communicated to the student, with a chance to apply the gained insight in an edit, or perhaps a new composition assignment.

In all this (remind yourself) you are assessing how well an assertion has been demonstrated. Of course you can do this, or you could not make way in the discipline you teach. You are looking for the same kind of evidence you use to determine what is sound and unsound about assertions in your field.

You are also (again remind yourself) far from assessing everything assessable about a composition. But what you have your hands on is what you need to guide your student toward more effective, more powerful thinking. Good thinking, remember, is creating effective, justifiable assertions. The composition delivers to you an assertion with its justification, and your careful critique will show the student what is or is not effective about it, what is or is not justified.

As to the rest of the job — full assessment of a composition — you must be the judge of how much of it to embrace. What remains is everything about the composition that influences the experience of the reader. There may be a sound assertion with a solid demonstration in there, but does it take an autopsy to reveal them, or do they leap at you with grace and power? Is the composition legible? Does the grammar and spelling speed or inhibit the message? Is there craftsmanship here that respects and rewards the worn and tired reader? It is in light of these concerns that a sound assertion solidly demonstrated can, in its full role as *composition*, earn a failing grade.

These are unavoidable concerns for the composition teacher, but should they be yours? Your time and resource and goal as teacher must decide, but we can present a brief, two-part case for you to consider.

First, "I don't know how" is questionable reason to beg off. You likely have more sense of what helps or hinders effective written work than you credit yourself, and if the question comes to interest you, that sense will grow rapidly. Besides, your goal of fully effective composition is not remote; it does not hinge on the production of deathless prose. You are interested in written performance within reasonable range of your students.

Second, realize that to suspend concern for such things as spelling and usage in your teaching is to create a highly artificial and maybe seriously misleading environment. Wherever the written word counts, that suspension is not tolerated. You risk developing wielders of thought to whom no one will attend.

But whatever responsibility you elect for its total form, use composition to expose and direct the mind's key work of demonstrating assertion. And while you're developing the student's wherewithal for that work, encourage a taste for it. Help them see how undemonstrated assertion assaults our society. With its daily doses of triviality it is the road to terminal boredom. In the mouths of demagogues and bigots it explodes us into monstrous lethal violence. It befouls each vital social, economic, and political question.

These, however, are the extremes, the crimson pox. To measure the depth of the disease, spend a day, even an hour, listening — to friends, husband, wife, girlfriend, boyfriend — even self. Finally, mark a pathetic note — the attempts to substitute sincerity for demonstration. ("I *really, honestly* feel with all my heart the world is flat.")

Please do try this little exercise, because without demonstration all assertions are mere air. Even this one.

The File

You might begin by discussing the "naturalness" of the composition process in oral communication. Examples you could provide and the many that would flow from class members once they understood the concept would show that assertions without demonstration mean almost nothing. Try this, for example: Tell class members to write on a slip of scratch paper in response to a question you will ask *only* a number; then say, " 'It's cold outside,' the woman said." Ask the class to write the number of degrees Fahrenheit. Obviously, accurate answers could only result from details that would demonstrate the assertion: What time of year is it? Where is the speaker? How old is she? How is she clothed? What's her state of health?

A rough day at the office, the high price of food, a narrow escape on the freeway, a swinging party, supporting Miss X or Mr. Y for political office, a beautiful new recording, an interesting movie are a few of the thousands of seeds of assertions in everyday conversations that will never sprout durable meaning without demonstration.

What at first glance seems to be a familiar form of oral communication is a phenomena of high-tech composing: the TV news. The newscaster *asserts* the scripted heart of the story and the camera demonstrates it. ("There's more trouble in the Middle East today. . . .")

When you are ready to begin composing in writing, introduce the basic process (C = A + d) and delay discussion of precomposition and post-composition until there has been practice and experience in composing.

1. Write fragment demonstrations of the following assertions—at least five "particulars":
   A. The Detroit Tigers are strong down the middle.
      (Possible response: Catcher Nokes' strong arm and home-run punch, Whitaker and Trammel turning double plays, Whitaker as leadoff hitter, Trammel batting cleanup, the defense and offense of centerfielder Chet Lemon).
   B. There are several items in a single dinner place setting.
   C. Professional wrestlers are the clowns of the sports circus.
   D. Many kinds of people love rock music.
   E. A variety of people visit the Mall.
   F. The truck driver had interesting eyes.
   G. Brownies are easy to make.

2. Write assertions to fit the following sets of fragmented demonstrations:
   A. Harry, the canary, Ziggy the gerbil, Antonia the goldfish, Elegantè the cat.
   B. Scattered baseball cards, a piece of driftwood, a Mars bar wrapper, one red sock, a torn tee shirt, a banana.
   C. A stereo playing, an open three-ring notebook, two books, three sharpened pencils, a ball-point pen, a half-empty diet Pepsi, a telephone being dialed.
   D. An empty birdbath, a squirrel sitting on a fence post, a smoky haze, geese flying south.

3. (Don't overlook *example* as a means of demonstrating. It gives students a chance for some fun with hyperbole, and it is a good vehicle for simple narrative. If you are courageous, you might offer this chestnut—generally credited to Henny Youngman: "It's really hot! How hot is it? Yesterday I saw a dog chasing a cat, and they were both walking.")
   Demonstrate the following by example:
   A. Funny things happen when you're a twin.
   B. Flat tires are more than bad luck.
   C. Eating dinner at our house is not always fun.
   D. My mother (father, aunt, cousin, boyfriend, etc.) is the kindest person I know.
   E. Brushes with greatness are exhilarating.

THE FILE

THE FILE

THE FILE

CHAPTER 10

TWO SPECTIVES — RETRO AND PER

Forethought

You needn't take this chapter seriously. In fact, you needn't take it at all. This is the book's one throw-away; you can quickly thumb it and go on to Chapter 11. Or you can use it — whole or in part — to rest, reflect, and recoup.

We've come a fair way through this guide, uncorking most of the issues and most of the instructional techniques we will encounter in its full course. We're about to shift our perspective a little as we begin to consider the secondary/collegiate mission, and it could help to recollect where we've been.

What better way than a surprise quiz?

You know the routine — all books off the desks. No talking once the test begins. All questions are true/false or multiple choice. The test will be scored right minus one-half wrong so that random guessing will be penalized. Course value is one-quarter of your final grade.

Any questions? You have 45 minutes. Please begin.

UP-TO-HERE QUIZ

Guidelines

1. The book, if it is successful, will enable the dedicated teacher to begin a thinking skills program in her classroom.

2. All necessary "equipment" for a thinking skills program is here included.

3. Everyone has a reasonably good idea of how he or she thinks.

4. Good thinking is automatic — not an integrating of distinct mental operations.

Chapter 1

5. Teaching thinking skills is another unnecessary increment to any teacher's busy schedule.

6. Thinking skills can be taught.

7. Thinking skills cannot be taught.

8. Some thinking skills the schools have always taught.

9. In the context of thinking skills, the terms *respondent* and *operant* are roughly equivalent to *passive* and *active*.

10. An analysis of classroom instruction suggests that the proportion of respondent to operant thinking called for is about (a) half and half, (b) two to one, (c) ten to one, (d) a hundred to one.

11. The main role of a good teacher is to dispense facts and information about her subject.

12. The good teacher never challenges her students toward use and mastery of the thought that gives life to her discipline.

13. Knowledge (as opposed to information) is come by only through a subtle interplay between respondent and operant skills.

14. In the sense of coming to both operant and respondent skills, student minds are what their mentors make of them.

Chapter 2

15. One problem with determining the thinking skills is a superficial, "commonsense" view of the mind's work.

16. An epistemologist is one involved in the theory of knowledge.

17. A major difference between the epistemologist's view of the mind and that of recent thinking skill literature is that recent literature nominates far fewer basic skills.

18. Quine and others representing a reductionist's view of the mind's capabilities mention as few as (a) one (b) three (c) five (d) seven (e) nine.

19. An explanation for the relatively small number of the mind's capabilities may be based on (a) reaction (b) repression (c) recursion (d) revision (e) retention.

20. Many "thinking skills" lists would be more accurately described as "thinking activities" lists.

21. Describing a child's early mental constructs, Vygotsky speaks of (a) numerators and denominators (b) spirits and substances (c) mounds and compounds (d) heaps and complexes (e) subjects and predicates.

22. The mind often settles for less than concepts.

23. The principal task of the TS instructor is to acquaint her students with the small set of core abilities the student already possesses and, quite important, to encourage the use of these abilities.

24. The small set of core thinking abilities is referred to as (a) respondent skills (b) generic skills (c) germane skills (d) complex skills (e) compound skills.

25. "Sustained analysis" is the capacity to identify components of a situation.

26. "Suspension of closure" is the capacity to evaluate all problem factors before shaping a solution.

27. Generic thinking skills are a set of archetypal ways the mind deploys when it effectively does its best work.

28. The absence of the generic skills does not always correlate with poor mental performance.

29. The core abilities of the mind are to remember, to discern, and to (a) predicate (b) hyphenate (c) objectify (d) subjectify (e) neutralize.

30. The generic skills support the mind's core abilities.

Chapter 3

31. The first reaction most people have to problems is to try to avoid them.

32. A problem is ignored usually because of laziness.

33. Frustrated acknowledgment and symbolic gestures are frequently brought into play when a problem occurs.

34. Operant thinking is unusual among learners because of a bias against it and an inability to do it.

35. Even our capable problem solver, Joanne, initially blushed and lacked confidence.

36. Using her finger on the blackboard was an unsatisfactory gesture in Joanne's problem solving.

37. The "if. . . then" form of the problem alerted Joanne to a similarity with other problems.

38. Although Joanne is an outstanding graduate student, capable sixth graders follow a very similar system.

39. The thinking skills teacher aims to bring her students to a confident proficiency in the use of the generic thinking skills.

40. There are strong similarities between a coach and a thinking skills instructor.

41. Correct answers are accurate indicators of capable thinking.

42. A good general rule for the TS instructor is to ask rather than to tell.

43. There are how many "teaching strategies" discussed in Chapter 3? (a) 3   (b) 5   (c) 7   (d) 9   (e) 11.

44. An exception to the learner's conservatism is the use of operant skills in play.

Chapter 4

45. As regards teaching generic skills at the primary level, the teacher should move with restraint.

46. For primary students, "Selective Attention" might be referred to as "pointing out."

47. Similarly, "Analoging" might become "likening," or "It's Like."

48. Before testing significance or assigning value, the mind must (a) relax (b) reiterate (c) fashion (d) focus (e) ferment.

49. "Sustained Analysis" is "taking apart."

50. "Analoging" is "never giving up."

51. The TS teacher develops a taste often unusual among her colleagues: She trains herself to credit the *considered* answer over the *quickest* answer.

52. Autocensorship asks the young thinker to try out his decision and to evaluate its consequences.

53. If a teacher relies too heavily on workbooks to exercise the generic skills, her students will probably view these skills as "those we use in workbooks."

54. If a teacher's students have a feel for and a satisfaction using the generic thinking skills, she is doing a very good job.

55. On a gloomy Tuesday in February, the young second-grade teacher walked into class with a pink elephant pinned to the back of his sports jacket. He acted as though he didn't know it was there.

It's likely that he is (a) about to review the alphabet and focus on the letter *e* (b) letting his class "play-teach" by making himself the major distraction in his class.

56. "Show and Tell," a good TS activity, has a bonus in allowing the teacher insights into her students' special interests and values.

57. A rewarding adjunct to "show and tell" is to ask each student what he would bring if he could bring anything in the world he wanted to.

58. A valuable day-after follow up to "show and tell" is to ask each child what interested/amused/frightened/surprised him or her.

59. A practical reason for "show and tell" is that the teacher doesn't have to spend a lot of time on a lesson plan.

60. "Taking Apart" means breaking down a thing or concept into its component parts.

61. Parents and others usually give the child good models of analysis.

62. "Unscrambling" is a good stimulus to analytic skill.

63. A generality is "taken apart" by examples.

64. "Comparing and Contrasting" games using student-suggested articles (pencil–pen, tv–book, door–window) are ways to exercise thinking skills and integrate students' lives with classroom experience.

65. Student hosted guessing games ("What am I thinking about — its like a mirror?) are not good ways of gaining analoging skills.

66. The main value of "Comparing or Contrasting" games is that they provide new sets of experience.

67. "Another Way" skills may be developed during story time.

68. Trying out wrong answers is a poor teaching technique.

69. "Try Out" exercises are an exception to the thinking skill instruction rule that the considered error is better than the rapid one.

70. In teacher response to student answers, which of the following is superlative? (a) "Very good" (b) "Good thinking" (c) "Correct."

71. In the File, a Take Apart exercise asks you to "take apart" one dollar into the fewest number of all coins but including each denomination (excepting, of course, the silver dollar). The answer is (a) 5 (b) 7 (c) 10 (d) 13 (e) 15.

72. A double-or triple-single question would be a good technique for the It's Like" 20 questions game (e.g., Is it a living American pop star? Is it an existing man-made structure?)

Chapter 5

73. A major difference between TS instruction in the primary and intermediate years will be an emphasis on student consciousness of the skills in the latter.

74. One important reason for making students "owners" of their TS is that we want those students to think effectively in situations other than those designed and controlled in the classroom.

75. No real skill needs to be modified when it is applied to an unlearned situation.

76. TS teachers need to ask themselves who really owns the skill being developed in students.

77. In the intermediate years the TS teacher has done a satisfactory job if he has coached well good examples of satisfactory thinking performance.

78. Another reason for students being conscious of their own thinking performance is to allow the teacher access to thought processes.

79. Two techniques especially suited to introducing students to their own thinking are (a) vocalization and special writing (b) vocalization and memorization (c) special writing and random testing.

80. It is important that the TS instructor take courses in composition.

81. For the TS teacher a useful analysis of writing is (a) descriptive and expository (b) personal and impersonal (c) recording and composing.

82. Note-making is a major form of recording.

83. The great bulk of consciousness deals with the instant past.

84. Memory is the only access to experience.

85. Lists of various kinds (grocery, Christmas card, birthday, etc.) bolster memory.

86. Note-making, a symbolic recording of events, is a kind of ultimate list.

87. Clearly, note-making enhances taking notice.

88. The TS teacher can help students enhance their own attentiveness by modeling physical acts that aid in concentration.

89. Recording is a "single-pole" concern in that the note maker works only for his own anticipated use.

90. Composing is "bipolar" in the sense that the writer wants to influence a reader.

91. Notes are "wrong" only when a student cannot decipher his own work.

92. There is no essential difference between "note-taking" and "note-making."

93. The veteran TS instructor spends much time with student-made notes.

94. The ultimate reward of a competent student note maker is an active noticing mind.

Chapter 6

95. ETSI is an acronym for (a) extensive teaching skill instruction (b) exhaustive thinking skill instruction (c) exhausting thinking skill instruction (d) explicit thinking skill instruction.

96. The TS instructor equips the learner with three kinds of control or "dominance."

97. Thinking can improve thinking ability.

98. One very good acquisition of the young, learning thinker is "task assessment."

99. One's past experience is "out of bounds" in the sense that it cannot be affected by newly acquired thinking skills.

100. Faced with classes that have mixed experience, the TS instructor must make major adjustments.

101. In the example problem ("Cathy knows French and German . . ."), the problem and its solution dominate.

102. Teacher modeling of her own thinking has little effect on her students.

103. A teacher must never model an unsound approach to a problem.

104. Rather than theorize about the nature of the thinking skills, a good teacher initially shows what the skills do and how they do it.

105. Modeling is a poor way to illustrate the importance of confidence in problem solving.

106. The effective ETSI teacher avoids providing a "how to" list for problem solution.

107. In general, a lesson plan outline for the introductory phase of ETSI would change little from the third grade through graduate school.

Chapter 7

108. The main purpose of ETSI is to develop intelligence test problem-solving skills.

109. IQ test-type problems represent the kind of work the mind usually faces.

110. Problems are tasks that hide their mode of resolution.

111. The ETSI instructor always sets her problem solvers on the trail of the most powerful solution.

112. You know your students are getting the knack when their problem protocols exhibit uniformity.

113. It's important for the problem solver, even when she has a sound solution, to seek an alternative.

114. The main virtue of working in two-member teams is the security and support of sharing.

115. It's important for the ETSI teacher to script his classroom problem solving so as to minimize his own errors.

116. A prime goal of the ETSI teacher is to have students assume her "coach/demonstrator" role.

Chapter 8

117. Problem-free learning for students should be a primary instructional goal.

118. Modern texts with built-in thinking skill aids greatly simplify the TS teacher's task.

119. The social science teacher "taught questions" primarily to (a) review material (b) stimulate interest (c) exercise respondent skills (d) deepen concepts.

120. Math is difficult to teach because students have so little prior experience with it.

121. Students need to master the discipline of method before they can "do" science.

122. The "skill/content mix" refers to the operations you want students to master and the information you want them to possess.

123. For any given course you teach, the skill/content mix is predetermined.

124. You teach a skill most effectively by ignoring prior student use of it.

125. The best way to develop unprecedented skills is to train students in them.

126. To "game" or "model" something is to project that thing's complexities.

127. You can't "operate" in a desirable way before you've mastered the "givens."

128. Despite their more complex lesson plans, TS teachers have greater need to remain flexible and adaptable.

129. Gaming and modeling are useful ways to adapt students to unfamiliar operations.

Chapter 9

130. Because writing is basically putting already formed thoughts on paper, the thinking skills teacher can largely ignore it.

131. Assertions are general statements.

132. "Jury In" assertions are those that (a) we like (b) are well expressed (c) are forceful (d) are evidenced.

133. "Jury Out" assertions are those (a) we reject (b) have yet to evidence (c) we disagree with (d) we don't understand.

134. Assertions without evidence are (a) less cumbersome (b) not worth considering (c) never accepted (d) always wrong.

135. Assertions with evidence are (a) always right (b) dependable (c) worth considering (d) unshakable.

136. A student's assertion should be accepted when it is (a) correct (b) well expressed (c) well intended (d) well evidenced.

137. C = A + d stands for "Composition equals Accuracy plus dedication."

138. "It's a cold day" is (a) assertion (b) demonstration (c) composition.

139. In light of Q. 138, "There are goosebumps over my whole body" is (a) assertion (b) demonstration (c) composition.

140. Skill with the mechanics of writing (e.g., spelling, grammar) is a sound gauge of composition quality.

141. The mechanics of writing are unimportant.

142. Confusion may result from the ambiguity of the word *thesis*.

143. In the *precomposition* stage of writing, successful student writers align assertions with their own experiences to see how the assertions might be *demonstrated*.

144. Because their fields do not rely on composition, math and science teachers find it difficult to use.

145. Demonstration is the problem in writing compositions; making the assertion is easy.

146. In composing effectively for the teacher, it is important that students understand what will serve as acceptable evidence.

147. Frequent writing will improve thinking.

148. Writing about the generic skills will improve thinking.

149. If you aren't an English teacher, it's safe to ignore writing mechanics.

150. Test-taking is not a useful learning experience.

ANSWERS

Guidelines

    1. T
    2. T
    3. F
    4. F

Chapter 1

    5. F
    6. T
    7. F
    8. T
    9. T
  10. (d)
  11. F
  12. F
  13. T
  14. T

Chapter 2

  15. T
  16. T
  17. F

18. (b) It's probably useful to remind yourself of the mind's core abilities—to remember, to discern, and to predicate—and of the generic skills that emanate from them.

19. (c) Note the concept of recursion. It's a key one that is taken up again.

20. T

21. (d) As terms to describe mental ability less than conceptual, Vygotsky's terms—*heaps, complexes,* and *pseudo-concepts* are quite useful.

22. T

23. T   Make a note here. The teacher's role is *not* to require memorization and reiteration: Rather, his role is the subtler one of modeling the use of skills and, as quickly as possible, making of the student a skill user.

24. (b)

25. T

26. T

27. T   Again, a reminder is useful. One convenient (and valid) method of ascertaining the generic thinking skills is to analyze the behavior of those who consistently fail as problem solvers. Such analysis reveals random attention, haphazard scanning of problems, failure to test known relationships, etc. These, of course, are behaviors (disabilities?) diametrically opposed to the generic skills.

28. F

29. (a)

30. T

Chapter 3

31. T

32. F

33. T

34. T

35. F

36. F

37. T

38. T

39. T

40. T

41. F

42. T

43. (c) You have a perfect right here to ask, "How am I supposed to remember that there are seven teaching strategies discussed?"

The truth is that you're not. This question is to remind you that the strategies are discussed, to urge you to thumb back and slip one or two on, and to remember how your students who are using their operant skills on a test you might give would react to a similar question.

44. T

Chapter 4

45. T
46. T
47. T
48. (d)
49. T
50. F   Analoging is, of course, a major tool with which the mind compares and contrasts its present focus with all its previous experience.

A good stimulant for the tired teacher is to face her young thinkers with things that are similar but different (i.e., a camel and a horse, a bicycle and a motorcycle), and then without coaching to watch the sparks fly as the operant analoging begins to take over.

51. T   No one should miss this question, but the concept is so important that you may need to remind yourself of it.

52. T
53. T
54. T   In fact, very, very T.
55. (b)
56. T
57. T
58. T
59. F
60. T   Note here that any complex unit may be "broken down," but the analyzer often needs to explain his vantage point. "It's cold," for example, may be analyzed in terms of the speaker's sensory perception of cold—red nose, smarting eyes, tingling toes, etc. It also may be analyzed from a meteorologist's perspective—a temperature of 9°F., a wind of 10 miles per hour, cloudiness, etc.

61. F   Note here that the TS teacher must *undo* the child's rote response tendencies to analysis, tendencies that the child unfortunately learns from his parents.

62. T
63. T
64. T
65. F
66. F   Note here that these skills are very valuable—but in letting students draw upon the experience they already have.

67. T (Suppose Cinderella didn't lose her slipper!)

68. F
69. F   Did you try out your own answer to this question?
70. (b) If you missed this, stop for awhile and reappraise.
71. (c)
72. T

Chapter 5

73. T
74. T
75. F
76. T
77. F   Note that the coaching analogy breaks down at this point; The TS teacher's ultimate job is not to coach performance, but to create self-coachers.
78. T
79. (a)
80. F
81. (c)
82. T
83. T
84. F   Instinct and habit are other accesses, but the question is perhaps unfair in that the TS instructor is in the main concerned with memory, not habit and instinct.
85. T
86. T
87. T
88. T
89. T
90. T
91. T
92. F
93. T
94. T

Chapter 6

95. T
96. T
97. T   This seeming *reduction* is defended fully in Chapter Six. The key word again is *recursive*.
98. T

99. F   Note here that there is a new governance of even past experience when that experience is reinterpreted by means of newly acquired thinking skills.

100. F

101. F   Throughout ETSI the *problem* is little more than context for the real work: student discrimination about the capacity to direct thinking behavior.

102. F

103. F

104. T

105. F

106. T

107. T   Admittedly, this idea is startling but note that through it all the student is being asked to take a close look at how he thinks, and for most students this is a rare and fascinating activity.

Chapter 7

108. F

109. F

110. T

111. F

112. F   Rather, you know you're molding them to recipe.

113. T

114. F

115. F   Only if the show makes summer stock.

116. T

Chapter 8

117. F

118. F   Not an iota, though they may enhance resources for it.

119. (d) Also, one should add, to replace *fear of* with *interest in* questions.

120. F   This would be T if we replaced "have" with "are conscious of."

121. F

122. T

123. F   Adding "by you" would give this a T.

124. F

125. F   . . . at least for the TS teacher.

126. F   Quite the contrary. It is to enhance salience by making simpler.

127. F   Remember that you can operate similarly with similar givens.

128. T   Sorry.

129. T

Chapter 9

130. F
131. F   Too vague. They are predications; sometimes general, sometimes specific.
132. (d)
133. (b)
134. (b)
135. (c)
136. (d)   It's useful to realize that "correct" is just a convenient surrogate. We accept "correctness" as a sign of having been well evidenced.
137. F
138. (a)
139. (b)
140. F
141. F
142. T
143. T
144. F   The reliance is there, but goes customarily unremarked.
145. F
146. T
147. F   An apparent truism, this is too dangerous to permit. Only carefully *assessed* writing can improve thinking.
148. F   It hasn't helped us much.
149. F   This is *always* risky.
150. T or F   This is your freebe.

CHAPTER 11

THE SECONDARY/COLLEGIATE AGENDA

Forethought

We open our segment on secondary and collegiate thinking skill instruction with this preview chapter. What we want to preview is a set of thinking skill issues and themes that arise as we approach the last two learner populations we plan to consider.

Secondary and collegiate students are seldom lumped together. They don't appear to have much in common and educators generally examine them separately. But in this chapter we inspect a very basic concern that rises with secondary students and abides throughout the college years, so we are examining learner needs that these populations share.

This secondary-collegiate grouping embraces a good deal of human development. It appears to include everyone from the sixth grader through the college senior. Actually, it's worse than that. The college senior marks a purely arbitrary limit within a far larger population responsive to the thinking skill issues we examine. Anyone either closely approaching, entering, or passing through adulthood fits the bill.

Such a large target population could be alarming. We might expect things to get extremely complicated as we try to embrace thinking skill needs that touch the bulk of mankind. For anyone apprehensive about this, there is some good and some bad news.

The bad news is that the thinking skill instructor's job does grow more complicated as we enter the secondary-collegiate domain.

The good news is that it gets more complicated in a special kind of way that prevents it from really getting much harder. In one sense it even gets easier.

Things grow more complicated during the secondary–collegiate period because new learner needs arise as it begins. In themselves, none of these new needs will be more difficult or demanding to address than those the thinking skill instructor has already confronted. In fact, these late-flowering needs tend to be considerably easier to handle than earlier ones. If we could limit thinking skill concerns to this new batch, we could say the job had gotten easier. The problem is that we don't get to ignore any of the earlier needs as we turn to the new ones. We end up responsible for the whole augmented range.

For example, you will have no trouble finding secondary or college-level students who've encountered little if any prior emphasis on operant skill development. It is quite possible that such students would benefit most if they began with a program that concentrated on some of our earliest elementary thinking skill objectives. This implies that the secondary or college-level thinking skill instructor should be in touch with those elementary objectives and savvy about helping older students approach them.

At the other extreme, we can encounter students who display as much facility in employing the generic skills as we've so far sought to develop and are therefore ready to go further. It is this issue of how to take such able students further that will add most of what's new to your repertoire as a thinking skill instructor. It isn't really harder *to take students further, but it is an added and significantly different task.*

We examine this difference in detail over the next few chapters, but we need to isolate and understand its basis now. We can summarize it as a certain kind of shift in the thinking skill instructor's emphasis—a shift away from skill consciousness on the learner's part toward task *consciousness. But such a curt summary doesn't tell us much about what kind of a shift this really is, what prompts it, or why we wait until the secondary years to make it.*

All this should grow clearer as we examine what kind of thinking skill agenda our secondary–collegiate population raises.

FACING THE NEW POPULATION

For everyone—students, prospective thinking skill instructors, subject matter teachers—the step from elementary to secondary education is enough to tax a seven-league boot. Yet on the face of it we're discussing a simple advance from one grade to the next. It's hard to credit a sudden rush of change to such a humble increment, but extensive changes do come to a head at this point, and we need to trace some of them to see how they shape secondary thinking skill concerns.

As we consider the students, three main things have occurred that make middle school or junior high a new proposition. The first is a certain loss of innocence. To a degree never true before, these students are accomplished veterans, and they have begun to see themselves in that light. They have overcome and left behind them the years-long enterprise of elementary education. Schooling, for them, has lost most of its surprises. They know the ropes. They've seen and come to terms with a good number of teachers. They enter classrooms now with a calculating eye.

Second, these are students propelled and often dismayed by an onrush of the genes. They are coping with bodies gone wild with new growth and glandular imbalance; bodies rushing toward maturity as if tomorrow will be too late. At times they hardly recognize themselves and their new urges.

Third, these metamorphosing veterans are tasting and cultivating a new independence. Never again will students belong as much to their parents or their school, because there is an exciting third option — their peers. They've grown conscious of a society of their own, and dealing with it becomes an ascending priority. It doesn't help to point out that school is a primary occasion for that society. In the student's mind it comes more and more to be a case of "them" and "us." Henceforth, classwork gets a smaller cut of the student's consciousness. So much else is going on.

These three changes ground much of the tumultuous, know-it-all quality of the middle schooler and help account for the increasingly adversarial student–teacher relationship in those early secondary years. By high school, there's been a coming-to-terms, a new equilibrium. Lines have been drawn that neither side tends to cross. The accommodations lead to a kind of wary truce. In class, it's the teacher's thing. Outside, it's the students'.

The new dynamics of the secondary student obviously influence the thinking skill instructor's efforts, as they do that of any teacher. The student has less psychological space available for instruction just as the teaching pace — goaded by a sense of the impossibly vast job of educating teens — tends to increase. As students come to invest a smaller and more proscribed portion of themselves in schoolwork, teachers face a choice. They either settle for less or work very hard to counter the student retreat from involvement.

While this competition for student involvement heightens, other pressures conspire to crowd out thinking skill concern. There is, for instance, a tacit feeling that the elementary — and avowedly developmental — phase of education has ended, and that schooling should now concentrate properly on subject matter. Any thinking skill emphasis will have to go to much greater lengths to justify a claim on already oversubscribed secondary instructional time.

PLAUSIBLE PRIORITIES

As the thinking skill instructor anxiously searches for a context in this tight market, two possibilities stand out.

The first is in direct support of the subject matter teacher's increasing emphasis on teaching a discipline. Shouldn't the thinking skill instructor follow suit and concentrate on developing good thinking in the subject matter field? The individual teacher looking for a synthesis of roles ought to find this an especially appealing option, because the thinking concern here so nicely supports the subject matter focus.

The second possibility resides in secondary education's final and overarching "developmental" mission, which is to foster a productive and responsible citizenry. We may think of this mission as rooted in vocational and social studies, but it is really a synthesis of everything the school does to achieve a student body that is on the one hand employable, and on the other informed about, concerned with, and involved in its contemporary world. Why not add to this synthesis an emphasis on practical thinking skills for the real world?

Here are two possible orientations. We can concentrate on getting students to improve thinking skills in dealing with their classroom subjects. Or we can emphasize developing those skills for their utility in real life. Both orientations have their appeal. Good motives prompt them, they adapt well to interests dominant in the established secondary agenda, and they wear their utility for students on their sleeves. But neither is really sound, and either will tend to set you off on the wrong foot.

We've led you briefly down a primrose path in proposing these two options. We've done so because they represent goals frequently pursued by thinking skill programs and often counseled in the thinking skill literature, so the question of their adequacy is important. If there is weakness here, exposing it will help us identify what our core thinking skill focus ought to be.

REAL PRIORITIES (PERFORMANCE VERSUS CAPABILITY)

If our chief focus is to be neither good academic thinking nor good real-life thinking, what could it be? And why doesn't this better focus leap out at us? Why does it give ground to these more popular options and itself remain obscure?

Oddly enough, what obscures the needed focus most is a widespread devaluation of the classroom. We've come to such a poor level of esteem for what the classroom is capable of doing that we no longer recognize its distinctive potential.

One sign of this low esteem is the well-worn and misleading real-life/ classroom distinction. Classrooms, the feeling goes, are somehow artificial and not to be confused with "real life." You "play" at reality in classrooms; it's where those who can't "do" go to either learn or teach. We tend to project a feeling that classrooms don't have to own up and face the real test, as in, "That maybe OK in the classroom, but what's it got to do with real life?"

This puts an unjustifiable face on classrooms. The dynamic of the classroom is simply the dynamic of one person assisting another's growth, which is as fundamental, real, and essential as anything else mankind does. The classroom is an artifact in the sense that it is planned, organized, and regulated, but so are all the other wholesome fruits of society or culture we count as "real." Perhaps what makes the classroom different is its intrusive insistence on growth. Nowhere is our own development a more constant and central issue than it is in the classroom. Too bad we allow a connotation of dilution, weakness, and artificiality. We should have insisted that "classroom" connote intense rather than superficial existence.

There is an important secret to the kind of intensity the classroom can achieve, and that secret holds the key to what the thinking skill instructor's focus should be. Even when they can't consciously label this secret, exceptional teachers evidence it. The secret is that there is a goal in teaching beyond eliciting performance. For any learner, this secret insists, performance is not the point. Performance is a required step toward improving ability. Improving ability is the point.

The real purpose of performance for a *learner* is to *reform* that learner's capability. It is in carrying performance back to the student and insuring this reformation that the good teacher excels. It is also this little step that unveils the radical potential of the classroom.

If *reforming the student's ability* is our real goal, getting good academic performance, good "real-life" performance, or some combination of the two out of the student can't be our prime focus. We must remind ourselves of the pitfall that awaits single-minded concentration on performance, namely that there are countless ways to deliver performance other than by inculcating individual ability.

Once we slip and aim at applied thinking skill, we run the risk of confusing performance and capability. Quarterbacks incapable of designing a good offensive play win football games. Their performance has been orchestrated by someone else: a capable designer. It is easy to do the same thing with students when our aim is to draw from them some performance. We tend to secure the outcome by constraining and guiding the steps. We don't get good thinking, but we do get good performance. In effect, *our* skill has orchestrated the outcome. We risk overriding rather than developing student skill when what we simply want is results.

In light of the thinking skill instructor's agenda, the *result* of *any* performance is itself *always* an inadequate measure of capability. He must take the performance itself carefully and analytically to pieces — as we saw him do in Chapter 7 — before it begins to speak to him of capability. On the other hand, *any* performance so examined can tell us something of its author's capability and gain us access to it. *Performance*, for the thinking skill instructor, is occasion to get elbow-deep in *process*.

So the thinking skill instructor's primary focus has to be on the *individual student's capacity to think*. The handling of classroom tasks or "real-life" problems cannot be his chief concern. His chief concern has to be the learner's own facility in thinking, and it is not served well enough by simply assuring that an individual can solve a specific range of problems, in or out of classrooms. The thinking skill instructor needs to concentrate on each learner, and in light of his or her performance, ask these kinds of questions: "Can *she* skillfully deploy attention?" "Can *he* sustain analysis?" "Can *she* track likenesses?" "Can *he* suspend closure?" "Can *she* project consequences?" "Does *she* grasp that she commands these skills?" "Does *he* grasp he commands them?"

The thinking skill instructor — *as* thinking skill instructor — has his pure agenda here. He will go where he has to — inside the discipline, outside the discipline — to provoke and win affirmative answers. His core agenda is very focused, very narrow, and it does not define the thinking site. What body of lore or experience or problems might call upon the skills is a matter of indifference. Good thinking is not any subject matter's province. It is the individual mind's province.

We need to see that getting the mind to perform well in some context is quite different from using some context to expose and advance its capability. Perhaps an analogy will help. Tuning an engine for high-altitude driving is not the same as driving at high altitude for a fix on the engine's performance envelop. You do the first to get the best from what you've got. You do the second in seeking to improve what you've got.

Now we're close to the real wonder of classrooms. It doesn't reside in the fact that they can *invoke* ability. It resides in the fact that they can *reform* it.

THE CLASSROOM POTENTIAL

As a thinking skill instructor, the teacher is free to drive the student's mind through any terrain — the subject field, peer issues, work situations, story problems, pop art, politics, what have you—that can reveal that mind's performance envelop. She is not diluting her subject matter or jumbling her syllabus by doing this. Her sights are fixed on the student as thinker and her syllabus is prying that object into the light.

As a subject matter specialist, the teacher's priority is to bring the student to a mastery of the course content. That content governs the syllabus. You can't toy lightly with that syllabus without jeopardizing the aim of the course. And, quite rightly, this goal emphasizes the result, and not the nurture, of skillful thought.

So we have two quite different focuses, or vectors for instruction. One faces the student and her resources; the other faces the subject matter and its intricacies. The problem for the secondary/collegiate teacher seems to be how to face both ways.

The artful teacher knows that there is a point where concern for the student's capabilities and concern for the subject matter naturally converge, and she focuses on that point. That point is the classroom itself. To see the classroom aright—to see it as the capable professional teacher sees it—you need a special kind of binocular vision. Tune one eye sharp to student ability. Adjust the other to content mastery. What you see now is the classroom in full depth and true dimension. It is the place where ability, discovering itself in content, strives to become mastery.

We are back to the *intense* quality of life a classroom can sustain and the concentration it requires of the teacher. There are many settings in life where concern for the individual dominates: the family, rap sessions with pals, the counselor's office, church, outings with friends. There are equally as many where concern for performance dominates: work, sports, competition, any arena dedicated to achievement. There are very few—chief among them the classroom—where both can be fostered in light of each other. As students strive to perform in the subject field, the teacher scrutinizes their exertions. Where individual exertions are flawed, she concentrates on setting them right. As capabilities strengthen, she heightens the subject matter challenge. To and fro she weaves this double emphasis.

An observer unaware of this duality will seem to see contradictions in the teacher's performance. Vis-a-vis the student's operant behavior, she is sensitive and open, praising and encouraging even when student effort is feeble. She must get the student to expose ability, to commit, to act, and no issue, no experience, no topic is barred that can lead fittingly to such exposure. Vis-a-vis the subject matter, she is demanding and inflexible. The dynamics of the discipline, its rules and requirements, cannot be waived. Here she is quick to mark what is irrelevant or inadmissible. "Kind of" or "almost" or "close" isn't adequate. She seems at once empathetic and unapproachable, taskmaster and facilitator, martinet and confidant. Her role shifts and resolves around her emphasis. The shifts are quicksilver, yet many of the students, intent and also shifting, understand. Everyone is concentrating, because as compared to almost anywhere else, twice as much goes on in the classroom of an able teacher

This kind of teaching is hard work; exhausting. Conducting "classwork" here involves plunging into and fostering the learning dynamics of a score of individuals while prompting their progress in a subject field. Outside a classroom, hardly anyone would be mad enough to try it. Many teachers have little private rituals that initiate the needed concentration – help them get "up" for it. They are preparing for a venture totally at odds with the sense of classrooms as places where reality is somehow diluted.

Simply doling out subject matter, or getting students to feel good about you and themselves, is not hard work, and there is nothing intense about it. Teachers satisfied with such goals invigorate the view that classrooms are places where reality goes limp.

Employing student performance to reform individual capability is un-avoidably hard work, but in the hands of teachers who do this work, the classroom becomes a place that can spark the student's most concentrated living. Here, as nowhere else, the student can wield, probe, and gain control of her most truly personal possession: her ability. It is sometimes fashion-able to explore settings outside the classroom in hopes of finding one more stimulating to thought, and perhaps the development of thinking skill. A similar impulse tends to cram the classroom with new gadgets and tech-niques. Mistrust both impulses. As it stands, the classroom has limitless potential for confronting students with their own performance, and that is the confrontation the thinking skill instructor needs to guide. Classrooms are good places for the student to grope toward this discovery of new capacities to act. Make sure that any tinkering with the setting or addition of gadgets doesn't defer rather than promote this tough process.

There is another point we need to make about placing the prime focus on reforming individual capability rather than securing performance. If you stop with performance, you interrupt the recursive process that advances skill. If you understand that the value of performance for learning lies in its feedback and use that feedback to reform capability, you encourage that skill-enhancing process. We see how this works more clearly by recalling some things about recursion.

RECURSION AGAIN

Recursiveness, we said, was the capacity of certain functions to produce new output when operating on their own prior output. We asserted that the mind exhibits this quality, and it is not very hard to find traces of it in many of the mind's products. Take, for instance, the hierarchic character of so much of our knowledge.

An individual picks up a seashell and studies it carefully, making notes. He does likewise with a different shell, and then another. Eventually he has a collection of notes on shells. At some point he turns his analytic skills on his analyses themselves, and malacology begins to take shape. The deft arithmetician, skilled at characterizing and manipulating things numerically, begins to probe what numbers themselves have in common, and algebra is born. An individual assesses a novel, then several others. He then assesses his assessments and begins to distinguish literary schools and trends. Knowledge begins in the encounter with singular, immediate, ostensive events, which we strive to discriminate and characterize. It flourishes as we further discriminate among those characterizations. Growth in knowledge requires a shift in focus. The movement is away from raw experience and increasingly toward our ways of modeling and symbolizing it. We point to this trend when we note the tendency of thought to grow "abstract."

The trend has a very practical point, which is to advantage us in future dealings with raw experience. Thanks to all that modeling, fiddling with, and fine-tuning of his characterizations, the malacologist picks up a new shell with a highly durable and almost instant sense of what is ordinary and what is distinctive about it. The algebraist saves hours and hours of arithmetic manipulation with his shorthand grasp of how numbers behave. The critic adroitly notes a new novel's promise or lack of it. Thought, by plucking at itself, by recursively entertaining its own work, improves its grip on experience.

In this hierarchic movement of the mind—from a focus on things to a focus on characterizations of things, then to characterizations of characterizations, and back again—there is an unexpected and often unnoted stability. What is stable are the processes by which the mind makes its moves, the processes we've labeled generic skills. They are at work throughout the hierarchy. This stability is unexpected because we aren't tuned to thinking of process as stable. Process impresses us more with its flux. Because we aren't inclined to look for stability in process, we have a tendency to give a process a new name every time we encounter it in a new setting. Remember all those thinking skill lists that were really activity lists?

We have hundreds of names for taking things apart. Some are more general, like *winnow, dismember, separate, segment, dissect, divide, partition, sift, assay, diagnose, analyze*. Others label more specialized occasions and contexts, like *docimasy, titration, parsing, scansion*. But whatever the label, the act invariably employs the capacity to discriminate and delineate. It is that capacity, variously harnessed and labeled, that we beckon when we talk of "sustained analysis" as a generic skill. It not only operates *at* the various levels to which thought abstracts itself from the experienced event; it—in conjunction with other generic skills—*produces* those abstractions. Recursively.

All this applies to our other generic skills. We have multitudes of ways of describing and labeling selective attention, analoging, suspension of closure, and autocensorship. All of these reference important capabilities that the mind invokes again and again in the business of fashioning, applying, checking, and revising the constructs it employs in dealing with purpose and experience. But our labeling grows really profligate when we describe especially useful, durable, and recurrent interactions of these skills. Think of the deluge of terms we use to describe mental behavior when the mind computes, forecasts, calibrates, controls, deduces, induces, infers, generalizes, hypothesizes, synthesizes, or verifies. Yet any mental performance characterized by these or cognate labels can be effectively described by a protocol involving—singly or in some combination—selective attention, sustained analysis, analoging, suspension of closure, and autocensorship.

The generic skills are, in short, mainsprings of recursion. They are durable mental processes that, when applied to mental output, deliver new output. The *reapplication* of these processes—the reassessment, readjustment, reintegration, and refinement they invoke—is what transforms old insight into new.

This same recursive process transforms old *skill* into new. Roll some past performance by the generic skills and the resulting assessment can foster considerations that will improve subsequent effort. We say "can" instead of "will" because neither thought nor skill is revised unless something urges its improvement. There must be some impulse to grasp better or do better, and there lies the problem with making a fixed performance or level of performance a thinking skill goal.

If my goal is to deliver a performance, I'm finished when the performance is accepted. If my goal is to *improve my ability to perform*, each performance is an occasion for further assessment and refinement—for, in effect, a recursion toward greater skill. Olympic contenders sometimes comment on the stunned emptiness that follows the joy of their final gold-winning performance. This is not at all what they experienced after the immediately prior trial. *That* period was filled with replay and critical scrutiny to uncover what this penultimate performance might reveal about improving the all-important final one.

The thinking skill instructor wants students to view every performance as penultimate in this sense—to view each, that is, with an eye to enhancing the next. That's why his prime focus is not on one or another kind of performance, but rather on getting students to reform capability in light of performance—which is another way of saying to *develop skill*.

Of course, to reform capability in light of performance, the mind must first perform. The learner has to engage tasks that require thinking. We could, in fact, describe the bulk of the thinking skill instructor's effort so far as one of confronting the learner with a measured sequence of appropriate thinking tasks. And that description leads to a key question. Appropriate how? What has guided our task selection to this point?

So far, we have carefully picked tasks that would introduce learners to, and familiarize them with, their own thinking capabilities. Especially during initial ETSI, we've selected tasks that awaken skill consciousness.

SKILL CONSCIOUSNESS

It's good to remember that you can only become skilled where there are options. If you are *compelled* to act a certain way because there is no option, your action doesn't merit description as skilled. It is when you constantly produce highly effective behavior while aswim in alternatives that you earn the label *skilled*. Obviously, then, to become skilled you need to recognize your options well enough to deal with them selectively.

Everything we've done so far in this book has been an effort to get the learner to recognize his thinking options so he can deal with them selectively.

The heart of that effort has been to get the learner to *differentiate a set of her own core thinking abilities*—to become conscious of her own discrete set of basic cognitive tools. We've insisted that she arrive at this consciousness not through someone's description of the tools, but by *wielding* them. We want students to learn the generic thinking skill options *by invoking them and experiencing the distinctive work they do*. This really does entail *using* the skills, which delivers an otherwise inaccessible feel for them, just as you learn something about a bicep while doing burn-out curls that you will not learn memorizing a muscle schematic.

We've aimed at getting our students to uncover their thinking skills while those skills are in harness—to catch their capabilities red-handed, so to speak. They have a tested and established sense that those capabilities can be controlled and enhanced and are demonstrably useful. We've brought students to an awareness of their own skills as governable and developable.

Let's make absolutely sure we grasp why we've done this, by placing ourselves in the shoes of the learner seeking thinking skill. As such a learner, the most important need I have is a validated image of myself as an operant thinker. This means I must be able to see myself as someone with a repertoire of mental abilities that I can elect to apply to situations in various ways, thereby effecting desirable change. That lets me count my thinking as *efficacious* and therefore worth taking seriously.

This kind of self-consciousness is critical to me as a thinker because it places me in charge of my thinking ability. There are limitations and qualifications, but basically I've discovered that I author my own thinking performance, and by improving that performance, my own skill as well.

Bringing the student — any student of any age or educational level beyond elementary — to this vantage has to be the thinking skill instructor's prime goal. Ideally, no *other* thinking skill goal should be pursued before this one is achieved *unless* it aims at this one. Nothing in this guide to this point has violated that principle.

Once this skill consciousness *has* been achieved — once the learner has this kind of working (theoretical won't do) discrimination about his or her thinking abilities — the major and most critical phase of thinking skill instruction for that learner is concluded. Does that mean that the learner has now achieved most of his or her thinking skill? Hardly.

In fact, at this point, when we would be justified in celebrating completion of the hardest part of our task as thinking skill instructors, our students may be incapable of exhibiting the quality of thought that characterizes a thinker as truly skillful. The good thinker understands himself as operant, but the skillful thinker takes this understanding a step further. He uses it to form an increasingly sharp sense of the world as *operable* (i.e., *responsive* to his skills). The skillful thinker manages to parlay skill consciousness into a growing task consciousness.

TASK CONSCIOUSNESS

We've devoted all kinds of time to developing generic skills in our students, and to fostering some discretion and control in using those skills. Must we now rush off and start prodding students toward something called "task consciousness?"

It really is crucial that we distinguish here between a new mission and a shift of emphasis. What we are about to do is shift emphasis. As a thinking skill instructor, you are always striving to enhance cognition, and you can think of cognition as a continuum, with "skills" at one end and "tasks" at the other. "Task" is what the active mind is doing and "skill" is what it is doing it with. We can emphasize one or the other, but we can't approach one without involving the other.

Remember that we achieved our "skill consciousness" by assigning students carefully selected tasks. We picked tasks that were as clear, transparent, simple, and unconfusing as possible — tasks that would draw minimal attention to themselves in favor of showcasing the discovery and exploration of skill. For a time we employed tasks to illuminate skill. Now we will strive to have our students employ skill in ways that illuminate and manage increasingly demanding tasks. We will be giving task an attention we had earlier reserved for skill.

It is a kind of *task consciousness* that we finally need to develop. We will see that the skillful thinker does not passively accept tasks. She has to actively assess and constitute the task as *operable,* which means in light of the operations its completion entails. Even more to the point, she has to see the task in light of what it would demand of *her*—what options she might consider and choices she need make to bring about completion.

Achieving what we've called skill consciousness was a major step toward making our students operant thinkers. That transition grows secure as students grow practiced in apprehending *tasks* as operable, which means vulnerable to resolution by skills appropriately applied. We are guiding the same process here, whether emphasizing skill consciousness or task consciousness. We're just prodding different ends of it at different times.

We should remember, however, that our choice of sequence—first emphasize skill consciousness, then emphasize task consciousness—is not arbitrary. I have to be able to selectively call on my own skills if I'm to be responsible for a task. If I can't do that, someone *else* will call on my skills selectively in light of *his* sense of the task. I will have performed the task by instruction, or recipe. I will have been trained to perform, and my capacity to think will be at best a minor sponsor of that performance.

Perhaps this sequence will make more sense if we look at what might serve as a model of thinking skill growth.

A Skill Growth Model

We begin with a learner (the dot), and we will let the learner's position represent some level of thinking skill, it matters not high or low:

Enlisting those skills in a way that employs and illuminates them, we lead the learner to experience him or herself as operant. Here we raise the kind of "skill consciousness" that comes from exercising the generic skills:

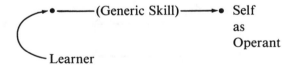

This operant self is confronted with a task that is to some degree unprecedented, and is encouraged to treat it as operable. Feedback modifies ineffective performance toward increasing effectiveness.

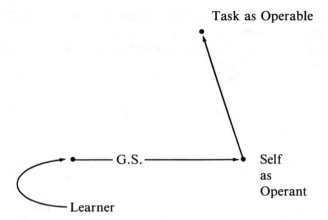

Effective performance confirms perceptions of self as operant and task as operable. This validates a capacity for control that produces effective behavior which is to some degree without precedent, thus heightening the thinker's basis for discretion regarding future unprecedented tasks: Enhanced control of this kind represents incremental gain in skill.

The thinking skill instructor leads this process through various recursions, transferring ownership to the student wherever possible as quickly as possible.

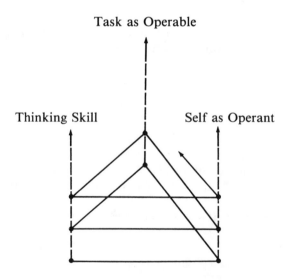

Our recursing spire (an *a*spiration?) captures a number of correlations we want to affirm and enhance. As we come to see ourselves as more operant — capable of disposing ourselves in more ways to influence affairs — we see the world and its events as more *operable*. As we perform, some of our operations are ratified as productive. Others are modified, and still others perhaps rejected. We arrive at greater *informed discretion* respecting our next performance, which translates into an increment of skill. As our skill rises, our perception of self as operant gains clarity. A better sense of our effects sharpens our assessment of how to address the task (i.e., in what ways the task is operable). Crisper tuning to the task improves performance feedback. That, in turn, improves control, which is to say skill. Finally, we have our three arrows vectoring upward. They tell us that thinking skill tends to increase with command of our own agency in a world increasingly viewed as operable.

This is the kind of recursion the thinking skill instructor tries to encourage. Accurately, if not happily, our sketch with its triangular shapes suggests that the process doesn't just tend to roll along on its own. Each leg usually requires deliberate guidance and emphasis, first by the thinking skill instructor, eventually by the skillful thinker him or herself. This should not surprise us. Good thinking, essentially a process of control, opposes entropy. The results of good thinking may lighten our load, but the process itself remains an uphill climb.

A NEW LIGHT

We pursue this emphasis on task consciousness in some useful detail over our next few chapters, and we see that it mostly involves doing a great deal of what we've done before. But treating old issues in a new light will give some of them a fascinating new profile.

We see, for instance, that imagination is an incredibly powerful factor in shaping task consciousness and, ultimately, thinking skill. We discover that imagination — author of the flighty and frivolous, source of the daydream and all wishful thinking — is the font of accurate, powerful task assessment and execution. We see that one kind of imagination in particular is indispensable to the chief enterprise of thought.

What is this chief enterprise? Thinking, and all the skill it can summon and accrue, is dedicated to composing human action. We will be trying to develop task consciousness in minds so they can compose human action more effectively.

In the final analysis, you see, the teacher never escapes the issue of composition. All products of thought are *compositions* in a broader and deeper sense than we reserve for products of the pen or word processor. We are going to foster a kind of task consciousness in our students that will make them better composers.

THE FILE

THE FILE

THE FILE

CHAPTER 12

EXTENDING ETSI

Forethought

Progress in thinking skill development could be described as a move from one kind of unconsciousness to another.

Students usually begin oblivious of their thinking capabilities, with little or no sense of what might constitute a thinking skill. Instruction quickly informs them, but as students gain experience using these now-identified skills, their need to think about them diminishes. Eventually a new unconsciousness reigns.

It's a little like learning how to somersault. It is important to tuck your head in, we are told, and we make a point of doing so as we learn. But eventually we come to tuck our heads without thinking.

This kind of acquired unconsciousness is generally a blessing. It enables us to clear our minds of endless performance discriminations we once had to make and master but can now happily consign to the realm of the conditioned and habitual. In place of awareness, we have an automatic mastery that vastly facilitates performance. The concert pianist does not retrace his initial struggles with hitting the right keys and producing scales and chord patterns as he practices his new piece. That mastery is now ingrained; he simply calls on it.

The process of digesting and ingraining conscious behavior to the point of losing consciousness of it is, in fact, a central feature of our most important, most durable learning. We bring our abilities to bear on mastering some complex new performance. We succeed when we can number control of that new performance among those abilities.

The thing we sought to learn has been incorporated *and is now part of our behavioral repertoire.*

This process of incorporation (as well as its erosive converse; a kind of dis-*incorporation due largely to forgetfulness and lack of use) seems continuous. In fact, if we looked carefully at individual performance, it might lead us to conclude that people never consciously do the same thing the same way twice. Consciousness tends to be heightened the first time we attempt something. On our second try, consciousness begins to shift away from elements of the task that went without a hitch to those still troublesome: The facets of our first performance that went well are already on semiautomatic. As repetition grows, less and less of the performance requires deliberation; more and more involves triggering proven behaviors.*

It may sound contradictory, but it is just this kind of "routinizing" that keeps us responsive and flexible. Transferring the nonproblematic elements of performance to automatic enables the performer to adjust quickly to any distinctive *feature (perhaps new task elements; perhaps new criteria) of an upcoming task. The performer doesn't have to reconceive his entire response each time, but only those elements of response that confront* differences *in task. Our second kind of unconsciousness empowers us to deal economically and easily with similar but somewhat variant tasks, which are the kind life usually poses. Frequently when people label a performance* skilled, *they are applauding this capacity for minimal adaptation to suite just the case in hand.*

We bring all this up in our Forethought because we are a little anxious about some of our terminology. We've used the terms skill consciousness *and* task consciousness *with some frequency recently. Those terms, we fear, may attract unwanted connotations from their better known, more powerful cousin,* self-consciousness. *It would be a grave disservice if we somehow nourished the idea that the height of thinking skill achievement is an intense self-consciousness about deploying one's own generic skills.*

Our greatest hope for the student who achieves a sound working consciousness of his or her generic skills is that frequent employment of those skills would quickly make that consciousness redundant — on all but specially demanding occasions.

The skillful thinker is one who unconsciously supports a great deal of good thinking behavior. She has tasted the utility of the generic skills, and she knows these are unavoidable ingredients of thoughtful performance. But it isn't accurate to think of her as having to consciously prod these skills into action from a dead stop whenever she wants to think effectively. Better to view the skillful thinker as unconsciously predisposed to these behaviors. Thinking, for someone skillful, is attending selectively, sustaining inquiry, analoging, suspending closure, and reassessing.

So what we fought so hard to surface, we in a sense would now be happy to see submerge. We want the generic skills integral to thought, not focal in consciousness. We made them focal for a time only so that they could become integral. The truely skillful thinker shouldn't have to reflect on her capabilities in order to wield them. Her consciousness will be otherwise occupied — especially in executive control. She will be striving to proportion the work of the generic skills to the requirements of the task, and for this she needs a sharp and growing savvy about tasks. On the path from good thinking to increasingly skillful thought, task consciousness becomes an abiding concern.

We explore this new imperative — as it guides more advanced Explicit Thinking Skill Instruction — right here in this chapter, just as soon as we complete one more visit to our initial introductory ETSI imperative of developing skill consciousness.

As a thinking skill instructor at the secondary or collegiate level, odds are that most of your students will need exposure to their own thinking skills before you emphasize applying them to task, so a look at launching an introductory ETSI program at these levels is in order.

INITIAL ETSI AT THE SECONDARY/COLLEGIATE LEVEL

The secondary/collegiate instructor who wants to empower students by giving them a command of their thinking abilities needs to consider a beginning ETSI sequence as presented in Chapters 6 and 7. Everything in those two chapters fits the period from middle school through high school and college. Even the difficulty level of the sample problems suffice. So we invoke the "Do Not Pass Go" rule outlined on pages 110 and 111.

There are, however, three topics we need to explore. First, there are some modifications you might consider in launching ETSI. Then there is a new way of looking at what ETSI helps you accomplish. Finally, there is the issue of extending ETSI toward an emphasis on task.

Let's look at the modifications first. You might elect a useful and somewhat simpler approach to introducing your ETSI session. Remember that we called upon the Whimbey Analytical Skills Inventory (WASI) or some similar set of problems as a way of concluding and in part assessing our initial ETSI sequence. At the secondary level, you can profitably *begin* Explicit Thinking Skill Instruction by administering such a battery of problems.

Launching ETSI with a battery of three dozen or so IQ test items might intimidate intermediate elementary students, but it will pose no special strain on secondary or collegiate students, and it can provide the instructor with a useful gauge of both individual and aggregate class problem-solving ability. A careful look at individual performance on the WASI will give you a rough profile of a student's current skills and let you anticipate areas that need emphasis.

Beginning ETSI this way requires you to say very little—almost the less the better. After a brief introduction, you simply hand out one form of the WASI (saving the other form for a posttest) to your students and give them a class period to complete the test. In that single period, your class has generated a shared thinking experience and built a considerable history of thinking performance. You have on hand hundreds of problem-solving protocols, any of which can be captured and debriefed, and many examples of the use and disuse of those generic thinking skills you are about to introduce and explain.

As for the rest—quick involvement in paired problem-solving teams, the unflagging emphasis on vocalization, and the constant exposure to a growing range of thinking protocols—these ETSI priorities remain unchanged at the secondary or at any other level.

Sometimes things remain the same simply for want of imagination to change them, but we have a better reason for maintaining ETSI priorities. The ETSI emphasis we've established both surfaces and harnesses a powerful language process that very few people, regardless of age, realize they employ. It happens to be a process central to effective thinking, and ETSI helps us make the most of it.

ENLISTING INNER SPEECH

To grasp the real promise of the paired problem solving, the vocalization and the attention to protocol we counsel for ETSI, we need to consider a little more about some of the mind's covert business, particularly when it comes to using language.

All of us achieve speech well before we show up for school, and it is clear, from our earliest fumbling attempts, just what the point of this marvelous capability is. Speech is a vehicle for social exchange and interaction. By using words, we acknowledge society and also harness it in a way that is intensely important to us. It is from this commerce of words with others that our own distinctive shape emerges. One chief product of exchanging meanings with others is a growing sense of ourselves as a unique term in that process. Speech is a primary way of discovering and shaping our own individuality.

It isn't long before a portion of this inherently social vehicle—vocal speech — begins to be used in a distinctive way. The preschooler increasingly converses with no apparent interest in an audience. She makes assertions and asks questions out loud as she normally would in social speech but does not want or expect responses from anyone. She seems to be talking to herself.

Vygotsky notes that this "egocentric speech" dramatically increases when the preschooler faces a frustration or difficulty. For instance, a child prepares to draw but finds the necessary supplies lacking:

> The child would try to grasp and to remedy the situation in talking to himself: "Where's the pencil? I need a blue pencil. Never mind, I'll draw with the red one and wet it with water; it will become dark and look like blue."[16]

Social speech transmuted to egocentric speech becomes for the child a means of concentrating thought and facilitating problem solving. At about school age, however, egocentric speech wanes and finally seems to disappear. But appearance here is misleading. Actually, it has gone underground. Shorn of its vocal element, it becomes "inner speech," and in this form entrenches itself as a principle medium for the mind's work.

Researchers, using a variety of techniques to resurface inner speech, have been struck by its profound structural differences when compared with oral and written forms of language. The differences are great, although with occasion to reflect on the issue, we could surmise most of them. Inner speech is immensely abbreviated speech; an almost indecipherable shorthand. This shorthand consists almost exclusively of predicates: Because the employer of inner speech knows what he is talking about, he doesn't need to flag subjects. It is rapid, active, and resolution oriented. It makes small concession to phonetics or the cadences of sound. It is semantically fluid, dealing more with the cumulative sense of things than explicit word meanings. So the drastically abbreviated terms of inner speech alter their connotations and denotations as the user chooses. For the mind engrossed in its own work, it is a far more deft symbol system than the ones we must use when exchanging meanings with others.

But, as extensively as we use inner speech, and as useful as it is, its unself-conscious utility covers a multitude of sins. It rushes us quickly to and through the task by not calling attention to itself. We barely sense our deployment of inner speech, much less our habitual ways of deploying it. And habit, we all know, can be good or bad. Inner speech, in terms of which we do much of our thinking, disguises both the strengths and weaknesses of that thinking.

Until and unless, that is, we are forced to do something ETSI by design

---

[16]Vygotsky, *loc. cit.*, p. 16.

forces us to do: Translate inner speech into its overt ancestor; a kind of reconstituted egocentric speech. Here is the point of ETSI's insistence on vocalization. Vocalization compels us to cast a conscious and public light on our private means of negotiating life's problems. Now we can exercise inner speech in the open, testing it with and against the now-public inner speech of others for staying power and soundness of limb.

To bring our inner speech into the open, however, vocalization has to be immediate. If too much time passes between our inner processing of an issue and our vocal translation of that process, a good deal of glib editing can occur. To polish up and put a good face on our thinking performance is to make that performance finally even less accessible. The emphasis on paired teams in ETSI is designed to lower this risk. In the paired team, inner speech is pressed to become vocal as it occurs. Students involved in the paired problem-solving work quickly develop a fine sense of when someone's vocal translation of an ongoing inner process is relatively valid. Posturing is both pointless and difficult.

As ETSI progresses, the students will have produced and examined scores of problem-solving protocols. In doing this, they will have come to conscious terms with their own inner speech and noted there the employment and utility of the generic skills. They've also been made privy to the employment of selective attention, sustained analysis, analoging, suspension of closure, and autocensorship in the inner workings of a few dozen other minds. They've cracked a critical and previously hidden thinking nexus of their own and been given purchase on it by comparing it with a number of others similarly revealed. They consequently have both the access and the example required to achieve more powerful control of their own cognition.

These are reasons for ETSI's priorities, and they hold whatever the student's age or placement in the educational spectrum beyond the intermediate elementary years. Custom, upbringing, and psychological economy conspire to close a door on the individual's thinking processes. ETSI conspires to pry it open.

TASK CONSCIOUSNESS

Once students have met and acquainted themselves with their generic thinking skills in an initial 6-to-8-week ETSI sequence, they've completed a critical first step. What we need to examine now is where ETSI goes after this initial sequence, and we've suggested that it ought to move toward developing *task consciousness*. What might that be?

Task consciousness is the result of a set of dispositions we bring to pending work. The set probably takes on a distinctive blend in each of us, which time and experience influence. But in basic ways the task consciousness of the skillful thinker differs from that of the mediocre one. Good task consciousness vastly expands the role of thinking skill in shaping our behavior. Weak or malformed task consciousness gravely limits it.

The point is that we approach no task unpredisposed. We might casually think that only the requirements of the task dictate our response, but this is never so. What we bring to a task in terms of orientation and expectation determines its course at least as much as any other factor. Some of these expectations are very general and aren't shaped by the pending task at all, though they deeply influence how we will address it. These are expectations we've gradually formed about what kind of world we're in, how best to relate to it, and what kinds of things it is likely to hand us. Collectively, these expectations can either enhance or diminish our reliance on, and hence employment of, skillful thought. That is why the thinking skill instructor will want to underscore the task consciousness of the skillful thinker and demonstrate to students the radical difference it can make in performance.

For a sense of where we're headed, we look quickly at three important elements of task consciousness here, together with the key disposition that makes them useful. We see them up close later, when we explore how to enhance them during extended ETSI.

Keep in mind that by "task" we mean a conscious attempt to meet some need. For our purposes, any effort to establish a desired state of affairs through selective action is a task. A skillful thinker is disposed in special ways toward (1) the features, (2) the composition, and (3) the execution of any task.

DISPOSTION TOWARD TASK

There is something distinctive about the way a skillful thinker approaches the whole business of performing tasks, and a few observations about the kinds of tasks we encounter help us grasp what it is.

Some of the tasks we embrace we elect ourselves, simply by deciding to address a need on our own initiative. But a good many others are handed to us ready-made; we're expected to accept them and perform. Our lives seem full of tasks we did not dream up but are, for various reasons and in various ways, compelled to take up.

Whether we devise it or receive it, the task itself falls somewhere on a scale from fully precedented to completely unprecedented. Perhaps it's never totally one way or the other, but we can generally classify any task as mainly something familiar that we know how to do or have seen done before (precedented), or something unfamiliar that we don't know how to do or haven't seen done before (unprecedented).

That gives us four rough categories of tasks:

1. Self-initiated tasks.
   A. Precedented.
   B. Unprecedented.
2. Received Tasks.
   A. Precedented.
   B. Unprecedented.

What is important about these categories is not how neatly and precisely they carve up the realm of tasks. It's easy to envision long arguments about where some given task would fit in such a simple schema. Regardless where a given task really fits, the schema lets us characterize important *attitudes* toward task.

The passive thinker, for instance, is best equipped to treat any task as though it were a 2. A. It is comforting to view a task as pre-established and required — as though it were a dictate of nature. You can then embrace it with a minimum of critical inspection and almost no personal responsibility, because "That's the way it is." And upon being confronted by such a task, it is only natural to look for precedent. To handle it in some established and sanctioned way again reduces responsibility, because "That's the way it's done." Should precedent not be forthcoming (i.e., things look like a 2. B.), the tendency is to demand that someone else establish it — in other words, show us how. If composing or devising the task oneself is a resort at all, it tends to be a very last one.

The operant thinker, on the other hand, tends to address any task as though it was a 1. B. Even if someone else saddles him with an amply precedented task, he will, when thinking skillfully, treat it as though he's responsible, as though he initiated it, and as though he had to shape an unprecedented, best fit response. He does, in fact , make the task his own. He explores the situation that gave rise to the task. He tries to refine his sense of the task's goal: to clarify what and who's purpose(s) it is supposed to serve. Often there are multiple purposes — some of them cross — which need to be untangled and prioritized in some way. He looks at task completion in light of available resources, which are usually less than optimal. He wonders, and probably explores, whether some slightly redefined goal or modified approach could advance the purpose within means.

After such extensive exercise of task consciousness, the skillful thinker often appears to behave just like the passive one, because often the skillful thinker concludes that precedent suffices or excels in a given situation — nothing about the case warrants a fresh approach. But by having assessed the utility of precedent in that instance, and having decided on evidence that it's the best alternative, he has in effect distinctively composed his choice — made the task his own.

We have to remember that to the mind functioning skillfully nothing is inherently routine, or old hat, or past thinking about. At first everything is simply itself — a pristine, unequaled event — until it is compared and assessed, at which point it may well be deemed routine, old hat, or past thinking about. The passive mind avoids all this picky business of responsibly assessing things by simply taking somebody or something else's word for it — precedent, authority, what have you. The operant mind, on the other hand — believing its operations often make a difference and hence seeing itself as *responsible* in execution — insists on its own assessment.

There is a certain kind of confrontation that tends to accustom minds to this 1.B. bias — that gives them a feel for devising and handling tasks as evidence rather than precedent warrants. We've already encouraged that confrontation extensively in ETSI. The confrontation is with things called problems, and the process of devising a response without clear precedent is what we call problem solving. A problem, you recall, is a situation that compels a response without offering clear precedent for making one.

"Task consciousness" is knowing odds-on how to move and what to look for in the absence of clear precedent. It involves a kind of reconnaissance, a going out of oneself into the fabric of the problem, the issue, the situation to learn just what it requires, just what will suffice to meet the present need. This disposition toward such outward movement is what gives utility and focus to the task elements we consider next. Without that disposition — without the need to fashion our own precedent for action — what we are about to examine isn't worth thinking about.

TASK FEATURES

A key part of task consciousness is recognizing that tasks, whatever they might be, share certain common features, and that we approach tasks most skillfully by anticipating and managing those features in useful ways. All effective thinkers have some sense of these features, but quite often that's as far as it goes; they aren't usually singled out, named, and numbered. But because we want to consciously direct students to these key features, we need to name and number.

There are at least five features of any task that attract the skillful mind, because exploring them turns out to be fruitful in composing or assessing tasks:

1. All tasks arise in a context, and the context plays a crucial role in defining the task.

2. Purposes motivate every task.

3. All tasks have a terminus, or goal; some state that, when reached, defines the task as accomplished.

4. All tasks harbor change factors; elements of the situation that must change if the goal is to be achieved. Managing these requires a suitable approach, or where possible, an effective technique. If nothing requires change, there is no task.

5. The execution of any task consumes resources.

You might be prompted, on reading the preceding five features, to observe that they seem rather obvious. You would be right. They are rather obvious. Perhaps that is why their utility is so often missed. Skillful minds are especially attentive to these distinctive and distinguishing features of task because of a characteristic they share that is not so obvious: The five features are highly interdependent.

Alone, each of our five features does not seem — and in fact is not — especially revealing. But change an element in one feature, and something shifts in the other four. It is what each feature helps reveal about the others that makes it illuminating. In turn, we understand each feature best *in light* of the others. We build a better view of any task by sifting what we know of it through these perspectives, often uncovering flaws, misfits, and trouble spots that might otherwise slip by.

You can, for instance, ascribe all kinds of purposes to any given task. But in searching for a task's real motive (feature 2), it helps to inspect its goal (feature 3), because the situation we will accept as completion of a task is an important and clarifying measure of its purpose. Imagine, for instance, a union/management tug-of-war over an 8% wage increase. Both sides invoke social and economic justice. Suppose the union would be totally satisfied if it gained the increase while deflecting all attempts to adjust wage to performance. We now have a more precise sense of the kind and degree of socioeconomic justice motivating that side.

Or try understanding goals (feature 3) in light of resource requirements (feature 5). Though they might seem alike, the goal of making illicit drug use impossible is not the same as the goal of making it very difficult or largely unprofitable. The resources required for the former will differ drastically in magnitude and kind from those needed by the latter. Contrariwise, some goals that at first glance appear vastly incompatible can in significant ways be remarkably alike. Scrutinize their components, and a more conservative communism begins to look suspiciously like a more liberal socialism, much as a half empty glass strongly resembles a half full one.

We could go on. If you really want a sense of the resources a task will require (5), try contrasting the situation that spawned the task (1) with the one that will satisfy it (3). You sort of subtract (1) from (3), which highlights the change factors and clarifies suitable techniques (4) and gives you a basis for estimating what the operation will require (5).

It is in attending *selectively* to these features of any task that we develop an increasingly sharp sense of what the task entails. The really skillful thinker is scouting these features even before the task is fully specified. The passive mind, on the other hand, often couldn't care less and readily accepts as salient or important whatever is so labeled. We saw, when we discussed Disposition Toward Task, that this is largely because of the very different orientations the skillful and the passive thinker tend to assume respecting tasks.

Having formed an acute sense of the task by examining its features, the skillful thinker must now determine what to do. She needs to decide how in fact she will operate, and to do that she will employ two resources in ways quite distinct from those of the passive thinker, who will tend not to employ them at all. She will use (1) imagination together with (2) prior knowledge — and the more systematic that prior knowledge, the better.

TASK COMPOSITION

Without imagination, the only tasks we could perform would be highly precedented received ones. If someone didn't detail the task and tell us — step by step, with the precision of a computer programmer — how to execute, we couldn't — either literally or figuratively — imagine what to do.

Among other things, imagination is the mind's surrogate for precedent. If it hasn't actually happened before, imagination lets us examine things as though it had. The less precedented a task and the more we assume responsibility for it, the more critically we depend on imagination.

We think of imagination as something flighty and frivolous, not as a basic implement in the hardheaded execution of mankind's affairs, which is what in fact it is. Perhaps we unconsciously suspect the truth when we stimulate imaginative childhood fancy, thereby encouraging a kind of early flapping of wings that must ultimately sustain serious flight. Imagination is the only vehicle that lets us cross the threshold of the future. We can't even plan our weekly calendar without it. How, without imagination to extrapolate the consequences, could we decide between alternatives? On the assumption that things will operate next mostly as they just did, we imagine everything beyond the immediate instant.

Nothing requires that imagination has to be vague, imprecise, or merely fanciful. Before the Sears Tower in Chicago began construction, thousands and thousands of architectural, mechanical, electrical, and other types of drawings, schemata, and specifications were our most precisely codified imaginings of what it would be like.

If and when our imaginings are sufficiently accurate, germane, and comprehensive, and when we execute them well — as was the case with the Sears Tower — what we plan to have happen often actually does. So when we want some special thing to occur, we strive for verisimilitude in our imagining. We want our imaginings to take everything possibly relevant into account.

An example of this perceptive imagining comes to mind, unfortunately without the names of the key players or the midwestern company in which it took place. The management is looking across a table spread with drawings of the new company facilities, whose foundations have already been laid. They are looking expectantly at a consultant, who says, "Make the hallways 12 feet wide." They do, thereby resolving a mare's nest of problems that have come to threaten both the company's reputation and its balance sheet.

With less than 100 employees, the company had been known as outstandingly responsive in serving the special needs of customers with high-quality goods delivered promptly. Success brought expansion. Now with near 300 employees, the company rewarded its product design staff with a suite of offices and a conference room. It did the same for the manufacturing staff, as well as other increasingly specialized groups. Customers began to have difficulties in getting special needs addressed. Some contracts, in frustration, went elsewhere.

Office suites and meeting rooms disappeared in the new building. There wasn't room with the 12-foot halls, so the surplus chairs and tables were placed out there. Like as not, when some of the manufacturing staff, lacking a good alternative, assembled in the hall to chat, a product engineer or orders department person or shop foreman would interrupt or even join in. Vigorous communication and interaction had come back, and things began to get done again. A closer look would reveal that work roles grew more fluid. There were fewer pure managers or pure workers. To get things done, workers would sometimes manage and managers sometimes execute, much as in the old days.

A consultant who always recommended 12-foot halls would justly and quickly be drummed from the corps, and perhaps this one never did again. But on this occasion, his perceptive imagining had taken important factors very well into account.

To insure this kind of accounting, the skillful thinker uses imagination in a variety of ways, but one is so special it's come to have a name of its own. We call it *empathy*, and it lets us incorporate a very critical fact, namely that events, besides affecting ourselves, impact on others. Through empathy, we savor that impact, often before it occurs. Empathy lets events do unto ourselves as they would do unto others.

Empathy — the business of putting on shoes and situations other than our own — is perhaps most easily understood by contemplating its absence. Having no empathy loses us every perspective save the egocentric one. We'd be condemned to see and do everything "My Way." Using empathy, there is no perspective against which we can't contrast and refine our own. In fact, empathy is one of the few sensibilities that can lead us to warrant some other perspective over our own. Thanks to empathy, we can weigh any task in light of the real or potential outcome it might have for anyone it actually or potentially touches. Nothing else quite so amplifies our common welfare, and nothing else gives us such a comprehensive grasp of the consequence of any act.

Thanks to empathy and our other marshallings of imagination, we can judge consequences before we act. We preassess. It is worth once more noting the bias of the operant mind that makes preassessment important. You have to believe that what you elect makes a difference. If your course of action makes a difference, you are responsible. If you are responsible, you'll want to examine the likely consequences.

To a very significant degree, what imagination builds is a function of what it builds with, and it has one exclusive source of material. The mind can only work with the knowledge it has acquired, and so the skillful thinker places a special premium on knowledge, particularly the systematic, disciplined kind.

At first it might seem that established knowledge — say, for instance, an academic discipline — is more prized by the passive than the operant mind. After all, where else would you find precedent save in established knowledge? And what about at least some traditions that depict the skillful thinker as someone independent — and generally scornful — of existing knowledge? We've all encountered sagas of the poorly schooled hero whose clear, direct, uncluttered mind penetrates to the heart of what befuddled academicians have obscured. The active, operant mind, we are sometimes led to think, is better off lean and not weighed down with all the dead baggage of established knowledge.

Poppycock. First of all, to the degree that it's passive, a mind can't comprehend an academic discipline's proper role. All disciplines share the goal of resolving — making clearer and more precise — our grasp of some phenomena. They generate and organize knowledge for its *utility* in that effort. We know utility is the key because disciplines also disintegrate and discard great chunks of knowledge and theory that cease being useful. Gathering everything disciplines have produced is a concern for the librarian or encyclopedist, not the disciplinarian.

While the passive mind confuses the academic discipline with these collections of its implements and fabrications and pokes through mounds of these for preshaped answers, the operant mind strives to use establish knowledge very much as the true disciplinarian must. Such a mind tries to insure that the mental constructs it employs apprehend things as fittingly and perceptively as possible. The fee for such insurance is simple. The skillful thinker needs to maintain implicit access to all her acquired knowledge all the time, and often she must add great new systematic chunks to what she's already absorbed. She is compelled to do this by something we could call the "Best Fit" impulse.

To get a feel for the Best Fit impulse, imagine yourself with a jigsaw puzzle whose picture you've never seen. You've cleared a spot for the puzzle on the table and you reach into the box, picking the first of a thousand pieces at random. Without other referents, you can't even raise the question of that piece's correct placement. Now suppose you've assembled all but the last piece, and you pick up the one-thousandth. Correct placement is a foregone and completely unambiguous conclusion. That piece's fit is precisely defined by its relationship to all the others. Notice that for any piece between the first and the last, difficulty of placement tends to decrease as the number of referents — pieces already placed — increase.

Whether a skillful mind is striving to comprehend, devise, or execute a task, it gauges that effort for "fit" against accumulated insight and experience. In effect, the skillful mind brings as much of its "assembled puzzle" to the "piece" as it can to determine a best fit.

There is, in skillful thinking, always a demand to do more than simply dispense with the isolated task or quench an immediate need. There is a kind of pressure to build coherence across as well as within our operations. A given sequence of acts or choices is judged not merely on how they work themselves, but on how well they enhance anything else of which they are a part — an inclination, a developed taste, a mechanical system, a comprehensive scientific theory, whatever the case might be. We can never be sure, when aspiring to this kind of "integrity" or "fit," just what type of knowledge or experience might prove relevant, or even pivotal. These are good grounds for not despising any defensible insight.

The skillful thinker also — perhaps primarily — respects established knowledge because so much of his success or failure has been defined in light of it. He has evidence that his capacity to think effectively is circumscribed by the extent of his knowledge. If his years and interests have ripened at all, he also knows that many of his concerns and enterprises can't even be expressed or perceived, let alone managed, apart from systematic knowledge. The more systematically we know, the more sensitive is the "puzzle" we can bring forward to gauge the suitability of the present piece; the better we can gauge "Best Fit."

TASK EXECUTION

The skillful thinker's disposition, his sensitivity to task elements, and his vigorous commitment to task composition all resolve and justify themselves in a distinctive kind of performance on task. That performance is distinctive by virtue of being *considered*: There is an ongoing monitoring during execution. Unlike the mindlessness exhibited when we "follow the bouncing ball," the skillful thinker brings a complex of sharpened anticipations to the task. These anticipations embrace the consequences of each increment of the task's progress. When what is expected to happen doesn't, the prepared thinker is instantly alerted to the anomaly and inclined to deal with it. He will try for minimal adjustment, but nevertheless he will adjust, where necessary, reflecting on and re-executing any or all previous steps. When the passive thinker acts, it is often rule, instruction, plan, or precedent that operates with little reconsideration. In the skillful thinker on task, the operant mind constantly arbitrates.

So here we've viewed key elements of task consciousness that influence the skillful thinker's performance. Task consciousness disposes attention to those features common to any task that best illuminate its demands. It inclines the thinker to assess those features *responsibly*, as if the thinker's decision mattered. This responsible assessment is achieved by extrapolating and imaginatively projecting consequences in light of established knowledge and past experience. These are critical dispositions for a mind that "operates" in the constructive sense. There is no particular reason for the passively disposed, precedent-content mind to favor any of them.

As thinking skills of the type we've been teaching only make sense if the mind has a constructive role, we want our students to acquire and exhibit these dispositions, and so we begin to shift our ETSI emphasis toward forming them.

TAKING ETSI TO TASK

We noted in the previous chapter that our emphasis on task consciousness would be just that—an emphasis, not a sudden new direction. As a matter of fact, we've invoked task consciousness frequently in our teaching to this point, and recalling how we did helps us increase the new emphasis properly.

Whenever we drew student attention toward a problem or issue, we stimulated task consciousness. Even when we prompt no more than a simple classification—say a student, inspecting a test item, comments, "Oh, this is a pattern recognition problem . . . "—we've occasioned some small movement into the task. The more we compel students to *discriminate* about the issue at hand, the more penetrating that movement becomes.

So far, however, we've largely been encouraging movement into a very hybrid, specialized kind of task. We've emphasized a subset of written problems wherein all the information required for solution *is contained or clearly implied within the problem statement*. In such circumstances, discrimination couldn't be more convenient, or less laborious. That, of course, was our point. We wanted to invoke and explore skills with the least possible distraction, and self-contained, clear, unequivocal problems allowed us to do that.

But the problems we generally create for ourselves or that life randomly hands us tend not to be of this type. They more likely arrive ill-formed, incoherent, and laced with ambiguity. For such problems, *discrimination* — sorting things out, making them clear, deciding what absent information is salient and how to come by it or get on without it, etc. — is often the more difficult and labor-intensive part of solving a problem. In fact, it helps to think of such discrimination as addressing an activity quite distinct from what we usually label problem solving.

The first thing any problem does when it confronts us is pose another problem related to, but distinct from, itself. This second problem is the very serious and substantial one of what to do about the first problem. There is the problem itself, with its own terms to be unraveled and met, and there is the pressure it projects for resolution; "What are you going to do about me?"

A variety of options attend this corollary problem. We elsewhere noted that a much favored option was to do nothing, which amounts to ignoring the initial problem. The truly skillful thinker, however, has developed a different tendency. What he wants to do first with the initial problem is *pose it advantageously*. The capable mind engages in considerable clarification and discrimination about what it is looking for before it looks for it.

There is a reason for this that we haven't time to demonstrate, but that we can suggest. When faced with a problem, the passive mind needs a protocol — a recipe — with some assured and acceptable probability of working — in effect, a sort of guarantee. How or why it works doesn't really matter. Assurance that it will does. The operant mind has to supply its own guarantees. If it doesn't *devise* the sequence of resolving behavior, it at least has to *see* how a proposed sequence is supposed to work — someone else's guarantee isn't enough. To see how a prospective solution *operates* requires much more precise discrimination than does accepting a solution on precedent. Evidence has a kind of salience and vitality for the operant mind that does not trouble the passive one. In fact, the soul of this task consciousness we want to develop is the impulse to *make evident* how best to operate.

Speaking of souls, our strategy for developing this task consciousness is itself going to be the soul of simplicity. We will continue to confront our students with problems, but they will be gradually less self-contained, less complete, more complex, and more ambiguous. They will, in short, require of the student greater and greater discrimination.

At this point it should become clear that our growing emphasis on task consciousness is going to cost us nothing by way of thinking skill development. It is, in fact, a sure road to continuing our skill development, and this becomes apparent if we reflect on what the emphasis demands.

We are going to be asking the student for more problem assessment, more probing discrimination of problem elements. This will require (1) more selective attention and (2) sustained analysis. More extensive comparing and contrasting of problem elements and scenarios will of course require more (3) analoging. Nor can you devise and affirm a better problem description, assign relevance to data, or nominate solutions without having (4) suspended closure and (5) engaged in autocensorship. The only path to improved task consciousness follows increased employment of the generic skills.

EXTENDED ETSI SAMPLES

Before we talk about how one designs an extended ETSI session, lets take a quick look at some vignettes of what is happening in several of them.

Sample #1. Location: a college freshman "learning" seminar. The teacher is a member of the Economics Department.

The teacher speaks to a somewhat self-conscious young man midway down the leftmost row. "All right, Charles. I see you're bursting to share that roll of wallpaper with us. Come tack it up.

"To tune us in, let me remind you all of the day we first explored a two-dimensional matrix. We discussed the rows and columns and the interesting little boxes they formed that let us specify a relationship between two things. Then came that black moment when I said, 'Ask me any question you want, and we'll see what a matrix can tell us about it.' Some audacious wag—I think it was Philipa over there—said 'What is English Literature?' Charles has been elected spokesman of our English Lit team, who have been laboring ever since toward an answer. The floor is yours, Charles."

Charles has unraveled and pinned up a very large chart. There are over 60 columns and at least as many rows. The columns have such headings as "Early (11th–13th Cen.) Vernac," "18th Novel," "Contemp. Poet. & Lyrics," "Contemp. Essay," "Lit. Crit.," "Early Amer. Novel," "Lit. Instruc.,"

"Compar. Eng. Germ. Lit.," and so forth. The rows display seemingly similar titles, like "18th Cent. Novel, Hist.," "Contemp. Lit., Crit.," but also distinctive ones like "Gramm. Anal.," "Semantic Anal.," "Compar. Ling." The overall heading for the columns is "Subject Area." For the rows it's "Author's Field." Charles explains that the chart is an effort to organize 2 years of articles listed in the International Periodical Index related to the field of English Literature. What it does is correlate the kinds of specialists working in the field of English Literature with the articles produced in various domains of the field.

"But does it tell you what English Literature is?" the teacher asks.

Charles says his team thinks it gives one kind of answer. Whether it does or doesn't, he and his team now know a lot more about English Literature than they had previously dreamt. They'd had no idea so many specialists were involved in the field, or that the study of literature was itself composed of so many specialties. The team, Charles reported, had discussed what English Literature was before it ever began the matrix assignment. They were fairly content to think of English Literature as everything ever written in English, period — with maybe some things subtracted, like shopping lists. Now they thought that English Literature, although it might be many things, is one thing for sure. It is a complicated field of study that attracts a surprising range of people with specialized know-how. Why, even chemists and physicists make contributions to English Literature. They analyze and date manuscripts.

A student not on the team asks Charles where they got the column and row headings. Charles grabs his head with both hands and shakes it. The headings, he allows, just about sank the team. Though they mainly used categories found in the index, they quickly discovered that each was no more than the best of an unsatisfactory set of options. They had counseled with a number of English teachers trying to get the headings straight. A lot of decisions were just about arbitrary. For instance, there are literary historians who specialize in the literatures of the various sciences. Should English Lit. include the literature of the sciences? Yes, from some points of view. No, from others. Partly, from still others. Flip a coin. The team decided to leave them out. And what about pop culture, which includes a lot of writing. Once comic books were clearly "out" when it came to literature. Now they teach courses on them. Flip again. The team left comic books out.

There were also problems assigning articles to the right boxes. With an English teacher's help, they had developed a rough rubric to spot key words in titles and précis, but there were always articles that fell in the cracks. The team had to leave a lot of the matrix rough in order to get it ready, but, Charles added, he felt the team had done a fair job with what might be considered the main body of English Literature.

Charles attended the discussion of weaknesses and shortcomings in better spirit than seemed warranted. He gave a breezy review of the correlation coefficients, pointing to the high numbers in boxes where field specialists wrote about their specialties and the many empty or low coefficient boxes elsewhere in their rows. He compared these to the greater spread of coefficients where the author's specialty was an analytic approach or technique. Then he dropped the bombshell he'd been saving and savoring.

"We — the team and me, uh, I — took our chart to Dr. Miller in the English Department. We talked about a lot of the things we've talked about here today. But he looked at the chart for quite awhile and asked us if we could bring it back and loan it to him." Charles can't completely suppress a proud grin. "He wants to take it to a meeting of the graduate faculty. He says the chart suggests some fields where some specialists are not doing much work, and it might help faculty direct masters and doctoral students to good areas for their theses."

The teacher resumes control after the short burst of clapping and calls of "All*right*!" "Way to *go*!" They explore further the limits and the utility of this matrixing, this special way of *taking note*. The class — the last one before Christmas break — ends.

On the first learning seminar session after break, one of the students asks if she can address the class. She explains that she became an India buff in a high school comparative civilization program. As she sketches a simple matrix on the board, she explains that she'd gotten to doodling on the long train trip home. The rows are the various states of India, and the columns are dominant castes. She could check the appropriate boxes from memory. When done, she thought she'd try to add what else she knew to the boxes, beginning with each state's chief economic output as she recalled it (agri-products, manufacture, mining, etc.). She could only recall major output for six states, but as she inspected her chart, she thought she saw some relationship between chief economic output and caste profile. "I *predicted* the major economic output for the states I didn't know," she reports. "I had a chance to talk to my high school teacher while I was home, and it turns out I was right in every case but one, and that was a toss-up." This pleased young lady has affirmed that organizing known information can produce new insight.[17]

Sample #2.   Location: 11th-grade High School thinking skills component (6 weeks) of a social studies program. Teacher's field is social studies, math minor.

The teacher greets her class. "Good afternoon. I hereby formally convene the Board of Solvology, Inc. It is our task today to receive and act upon the

---

[17]This sample is based roughly on the work and experiences of Professor Robin Hough, Economics Department, Oakland U., Rochester, Michigan, during a series of Freshmen Learning Seminars at that institution circa 1964, slightly embellished by a few of the author's experiences at that same time and place.

feasibility reports of our regional divisions. We will begin with the Director of our Near East Division. Miss Clarkston, if you please.' "

The class is round-tabled, so Miss Clarkston addresses the assemblage from her seat. "I'd like to refresh the Board on this item by reading the summary proposal it forwarded to our Division on the 18th of this month."

" 'Shah Ali Mullah of the new Emirate of Sandabad has established political stability in his tumultuous new land. He is a leader of immense vision and total dedication to his people, whom he wants to raise from abject poverty and ignorance to a place of high integrity and ability in the eyes of all nations. He will direct the income from massive new oil resources to this end.' "

" 'A key element of his 5-year plan entails the abolition of hunger. He desires a system for the distribution of free food to his population of 1,500,000, so that energies now consumed in the struggle for survival can be directed to social and industrial development. He has requested that Solvology, Inc. design and produce free food-vending machines, together with a logistical support system, to meet this need.' "

" 'Sandabad's population is village based, with a mean size of 575 individuals per village. This mean is somewhat misleading, because Sandabad's five largest cities—running from approximately 200,000 to 80,000 in population—account for 700,000 of her inhabitants. Average distance between villages is 7 km. The Shah wishes reasonable access—half a day's travel—to a vending machine for any community of 20 inhabitants and above.' "

" 'The Shah has reserved resources of $200,000,000 for the first year, and $100,000,000 for each of 4 subsequent years, to establish and maintain the food distribution system.

" 'Please evaluate, by next scheduled Board meeting, the advisability of establishing a proposal development team.' "

On concluding her reading, Miss Clarkston informs the class that her group has arrived at a recommendation, based on several considerations:

1.   The mean village population divided into the population total tells us there are 2,609 towns. If you subtract the five large cities, the mean village population falls to 307.

2.   Assume we settle on a machine that can supply food for 300 people a day. We'd need 5,000 of them.

3.   Assume 3½ lbs. of unprocessed bulk food per person per day. Each machine would have to dispense 1,050 lbs of food per day.

4.   A call to a local vending machine supplier indicates that a machine which handles 100 lbs of product costs $2,000. Assuming a simple projection, our machines would cost about $21,000 each.

5.   Assume that the bulk food, including cost of delivery, would run 35 cents a pound.

Based on these assumptions, it would cost $105 million dollars for the machines alone. The remaining $95 million would provide food delivery for approximately 52 days. The $100 million for each subsequent year would provide only 54 days of food each year.

"Given these estimates," Miss Clarkston concludes, "our Division recommends that we reject consideration of the proposal unless the supporting funds can be increased something like six-fold. There is one problem, though. It isn't entirely clear whether the Shah expects the cost of the food itself to come out of his proposed program funds. If not, we think our supply costs would drop to about 10 cents a pound. So if he buys the food out of other funds, $95 million will deliver it for about 180 days."

"In that case, we would still recommend denial, but we could reconsider if the Shah could increase support two-fold."

The teacher thanks Miss Clarkston and opens discussion of the recommendation to the Board. The entire class acts as Board.

Sample #3. Location: 9th-grade composition course, first week of the thinking skill segment that occupies an initial 4 weeks.

Mr. Jacobs steps slowly around his class, now split into three teams actively debating the problem all teams have received:

"Sam has had hard times, but he's been working the past 6 months and has managed to scrape together $700. He needs to decide how to spend it."

"Sam's yard consists of one huge dead Elm and a pot-holed, crab grass lawn."

"The drier in the washer drier combo quit. The family has to clothes-line the wash."

"The bathroom shower tiles are falling out and the tub has a bad crack and a broken drain. The family has to use the shower stall in the basement."

"What should Sam do?"

As signs of lack of interest multiply, Mr. Jacobs queries the teams. He discovers a few firm opinions in each team, but no consensus. He suggests that a little more information might help and hands a slip to each team leader with a request that it be shared quietly within the team.

Team #1 gets the following:

"Sam's wife just found a job. What with day-caring the two kids and the long drive to and from work, she hasn't much time nights."

Team #2 receives this:

"The neighborhood improvement committee has given up asking and is circulating a petition to put township pressure on Sam and his eyesore property."

Team #3 gets the following:

"Sam's very arthritic mother-in-law will be moving into the bedroom next to his in 3 weeks."

This time, when Mr. Jacobs asks, Team #1 wants to replace the drier, Team #2 wants the yard tidied up, and Team #3 is after the bathroom.

"I'm pleased," Mr. Jacobs says, "that you've reached a decision, but I'm afraid none of you have the total picture. Let's all share what we know about Sam's predicament."

The teams are asked to advise in light of all three bits of new information. There are some fairly eloquent rationales for sticking to earlier decisions as well as for changing them, but consensus again appears to dwindle.

Mr. Jacobs prompts a discussion of what happened. First, there was no apparent reason to pick one decision over another. Then there was a reason. Then there were other reasons that confused that one. Mr. Jacobs asks what they think might help them break the deadlock. It is suggested, first halfheartedly and then with more insistence, that precious little is known about Sam and *his* priorities. Does he *care* what his neighbors think? Is he angry, resigned, or happy about his mother-in-law coming? Is he proud of or humiliated by his wife's new job?

The class assignment is a brief story — only a few pages — by each student. In it, they need to invent a Sam that acts in light of all the information but *convincingly* commits the $700 as their team proposed in its second deliberation.

Among other things, Mr. Jacobs plans to use some of these student products as illustrations in a discussion of story elements once he starts teaching composition.

DESIGNING EXTENDED ETSI

We return to these three samples after we've considered what they hold in common.

Each displays students engaged in a variety of tasks. The tasks are varied enough to accurately suggest that the subject matter employed in extended ETSI could be just about anything. Although perhaps not as apparent, the format of an extended ETSI sequence is equally variable. It might, for instance, be a 3-week unit devised and taught by an individual instructor as a "header" for a standard course, or several team-taught, full-semester courses that make up the required core of an entire academic program.

If so much about extended ETSI can vary, we need to be very careful in examining what must remain stable. An emphasis on doing tasks is one stable characteristic of all extended ETSI.

There are, however, different ways — some efficient and some inefficient — of getting someone to do a task. The ways extended ETSI favors may disappoint the efficiency expert.

One very efficient way to get someone to complete a task is to tell them what you want done and how to do it. It could be argued that the epitomy of this approach lies in the basic training programs of our military. A much less efficient approach from most perspectives is to outline not the task but the underlying need, and let the person formulate the task(s) in light of a growing, personally constructed comprehension of that need.

This uneconomical approach requires a great deal of thought. Confronting little more than a need to do something, the individual has to transform that compulsion into an actionable state of affairs. This calls for a "reaching in" to the situation to specify and clarify. It involves the kind of discerning and speaking of things left unspoken that we call analysis. As the situation and its dictates emerge, things that might be done — tasks — suggest themselves. These are mentally modeled and tried, and ultimately some subset of them elected. The whole process insists on an increasingly informed articulation of the need, and the selection/composition of suitable action to resolve it.

In our efficient approach to getting task completion, the learner's operant resources aren't called upon until the point of execution. In our second, uneconomical way, great wads of thoughtful activity are required prior to execution. Execution isn't even a last step, but occasion for more quantities of thought devoted to assessment. For many purposes, we would be foolish not to choose the first approach. But if we wish to strengthen thinking, there is no contest. Damn the economy for full use of the head.

Extended ETSI is therefore always an effort to establish a thinking intensive environment (recall our mention of TIE in Chapter 8), which *includes* the business of identifying and devising appropriate tasks. It is an environment in which the student must not only perform but *compose* his performance. In designing an extended ETSI sequence, the teacher's problem is to decide what kinds of performance he wishes to encourage, and to devise appropriate compulsions for these. But composing the performance is the students' preserve.

It is not too soon to mention that setting up an extended ETSI which demands that students compose their performance requires a major workload shift for the instructor. He can no longer simply concentrate on evaluating performance. Concern for performance, good or bad, is now ancillary. It still operates, but it comes second to a concern for *how the performance was composed*. This is a second stable feature of extended ETSI. The instructor sets things up so that *protocols of the composed performance* can be captured and reviewed. Knowing that a given student did well or did poorly in composing and completing a task is never enough if gain in thinking skill is the point. The "how" and "why" of performance has to be dismantled and inspected.

A third stable feature of extended ETSI has to do with the instructor's very careful specification of the kinds of "composing skills" he aims to develop. We need to distinguish clearly here between the subject matter you might employ and the skills you wish to develop.

We've suggested you can call on any subject matter, in or out of a given discipline. Often, students will respond much less timidly if they see the subject matter as related more closely to their own interest and experience than to a classical discipline, but that choice is the instructor's. What is not optional is the instructor's clear sense of the kinds of thinking behaviors he wishes to strengthen and bolster as students encounter that subject matter.

Clarity about the kind of thinking behavior you want to enhance in a given extended ETSI sequence is critical. Some of the reasons are obvious. Your sense of what you want your students to achieve will be the key criterion in shaping your instruction. The firmer that sense, the surer the instruction. In our chapter on Evaluation we explore some other compelling, if less obvious, reasons for clarity in targeting the skills you want to strengthen.

But when we ask what composing skills *can* or *should* be targeted, we face something of a problem. If we concentrate on what skills *can* be targeted, the answer is almost that the sky is the limit. Any productive sequence of cognitive behaviors that we feel will further empower the thinker *can* be an extended ETSI focus. This brings us to an observation you might choose to underline.

If there is a point where you can most easily adapt and employ some of the available thinking skills packages, this is it. Remember those activity lists that specified teaching objectives such as "Convergent Thinking," "Classification," "Conservation," "Extrapolation," "Generating Hypotheses," "Synthesis," and scores of others? We noted before that these are attempts to label noteworthy mental performances of proven utility in dealing with certain kinds of tasks. A thinking skills instructor might elect any one or any combination of such capabilities as a developmental goal for an extended ETSI sequence. Remember, however, that we are talking about what *can* and not what *should* be done. Reviewing the prepackaged material will not tell you what thinking behaviors you *should* target, but it can help you clarify your own thoughts on the subject and might suggest materials and approaches you can use.

Then what thinking behaviors *should* you target in your extended ETSI sequence? You will have to gauge that, largely in light of two kinds of considerations. The first set of considerations centers on the condition of the forthcoming students you will instruct. What kind of thinking skill and task sophistication will they likely bring with them? What kind of gaps in their thinking capability and task sensibility can you expect? If you had to rank order these, which would you count as most disabling at this point in their growth? The second set of considerations has to do with what they will confront when they leave you. If you are the only instructor they will encounter with an explicit concern for developing thinking skill, you might want to emphasize thinking behaviors of broad utility. If you are one in a sequence of thinking skill encounters, you will refine your choice in light of those others. If you are teaching in the context of a major, your choice will probably sway toward thinking behaviors of special utility for the kinds of tasks that major emphasizes. Choose to develop those thinking capabilities that appear to make the most sense in light of the condition of the students and the point you occupy in the path of their development.

In case you feel you've just been left hanging, you may be right, but no good alternative exists. A choice dictated by formula would be wrong on the face of it, even if there was such a formula. Extended ETSI must, above all, adapt to the condition of the students. Sometimes major adaptation takes place after the class has begun, and fine tuning always goes on. But it may help to realize that your choice of target thinking behaviors, whatever it might be, is not very likely to be far wrong, and where it does go wrong, the error will be relatively easy to flag and correct. The reason is that you have a sea anchor in the recursive nature of the generic skills.

It really is rather simple. Suppose you elect a target set X of thinking behaviors you want to develop. Your students can fruitfully compose those behaviors only through new interactions of the generic skills — selective attention, sustained analysis, analoging, suspension of closure, and auto-censorship. You get the students working and begin to examine their task protocols. If your students are consistently knocking the tasks cold with little sign of employing the generic skills, your target behaviors may be too simplistic, or already well within the students' realm of mastery. If the students constantly botch the job with weak employment of the generic skills, they are likely bewildered by tasks beyond them. If they make steady progress on task with high incidence of generic skill employment, there can't be too much wrong with your choice.

This brings us to the core of our insistence that clarity and precision — as much of both as can be had — about the thinking behaviors to be cultivated is an essential and stable feature of successful extended ETSI. It takes a precise anticipation of what you want if you expect to recognize when you aren't getting it. Vague, half-perceived and half-articulated objectives give no ground for assessing progress. They help you navigate about as well as a spent magnet.

Remember that this clarity and precision is meant primarily to guide *you*, the instructor. Once you have them, don't prematurely force them on your students. As much as you can, let the clarity and insight your students gain about those behaviors flow from their achievement of them, *followed* by your analysis. Forgive us, but here we counsel against beginning class by rehearsing a clinical listing of behavioral objectives.

We conclude with one more stable feature of successful extended ETSI sequences. You might think of this feature as a set of "surface" signs, indicators that the right kinds of things are going on. Their presence alone is not enough to insure successful extended ETSI, but absence of any of them is a warning sign. Students in extended ETSI *must* write, they *must* vocalize, and they *must* compose. The instructor *must* commit great energies to providing and stimulating assessment and feedback on these activities.

Notice the odd injunction to both *write* and *compose*, terms that usually signify about the same thing. Here they mostly mean two different things. For students in extended ETSI, the bulk of writing will be the extensive note-making employed in composing a task and capturing protocols. Composing refers to the student process of shaping and executing the task and can result in all sorts of outcomes other than a written composition. The two can converge when a theme or paper or report accompanies the task or constitutes its chief outcome, but it helps to keep the two requirements distinct. At times it's astonishing to see how much more at ease students become with words when it dawns on them that they are useful for things other than formal composition. On the other hand, it doesn't hurt for them to understand that even when they aren't wordsmithing, they are often composing in important ways.

We now have a list of stable features in extended ETSI. Extended ETSI:

1.   Establishes a thinking-intensive environment that requires task performance which includes the need to *compose* the task.
2.   Emphasizes capturing and evaluating *protocols* of student composed performance.
3.   Requires clear and careful specification of the thinking behaviors to be developed.
4.   Demands that students write, vocalize, and compose, and that the instructor prompts and produces analysis and review of these processes.

In a moment we look for these stable features in our samples, but it will help if we first outline a strategy for developing your own extended ETSI class exercises. We want to underline the strategy now so you can see how the instructors in our samples employed it.

EXTENDED ETSI DESIGN STRATEGY

Assume you've settled on a set of thinking behaviors you want to cultivate. You will have arrived at that set, in part, by considering a number of things you want your students to be able to do. In effect, you've considered a variety of tasks that harness and employ those behaviors. Concentrate on those tasks and try to compose a set of them which, if performed faultlessly by your students, would assure you they had mastered the target behaviors.

Now recall that if you completely specify those tasks to the students — show them exactly what to do each step of the way — *you* will have composed the tasks. What you need to do with your set of tasks is *de*compose them to an appropriate degree — deliberately remove that portion of insight, direction, and information which the students, *by thinking operantly*, can generate themselves.

One way of deciding what to obscure or omit is to reflect on our five Task Features. Remember that we said:

1. All tasks arise in a context, and the context plays a crucial role in defining the task.

2. Purposes motivate every task.

3. All tasks have a terminus, or goal; some state that, when reached, defines the task as accomplished.

4. All tasks harbor change factors, elements of the situation that must change if the goal is to be achieved. Dealing with these requires suitable technique(s) or at least a plan of action.

5. The execution of any task consumes resources.

In these terms, if you're after quick, faultless execution of a task by a student, you carefully detail its context, define its purpose, specify the desired outcome, explain what to do (itemize the factors that require change), and identify the necessary resources. If, on the other hand, you want operant thinking of some specific kind, you selectively obscure or withhold portions of this guidance — just those portions whose absence will call forth that kind of thinking. Ultimately, we are after students who can themselves discern the context, uncover purpose, set outcome, devise an action plan, and organize appropriate resources.

For instance, suppose I want to develop in students a capacity to act on estimation rather than balk in the face of inadequate information. Instead of saying, "we don't have enough information, so I want you to estimate to complete this task," I simply provide the inadequate information. Recall that we said our five task elements were interdependent. In scanning those elements, I may decide to add a constraint to the task context, such as, "We have one work day to submit the report," thereby fixing a compulsion for the student to proceed on estimation. One day won't leave him time to surface and elaborate new data. But now he will call on estimation not because I told him to. He will choose it for its inherent utility in these circumstances.

So as you design your extended ETSI exercises, juggle the task elements for a mix that will constrain but not compose the students' behavior. Again, avoid preorating about the desired behavior and overprogramming your students. There are good pedagogical grounds for this caution. It is always more effective to analyze and praise a behavior you've gotten a student to exhibit than to praise and analyze one you are leading her toward. In the former case, you will have her full sympathy and rapt attention. In the latter, you may simply build anxiety.

EXTENDED ETSI SAMPLE ANALYSIS

Sample #1 — Freshman Learning Seminar.   Our economics instructor began with a very clear sense of what he felt college freshmen generally lacked in thinking ability that he wished to remedy. It seemed to him that they could not correlate well. They were unpracticed in prizing and uncovering the stable relationships between things. They were ill acquainted with the fact that ferreting out those relationships is an invaluable route to new insight and understanding. They did not see that the bulk of statistics, mathematics generally, and all the other sciences are preoccupied with correlation. Nor can we fault our instructor if part of his motivation stems from the fact that you can't be a good economist without being an avid correlationist.

He saw the search for what two things have in common as a rough paradigm for correlation. There are a number of simple, ordinary approaches one can take in that search. But as the search grows more complex, wending through increasing numbers and kinds of things, it enlists more sophisticated techniques. Our instructor wanted to bring his freshmen a fair stretch up this path to sophistication, while stopping short of something like an introductory course in statistics. He felt, in fact, that a great deal of very useful correlation doesn't get done because it falls short of introductory statistics and no one pays it much attention. He decided he would assemble a type of "everyman's" tool kit of basic correlation aids, describe each in turn to his students, and see what they could do with them.

He handled the predicate (the heart of all correlation), Venn diagrams, simple charts and listings, free-form diagrams, flow charts, matrices of various kinds, and several other ways of organizing and depicting information. These different ways of organizing information — *of taking special note* — constituted the subject matter of the learning seminar.

Our sample takes place during the end of his treatment of two-dimensional matrices. He began that segment with what appeared to be an off-hand but was in fact a very careful description of the two-dimensional matrix. He emphasized *what it was* and *what it could do*, even demonstrating with, perhaps, something usual like columns on age and rows on health care costs, or maybe something less usual like rate of delivered pizza consumption in dorms against the daily menu. He did not lecture the students on how he wanted them to employ matrices. He wanted them to gain familiarity by trying to find uses on their own, and this led to his request that they "ask him any question, and we'll see how a matrix can help with an answer."

A set of questions was proposed by the class. Teams were formed and took their pick. As teams discussed how they might employ matrices on their chosen question, they kept track by taking notes. The instructor meanwhile circulated among the teams, helping to examine dead-ends, asking leading questions, providing resource tips, and encouraging where he could. When a team thought it had a feasible plan, it was presented to and inspected by the class. If the application seemed trivial or inept, or if the execution appeared unrealistic, it was back to the drawing board. When a team had defended its plan successfully, they were given the go-ahead to execute.

Through all of this, the instructor drew attention to team protocols whenever he felt the team or class would gain insight about effective ways of proceeding with the task. When a team got stuck, he might present an appropriate segment of the protocol to the class for discussion. When a team protocol revealed a particularly insightful or effective set of deliberations, he would bring this to the class' attention.

Midway through the execution phase, short written reports were required from each team outlining progress, key problems encountered, and next steps. These again were discussed in class, noting parallels and differences. As each project finished, that team organized a presentation to the class, and it was one of these we encountered in our sample.

The little note about the young lady who was an India buff was recounted ecstatically by the instructor to his colleagues. Technically, she had *misused* the two-dimensional matrix by scribbling extraneous information (economic output) in the coefficient boxes. This is what delighted the instructor; she had actually employed the array to foster her own insight, using it as a means and not some inviolable end. He applauded her sense that the matrix was there to help her operate.

After examining several simple correlation techniques, and while some team projects were still under way, the instructor launched a class project. It happened that the campus was undergoing expansion at this point — new dorms and other facilities were going up. The instructor sent the class out to uncover campus traffic patterns and document how bodies moved among the facilities on an average day. The students shadowed key intersections and facilities at various times during a 2-week period, taking counts and samples and employing a good variety of data collecting and correlating techniques. The completed study, pinpointing current bottlenecks and predicting how some of these would further constrict on completion of the

new construction, was delivered to the administration. Some actual modifications and adjustments of the new construction were attributed to this
report.

Let's quickly check this summary against our list of stable extended ETSI
features and see how the design strategy was employed.

No doubt these students are immersed in a problem-intensive environment with a constant compulsion to compose their tasks. There is call for
their generic skills whichever way they turn. They not only recount their
work protocols vocally and on paper but need to dissect and evaluate them
to clarify next steps. The instructor is quite clear about his desire to
strengthen his students in both motive and capacity to correlate. Writing,
vocalizing, and composing, together with assessing these behaviors, are
norms of class-related activity.

The instructor has tailored this operant environment by specifying one of
our five task features and leaving the other four largely unprescribed and in
need of student composition. Respecting the tasks he wants students to
compose, he has left (1) context, (2) purpose, (3) goal, and (5) resources
unspecified, and concentrated on acquainting them with (4) a set of
techniques that are useful in dealing with certain kinds of variables. The
students must elect, investigate, and organize four of the features around
their growing understanding of the fifth.

This approach can be remarkably effective in fostering student sense of
the strengths and limitations of a given technique. Students come quickly to
grips with what practically can be done with a method; how far it can be
usefully pushed, when and why it has to be modified or abandoned. And
they gain their feel for technique only by heightening their consciousness of
all the other interdependent task features. Students quickly learn that care
in delimiting the context, sharpening purpose, specifying goal, and
weighing resources all critically influence the usefulness of a technique.
Task consciousness is thoroughly stimulated by all this, and the instructor
maintains this stimulation by (a) compelling students to compose and
perform tasks and (b) insuring through his insistence on examining protocols that gains and problems arising in the process are attended to and
perceived by all.

It is important to see that our instructor's primary goal was *not* to convey
a profound understanding of correlation. It was to *get* students to correlate,
to operate in a distinctive way and experience the utility of doing so. He
wants to establish in them a sense of the utility of correlation and an
inclination to correlate when doing so holds promise. In short, he wants to
impart a cognitive skill and a certain kind of task disposition rather than
skill in a subject field. Those students with whom he succeeds will not as a
consequence pass an introductory statistics final, but they might surprise

some observers with their ready appetite for formal statistics when they encounter it.

One final note on Sample #1. As carefully as this instructor targeted his thinking behaviors in planning his Learning Seminar, there was a change, or more precisely, an addition midway through the course, and our analysis hasn't so far made this apparent. It happened while the instructor was doing some free-form diagramming on the chalk board. Actually, he was diagramming his own lecture on free-form diagramming, pointing to the gains in emphasis he was making with his circles and triangles and slashing arrows. A small group in the class were particularly insistent with their questions about the relative merits of schematizing one way or another. He decided he would set for them an added thinking behavior objective distinct from correlating, though kin to it: They were to foster and explore this business of schematizing. Eventually, this student team gained permission to attend large lecture sessions taught by a variety of departments. They would visit a lecture and strive to diagram the lecturer's strategy in organizing the information presented. The lecturer was then invited to a discussion with the team in which she or he would arbitrate different interpretations of the lecture strategy (not surprisingly, most instructors had assumed their "strategy" unconsciously), explore its strengths, and consider possible alternatives. It was, for everyone involved, stimulating evidence that careful schematizing can reveal hidden patterns. It also developed operant listening skills that enabled participating students to draw much more from a lecture than is usually gained.

The point here is that our instructor was willing to modify a carefully specified set of thinking behavior objectives in light of his students' unexpected readiness to grow in a promising direction. Student prepotency of this kind is not all that uncommon, and the sharp thinking skill instructor wisely tries to adopt and make the most of it.

Sample #2: 11th-Grade Solvologists.   In Sample 2, our instructor has a fairly broad range of thinking behaviors she wishes to advantage. She intends to teach social studies but wants to combat the largely passive reception and assimilation of information she feels is typical of students engaged in such study. Their tendency is to take social issues and problems at face value, leaving whatever elaboration might occur to the teacher. She wants to counter this tendency by encouraging them to root, if we can redirect Jerome Brunner's phrase, "beyond the information given." She wants them to understand that problem statements, particularly in the realm of social concern, are seldom even descriptively adequate. Often, the real source of the statement — not just an exacerbating media source — is itself oblivious to major elements of the problem, or else serious distortions and omissions occur in transmission, sometimes unintentionally, sometimes otherwise. There really is no alternative for a thinker short of striving to make sense of the issue him or herself. To do this requires a heightening of the whole range of task consciousness sensibilities, *not to solve the problem*, but merely to strip away its camouflage and expose its hidden portions for a less distorted view.

Actually, the use of "merely" in the prior sentence projects a conventional attitude, and sooner or later it dawns on us that convention here is misleading. We face no more abiding problem than the one of clarifying the problems we confront. There is nothing "mere" about our instructor's objective. She wants her students to develop the skills of clarifying problems, discriminating their elements, and recasting them in more revealing — hopefully actionable — form.

On the first day of class, the instructor tells her students that she is delighted to welcome such an august group of specialists aboard. They are the new staff of solvologists who have come to work at the head office, and the world can hardly wait for them to get going. They will do what the science of Solvology has trained them superbly to do, which is to solve especially demanding problems. In keeping with their training, they will work in three regional teams and three specialist teams (in this case, the teacher staffs her teams randomly while giving the class roster its initial reading). The three regional teams are Near East, Third World, and Superpower. The three specialist teams are Ethical–Developmental Analysis, Eco–Technical Analysis, and Political–Cultural Analysis. The Executive (instructor) usually forwards problems to the regional teams, whose preliminary report is reviewed when warranted by the specialist teams. They then append a specialists report. Collectively, the head office solvologists are responsible for the first and most critical phase of Solvology, Inc.'s work, which is to assess the problem carefully, state it in actionable form, and forward its recommendations for handling to the Planning and Implementation Division.

Without further ado, the instructor hands a written problem to one of the regional teams and asks them to deliberate it in open discussion before the class, Amplifying reasonable suggestions but leading them shamelessly ("John, I'm well aware of your brilliant work in the field of cost analysis. Do you think you might give us an estimate on what it would take to keep a dozen biologists on this for 6 months? And Suzanne, as a personnel expert, what about . . . ?"), she molds a reasoned and reasonable procedure for the team, seeking advice and comment from the rest of the class.

This instructor employs modeling in three senses. She is modeling the shifts in perspective the individual thinker must make by constituting them as *team* perspectives; ecological, cultural, technical, ethical, developmental, and political perspectives all have a voice. She models the critical presolution process of evaluating and clarifying a problem by staging it as a corporate task. And the instructor models the incoherence and ambiguity of real-world issues by composing problems for the teams that exhibit and selectively emphasize these traits. The generic skill employment her modeling stimulates is, however, not make believe; it is quite real. Again, oral and written reports capture the protocols that teams generate as they move to compose and complete their tasks.

The teams are well practiced by the time we arrive at our sample of Shah Ali Mullah's problem, and two things are worth noting at this point. One is that our instructor has cause to be pleased. The team shows some facility at getting behind problem statement verbiage in their team assessment. They understand something about making careful assumptions. Each of the Near East team's assumptions are open to challenge from more expert knowledge, but they made an effort to assume within a reasonable range, so that corrections aren't likely to throw their conclusions off drastically. Nor is the team afraid to estimate in light of available or reasonably accessible data, and they don't appear to be defensive about having their estimates questioned. They can catch ambiguities buried in the problem statement, as in the issue of who's buying the food. What pleases our instructor most is that they don't simply throw up their hands and complain as they encounter various glitches. They go on and do the best they can.

The other thing worth noting is the rich world of pedagogical options our instructor has created. If she chooses, she can stop the Ali Mullah problem following a general discussion of the team's report. Or she can go on to emphasize practically any feature of the problem clarification process. She could suggest there are signs that the Shah might increase funding to acceptable levels, and it would therefore be worthwhile to check out additional aspects of the food distribution scheme.

Analysts describe the cultural–ethnic mix of Sandabad as almost identical to that of Oman. With this in mind, are there ethical considerations, cultural taboos, or dietary constraints that might impinge on the scheme? If such a network were established, might it also serve to address other needs, like health care? Could world health funds be attracted? What are the developmental consequences of providing free food this way? Could it conflict with the goal of fostering an intelligent and responsible citizenry? Would there be problems in keeping the distribution fair and honest? Where would the food come from, and what impact would the acquisition process have on Sandabad's agrarian interests? Obviously, everyone in Sandabad doesn't need free food. Is there method or madness in the Shah's all-inclusiveness? And, oh yes, will we have to supply liquids? There are no end of possible assignments and considerations for the specialist teams, and the instructor can stage manage all kinds of occasions for integrating and resolving new insights.

The instructor will mine this potential carefully, ignoring most of it, but employing some where she sees relevant gain in strengthening task consciousness among this particular group of students. She might, if the signs are right, cap things by introducing a carefully proportioned here-and-now problem that the team can take some distance beyond formulation toward actual execution.

We leave a tracing of the stable features of extended ETSI in this sample to the reader, with just a few words on this instructor's use of the design strategy. She has chosen to specify all five task features for her students to some degree: context, purpose, goal, resources, and, perhaps least clearly, technique. But she's made it clear, in ways that the everyday world seldom does, that her specifications are neither complete nor dependable. *That* is the insight she wants to cultivate in her students' task consciousness. When the world cries "help," we shouldn't just leap forth and help. That cry is an assertion just like any other. It needs demonstration, and the onus of securing it is ours.

Sample #3: 9th-Grade Composition Course.   In Sample 3 we find an instructor who has for some time been troubled by the prevalence of mindless reading and mindless writing among his students. Too much of their performance is automatic and uninvolved. The writing is bland and monotonic, a passing on of information with all the discrimination and emotion of a teletype machine. He suspects that this may be why the punctuation is so bad. Meant to clarify emphasis, punctuation grows unsteady where there is none to clarify.

These students, our instructor suspects, think of reading as receiving information and writing as dispensing it. They don't understand that information stands on some purpose, some motivating source, and falls in its absence. Until that purpose is clear, the point, the utility, the value of the information isn't. Among other things, information without point is, as the metaphor predicts, dull, dull, dull.

The thinking behavior our instructor wants to develop is an inclination to seek purpose in received information and to deliver it in information composed to be dispensed. He has tried to get students to do these things by instructing them to, but they constantly misconstrue his admonition as some kind of rule they must follow when they read or write for class. They do not see this emphasis on purpose as an essential component of all organized thought, or as a key attribute in all effective task composition, so few of them have incorporated a consciousness of purpose in their nonegocentric thinking.

This time, our instructor chooses to get the students themselves to demonstrate. He proposes to them a situation in which the context, the factors that require change, the resources , and the goal (how to spend $700) are relatively clear, whereas significant elements of purpose are left obscure. Efforts to compose the situation are anemic. He adds information that ostensively suggests a plausible purpose, and composition grows stronger. When he then obscures this plausibility by adding more information, composition grows weaker. He keeps up the pressure until the students themselves identify and press for the missing source of purpose.

There are obvious ways our composition instructor might move from this exercise directly into his composition curriculum. He could show his students how managing purpose adds vitality of their story lines or essays or themes and contrast this output against the kind that is motivated only by an assignment deadline. But he wisely resists and conducts 3 more weeks of exercises designed to get students to see how information is molded by purpose, and to get them to do some of the molding themselves (two teams addressing the same situation with different purposes, for instance), until their own experience begins to root the insight.

He defers his course agenda a bit in hopes that more skillful, more task-sensitive thought will prompt more effective reading and writing.

We leave Sample 3 at this point, although acknowledging that it, perhaps better than our other samples, introduces a topic that deserves treatment on its own. In calling up Sam and his $700, our composition instructor has employed a very simple, stylized "case." Actually, all our samples have put some kind of carefully edited "case" before their students. Employing cases can be a powerful technique in thinking skill development. It could, in a sense that is far from trivial, be argued that all instruction that elicits operant behavior from a learner does so by confronting him or her with some kind of "case." It is worth a page or two to consider why the "case study" approach is a heaven-sent technique for the thinking skill instructor, and how he or she can best employ it.

CASE STUDIES IN EXTENDED ETSI

In instruction, the function of a case is to confront the learner with a situation that requires resolution. Way back at the beginning of this guide, we began confronting learners this way, but with highly stylized, one-sentence "cases" — word problems, pattern problems, math-story problems, etc. Then we began to move toward more complex cases whose resolution required more complex operant thought. We haven't yet arrived at what might be called the classic "case study" so familiar in graduate curricula that prepare for law, management, and medicine. Here, full-blown real-world situations are presented to the aspiring expert for resolution.

There is nothing to keep the thinking skill instructor from invoking the real-world case study. Doing so would be a logical extension and intensification of what we've already been doing. But there is one caution. We need to realize that some ways of employing the case study are not particularly helpful in developing thinking skill.

Dr. Mark Schlesinger has observed[18] that a great deal of case study instruction has theory demonstration and application as its aim. It goes like this. A theory (say of management) is proposed and developed. A case study is then presented, and it is the student's job to interpret the case in light of the theory. If the student does so effectively, the instructor can conclude that the student has achieved some skill in deploying the theory.

We wouldn't quibble with such an instructor's conclusion, but we would, as does Dr. Schlesinger, suggest that employing case studies this way does not engage or develop operant thinking skills as well as it might. Equipped with theory, the learner approaches a case study with a blueprint in hand. Often, the case study has been selected or subtly shaped to particularly suit this blueprint.

Suppose rather that the learner is led to the case study with nothing more than a compulsion to do something about it. If an obvious imbalance in the case itself won't fuel that compulsion, a pointed question or some instruction about what to optimize will. Now the learner works on the case, in the process trying various approaches and authoring some false starts. Finally he comes up with a resolution. At that point, he is asked to *generalize* his resolution (i.e., form a theory). Not having come with a theory, he leaves with one nascent and wriggling in his mind. Guess which approach demands of the learner more task consciousness and more levels of generic skill employment. Guess further which approach will give the thinking skill instructor access to the learner's own thinking protocols rather than protocols already prefabricated and patterned.

In passing, it is worth noting that the two approaches tend to develop different kinds of professionals. The theory application approach, pursued too vigorously, can preshape our view of things, and theory-driven viewing can distort the problem situation. While no one is theory free, we can strive to remain relatively theory open. The thinking skills approach to case study favors an effort to first make the problem situation cogent in its own terms. This can't always be done, but the effort to do so ought to precede rather than follow our attempts to apply theory.

As a thinking skill instructor, you will want to use the case study because it is an admirable stimulant in getting your students to generate extensive

---

[18]Dr. Mark Schlesinger, member of the Department of Essential Skills and Associate Dean of the College of Management, U. Mass., Boston, presented his concerns regarding the employment of case studies in an unpublished paper entitled "Case Analysis, Human Reasoning, and Organizational Problem Solving," delivered at the 1987 Annual Meeting of the Council for the Advancement of Experiential Learning.

sequences of thought. What you are after primarily is not resolution of the case, but access to the rich thinking sequences the case stimulates, so you can determine how well formed they are.

Here are examples of two "cases" Dr. Schlesinger has employed with students in an Essential Skills program within the College of Management at the University of Massachusetts, Boston. They are, please note, not classical case studies by a long shot, but short, highly stylized versions of their full-grown brethren. Dr. Schlesinger uses them on the one hand to generate and expose student thinking protocols that can then be addressed by the class, and on the other to exercise and mature the kind of task consciousness that will serve students next in more comprehensive case study, and finally in the world of work.

Our first sample looks like this:

College of Management   ESM 110 — Schlesinger
Department of Essential Skills   Fall, 1985

Paper #3

DATA ANALYSIS: THE JAILS OF TWO CITIES

THE CITY OF DAYTON
Police Department

TO: (Student's Name)   , Police Department Data Analyst
FROM: Mark Schlesinger, Chief of Police
SUBJECT: Update on the Crime Rate

As you may know, Helena Hanbasket, University of Dayton urban planning professor, caused a hullabaloo last week when she warned the City Council Dayton was going to become "another Atlanta." While she restricted her comments to building construction and the economy, certain members of the council—coincidentally coming up for reelection—have wondered aloud whether the comparison holds true for crime as well.

I need to respond to these folks. Please send me a report[1] by _____ . What data do you have? What conclusions do you draw?

I shall appreciate your being as detailed and accurate as possible. Thank you.

_____

[1] Based on *Beyond Problem Solving . . .* , p. 198. Write report as draft.

The reference note here is directing students to their own text copy of *Beyond Problem Solving* by Whimbey and Lockhead. The instruction will lead them to Problem 7 at the rear of a chapter entitled "Interpreting Graphs and Tables." The problem presents a small comparative crime statistics chart for two cities that includes 10 pieces of data with a few blanks. A series of questions requiring manipulation and interpretation of the data then follows. Although there is no injunction to do so, the wise student will work through these questions for a good grasp of the data before framing his assignment response.

A review of Dr. Schlesinger's various "case studies" would reveal no particular bias toward law enforcement issues. It does, however, happen that the assignment for Paper #5 again plays on that theme:

College of Management   ESM 110 — Schlesinger
Department of Essential Skills   Fall, 1985
                         Paper #5
              DRAFT DUE: _____

UNIVERSITY OF MASSACHUSETTS—BOSTON
Harbor Campus   Downtown Campus   Huntington Campus

     TO: __(Student Name)__ , Sergeant   DATE:_____
   FROM: Mark Schlesinger, Chief, Campus Police
SUBJECT: Priorities for allocating the SQR funds

You may be aware that the late Sharon Quincy Randolph, longtime friend of the University, left a specific bequest in honor of her son Brockton, a graduate of our Criminal Justice program. The bequest establishes a fund from which moneys may be drawn annually to combat specific forms of campus crime. Our normal operating funds, bound up in the budget and planning process, cannot reflect year-to-year fluctuations in types of crime, locations, etc. Ms. Randolph intended the Brockton Randolph bequest to remedy this problem by enabling the Department, at the Chief's discretion, to allocate the money in direct reponse to high-priority problem areas as they arise.

While I have the discretion to choose where to allocate the funds, I am responsible as well for basing that choice on the best available evidence. Please prepare an analysis of this past month's campus crime. In your report, I would appreciate your recommending a priority list of problem areas for my consideration. You need not concern yourself with methods to combat crime; we can confront that issue when we have a better sense of the priorities.

I look forward to your report.

An actual 1-month Campus Police Blotter, detailing over 60 events involving campus police personnel, accompanied this assignment. Unlike the data base provided for Paper #3, there is no charting or presifting of information. We see here one short step in a series of steps Dr. Schlesinger takes to place the responsibility for task composition increasingly in the hands of the students, thereby broadening and intensifying their employment of operant skills.

A FALSE CONCLUSION

That last paragraph could promote a happy — but grievously misleading — thought that may well have occurred to the reader by now. As we progress through extended ETSI with increasingly capable students, the strategy appears more and more to be one of "hands off." There is less prestructuring, less defining and channeling of student performance. It might appear, then, that extended ETSI grows easier to teach as you and your students progress.

Unfortunately, if you are really committed to *increase* skill, the opposite is true: It grows more difficult. In ETSI, whatever activity you divest yourself of and assign to students returns as a much magnified work load by the rear door. As you spend less time preshaping, channeling, and constraining assignments, time devoted to staying in tune with and assessing student performance on task burgeons. Always keep foremost in mind your primary reason for confronting students with "cases." You want access to more complex thinking protocols that, once you get them, you must process. You employ the "hands-off" strategy to increase the vitality and complexity of student thought. If there is to be any gain from this at all, you must then intensify "hands-on" respecting the thought you've stimulated. Earlier, we insisted that no worthwhile gain in student writing follows from having students generate volumes of unassessed composition. You can count on the same level of gain from volumes of unassessed thought. But performing the required assessment grows increasingly difficult in two senses, one obvious and one not.

Your analysis and guidance of student thought grows obviously more difficult as the thought grows more intricate and encompassing. As you approach assessing and discussing a more mature student protocol, there stirs an awareness at the back of your mind that the options and alternatives worth entertaining have increased geometrically. That awareness is unerringly correct, and difficult to ignore.

But the less obvious source of difficulty is even more treacherous. The students seem to be doing so well. Compared to similar groups you've taught, their performance is sterling. There appears to be little to justify pushing at them, and it is quite pleasant to watch them cycle the notable thinking gains they've so far achieved.

To be doctrinaire for a moment, there is no point to fostering extended ETSI that does not *develop* skill. There are dozens of less laborious ways to parade and exercise it. But given the difficulties of progressing, how does one continue?

Frankly, there very quickly comes a point where the individual thinking skill instructor cannot do it alone. The students themselves must take a hand in the job.

Here is where the little piece of jargon we coined—"developing a thinking-intensive environment"—needs clarifying. Analyzing, assessing, and restructuring protocols is the chief kind of thinking about which extended ETSI must remain intense. Solving the problem is always *second* in importance to assessing the consequent protocols. Regardless of your target behaviors, *it is the student's reconsideration of her employment of them* that will produce their refinement and incorporation—that will, in short, develop skill. Probing protocols, surfacing them, conceiving and trying alternatives have to be a class norm. Doing these things is everyone's active business in extended ETSI. In fact, when those activities are not central and vital, extended ETSI has drifted off and become something else.

Where the instructor succeeds in motivating students to actively engage this process of calling up protocol issues—by seeking their participation any time a protocol issue is raised and by carefully nurturing any impulse they exhibit to raise one—he is multiplying his own capacity to sense and discriminate. In no time at all, students will be proposing alternatives, catching out anomalies, and raising questions that could well have escaped the instructor. There are now a score or more assessors at work, rather than just one. The instructor begins to profitably *manage* assessment, rather than struggle to perform it all.

Better yet, student writing and discourse about student-generated thinking protocols will give the instructor valuable insight concerning the growth of student cognitive ability. The discussion about protocols is itself a new protocol that lays out evidence about where student strengths are forming and weaknesses still lie. This is the critical information you require to determine what to bring up and what to let lie among all those possible task consciousness topics.

We seem to have introduced this strategy of nurturing student assessment as a labor-saving device, but it is much more. If you follow it, you are actually elevating your extended ETSI sequence, whatever thinking behavior it targets, toward the intrinsic aim of all extended ETSI. In addition to the thinking behaviors you are developing to further the student's task composition, you are fostering the student's capacity and inclination to *assess those behaviors.* Now you have your hand on the ignition of a marvelous cognitive engine, which is a mind recursively assessing and reshaping what it has just done. Minds that do this are the kind that thinking skill instructors dream of—the kind that can engender self-prompted growth in thinking skill.

The File

Try to get a feel for where your students stand regarding the skills you've designed your extended ETSI sequence to develop. It's wise to check their facility with the behaviors you've targeted before you begin developing them.

Doing so doesn't have to be conspicuous, nor does it require a nationally recognized assessment instrument. For example, our instructor in Sample #1 might casually ask his class how they would make a case for an allowance increase—a simple instance of correlating need with resource. Everyone recommending an income/expense sheet would be one extreme. Everyone striving to plead special circumstances would be another. Whatever the result, our instructor would come away with some sense of the class' facility with the task consciousness and composing skills he wants to foster.

Our Sample #2 instructor might try for a class reaction to a recent social-issue editorial for a sense of where insights tend to fall on a scale from simplistic to probing. The instructor in Sample #3 could, in the same tone of voice, read two brief paragraphs to his class—one emphatic and effective, the other, equally sound in grammar and syntax, but wandering and confused. In choosing which they like best, the degree to which students fail to discriminate or elaborate their choice will give the instructor a clearer sense of what needs doing.

A little thought on how you might test the water with a group of students in light of your objectives will always serve you well.

THE FILE

THE FILE

THE FILE

CHAPTER 13

SECONDARY/COLLEGIATE PIE

Forethought

We return to a topic in this chapter that we first raised in Chapter 8, namely, how to teach your subject matter so that you may concurrently develop thinking skill. Much of what appears in Chapter 8 applies usefully to subject matter instruction at the secondary/ collegiate level. You would do well to consider that chapter again, and we will, in fact, revisit some of its key points here. But we also need to address a new concern, very much as we had to address a new concern when we moved from ETSI to extended ETSI. In that case, we shifted from an emphasis on skill consciousness to an emphasis on task consciousness. We need to explore a similar kind of shift in the realm of subject matter instruction.

With good reason, Chapter 8 concentrated mainly on how we could wield subject matter to provoke operant thinking—we were using subject matter as a means to awaken skill employment. Whether by means of ETSI or attentive subject matter instruction, this awakening has to be our first step. And there is no point in glossing over what the step requires; subject matter is here subordinate to the goal of eliciting desired thinking behavior from students. We are frankly more concerned with enticing thought than with mastering subject matter.

But that is only the first aim of the subject matter instructor bent on developing thinking skill. Getting students to unlimber and expand their thinking repertoire isn't enough. Since Chapter 8, we've argued that once thinking skills are in hand, full command of them comes only with their self-directed employment on task. It is in tending to this aim — generating task consciousness disposed to employ skill — that the subject matter instructor gets to reap what he has sown. The aim of this new goal, you see, is subject matter mastery — the kind that only composed operant thought can achieve. The subject matter instructor wants to foster task consciousness regarding the enterprises of his discipline.

It would be nice to conclude that by setting this second goal we've talked our way back home. Perhaps circuitously, but none the less finally, we've come to the traditionally sanctioned goal of teaching: subject matter mastery. We now want to do what teachers have always sought to do, but we want to do it because, done well, it will bring thinking skill to full flourish.

As good as this sounds, there may be a fly deep in the ointment. We've come home, yes, but in a way that could shake foundations. For some, the kind of subject matter mastery we're after may turn out to be the most intrusive and disconcerting element in this book, whereas others won't find cause therein to lift an eyebrow. That is because our goal discomfits some basic assumptions about what a discipline is.

We see disciplines as workrooms par excellence for operant thought — environments optimized in every way to serve and advance the construction of insight. When they are used as ornate barrels from whence insight is dispensed, we think their proper function has been suborned. Back in Chapter 2, we raised a fundamental problem with the view of teaching as a business of dispensing insight: Concepts can't simply be dispensed. Learners must themselves construct and employ them to gain functional possession. They have to want to make sense, and the attempt unlocks for them the supreme utility of the discipline. Your second thinking skill aim as a subject matter instructor is to get your students to experience your subject as a domain for making sense.

We suggest a final thought that might improve your feel for these two aims. We all know — occasionally from bitter experience — that any subject matter can be presented without a compulsion to think operantly. In pursuit of our first aim, the subject matter teacher deliberately confounds this option with careful strategy and sensitive teaching, all designed to elicit thinking. The students can't be faulted if they ascribe the demand for thoughtfulness, not to the subject matter, but to the insightful teacher. If they came to that conclusion, they would be no less than accurate — it was the teacher that demanded and stimulated thought. They know this by contrast with other teachers who largely didn't or don't.

With copious praise for teachers who have achieved so much, we need to observe that they still have a distance to go, and so we call up our second aim. This aim involves a kind of weaning. Students must be brought to see the subject matter—not the compelling instructor— as the fundamental stimulus for thought. They come to see this when they've been shown how to get their hands on a discipline; when they have composed and tested some of its insights, shaped and executed its tasks. The teacher who manages this transfer and gets student minds embroiled in her discipline is teaching thinking in a most enlightening way.

DEVELOPING THINKING ABILITY WHILE TEACHING A SUBJECT: TWO CHALLENGES

For the teacher of a subject who wants concurrently to develop thinking skills, two challenges need to be considered. Let's call them Challenge A and Challenge B. Challenge A is to develop operant thinking skill in your students as you teach your subject. Challenge B is to find suitable work in the discipline for the skills you are encouraging. The first challenge asks that you employ subject matter to achieve growth in student ability. The second wants you to engage this emerging ability in rewarding work within the discipline.

These two challenges may at first seem inseparable, one automatically invoking the other. One *does* imply the other, but that implication won't be realized unless actively pursued. Teachers often close with one of these challenges and fail to press the other.

For instance, a teacher might make the difficult decision that his students think so poorly he must give his subject matter priorities second place and concentrate on developing their ability to think. He embraces Challenge A. Another teacher, similarly motivated, will decide that the only way to get students to think is to present the discipline in more demanding ways. She embraces Challenge B.

Let's imagine that each teacher does an outstanding job. The teacher who accepted Challenge A has sparked a range of new analytical and problem-solving abilities among his students. In fact, they are equipped to do considerably more with their minds now than is likely to be required of them in the foreseeable curriculum. Perhaps this instructor will experience what we have. One of these empowered students returns after a few years. "Thanks," he says, "but you were wrong. I was excited about the skills we used in your class, but you said they would be a big help in our other classes. I never had to think that hard again." Thinking skills were aroused in this student, but their use seems contingent on the demands others make of him.

Use of the skills regardless of what others demand, but because there is warrant in the task itself, is what appears to be missing here.

Perhaps that is why some teachers embrace Challenge B and concentrate on fostering demanding tasks. Such a teacher's heightened demands for good thinking in the discipline will probably attract some responsive students. The cost is a number of other students, bewildered and sometimes resentful, who don't catch on or up. It isn't that they simply can't, but that they are ill disposed: Challenge A was not addressed. Among those students who do respond, there are a few who will likely form a special link to the discipline. In their experience, the discipline seems the only haven for a kind of strange, demanding, exhilarating use of the mind that doesn't seem much called for elsewhere. For such students, good thinking can come to be savored as an arcane and highly specialized activity suited to an elite enterprise.

In simple terms, the third option — embracing both challenges — involves consciously developing skills and consciously putting them to work. We take a look at what addressing both challenges requires.

Our approach is to present what could be considered an instructional planning guide. The guide takes the form of a series of templates. Each template outlines a perspective you should bring to your course planning if you want to teach your subject in a way that develops and employs operant thought. We call it a template because you can lay it over any subject you intend to teach, and it will still highlight issues that you need to consider if you want to advantage thinking skill.

We present these templates in two sets. Set I deals with Challenge A: the development of operant skill. Set II deals with Challenge B: putting those skills to work in your subject field.

INSTRUCTIONAL PLANNING TEMPLATES — SET I

As you examine each template, keep in mind the underlying principle that motivates all of them: *Wherever possible, make student gains in the subject field a product of operant rather than passive thought.* In short, you want your students to construct rather than simply receive required insight whenever they profitably can.

Template #1: Objectives Review. This first step involves a reconsideration of your course objectives. As best you can, analyze those objectives into elements of two types: the information you want your students to retain and the skills you want them to exhibit. Pages 134 through 138 in Chapter 8 address this process usefully, and it may help to refer to them.

Once you've divided your objectives into a set of "facts" and a set of "skills," take a look at your set of "facts." The aforementioned Chapter 8 reference explains that each of your facts can be treated either as a "given" or as a "product" of a set of operations. If it is an affirmation the student is supposed to accept, it is a "given;" if a student achieves it through a set of operations employing the generic skills, it is a "product." In which guise will you convey your facts to your students?

A bulk of the information you wish to convey will probably have to be handled as givens, but ask yourself if some of the more crucial items can't be achieved as products of problem-oriented student effort. While you entertain that question, look at your skill list. Might you arrange it so that students could achieve some of your content goals through an exercise of the skills you've targeted?

Suppose the following appears on your "facts" list:

6. Students should know the [pick a number] major influences that shaped the [pick a number] competing ideas of democracy that emerged during the French Revolution.

Glancing at your "skills" list, you find:

3. Students should be able to uncover, evidence, and prioritize significant causes of historical events.

Could you not arrange that students in your class gain 6 by performing 3? All you need to determine at this point is whether you could, not whether you should.

Continue your inspection and specially note those items in your "information" list that could be achieved by calling up items on your "skill" list. Remember, you aren't determining what you *should* do, but what you *could* do.

Now that you see some ways of achieving your content through the exercise of skill, concentrate on your skills list. Totally apart from your content goals, what kinds of student activity could you employ to foster those skills? Think of the kinds of assignments, exercises, team projects, modeling activities, games, and other forms of composed effort you've encountered, used, or heard of that might specially employ the skills on your list. Could some of these be tailored to address or use your content?

One point of this review is to make you aware, in detail, of the extensive flexibility inherent in any given set of course objectives. You can treat any fact in the course either as a "given" or a "product," and each choice you make in this regard will involve your students in different operations, in turn calling forth and exercising different skills.

That brings us to the central point of the review, which is to enable you to *see your course objectives as the terminus for a highly variable sequence of student operations*. There is no single path to your objectives; the possibilities are limitless. For 10 to 16 weeks, your students will generate a unique, complex sequence of activities. The whole point of that panorama of effort is to achieve the course objectives you've set. If you are interested in imparting skill, selecting, guiding, and molding those student operations should be your primary concern as an instructor. No other feature of your instruction will have as great an impact on thinking skill gains as how you manage these student operations.

All kinds of criteria can come to dominate your guidance of student effort. Unwanted ones will creep in unless you keep a sharp eye peeled. The path of minimum effort and dislocation to yourself and your students will be the one that enlists the simplest operations — a lot of memorizing and multiple choice. A much more demanding path — for yourself and your students — will enlist the more complex operations involved in operant thinking. You need to see this inherent flexibility you have in calling forth distinctive kinds of student operations in each phase of your course plan, and a content/skill mix review will sharpen your sense of these options. You might keep this little schema in mind:

Your Course

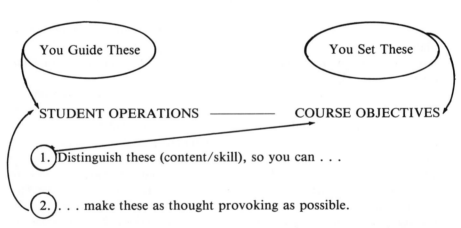

You Guide These

You Set These

STUDENT OPERATIONS ——————— COURSE OBJECTIVES

1. Distinguish these (content/skill), so you can . . .

2. . . . make these as thought provoking as possible.

Template #2: Student Inventory.   Your next step will be to move from this review of course objectives in light of possible student operations toward an actual plan of instruction. From the possibilities you've illumined in your review, you now begin to select the sequence of instructional steps you actually plan to take. To do this, however, you need additional data, because *course objectives alone, no matter how carefully defined, cannot determine your instructional plan.*

The problem is simply that goals, however carefully articulated, do not themselves specify means. The fact that I want you to meet me at 7738 North East Lake Terrace in Chicago will not, by itself, let me help you get there. To help you get there, I have to know where *you* are. I can't get you there from Phoenix the same way I would from Skokie.

Often, when we develop lesson plans or otherwise sketch out our courses for the secondary/collegiate level, we fudge about where the student is. In effect, we just assume they're all coming from Skokie and thereby lose any hope of a really well-tuned instructional plan.

What you need is an inventory of where your students are respecting your course objectives. You will need to take this inventory twice; once after you've reviewed your course objectives, and once again after your students have filed into their first class period and taken their seats.

We do, of course, employ some notions of where our students are, but these are seldom more substantial than an assumption that they'll be about where the last bunch was. Just a very little bit more insight about the condition of your students vis-a-vis your course objectives can pay surprising dividends in more effective instruction.

You will conduct your first student inventory before you ever meet your students. This is the simple process of imagining, based on available data and your own experience, where your forthcoming batch of students are likely to stand respecting your objectives. All we ask at this point is that you take this usual step as seriously and conscientiously as you can. Many times, the institution in which we teach can provide illuminating data about our incoming students. If so, review it. If you are inheriting your class from another teacher, talk to that teacher. Surmise as best you can the content/ skill equipment these students will bring with them, and this will give you some sense of the nature and extent of the distance you will have to take them to achieve your objectives. The sharper your estimate here, the more effectively you can set out an instructional plan. The instructional plan is, after all, your strategy for getting them from point A, where they are, to point B, where you want them to be.

After considering the remaining issues in our set of templates, you will approach your first class period with a carefully wrought, but still tentative, instructional plan. By "tentative," we do not mean uncertain. We mean that you see clear options along the way that you will select as you gain a better view of the state of your students.

Suppose, shortly after your students file into their first class period, you take an inventory that provides some insight on two questions. First, how familiar are they with the content you want to convey? Second, how familiar are they with the ways you will want them to deal with that content? The information you cull about these two questions will key final adjustments to your course plan.

If you find that your students are closer to your content goals than you had assumed, you can concentrate more on technique. If they are more familiar with technique than you thought, you can get them to employ it more extensively and embellish it further. If they have less content familiarity than you expected, you'll need to emphasize operations that will achieve that familiarity. If they are less adept at technique than you expected, you'll need to spend more time sequencing toward that adeptness. Resolving these issues will let you tailor limited class time more efficiently.

Notice that it is far more important to do this if you have thinking skill development in mind than if you don't. If absorption of course content regardless of student thinking capability is the goal, the student's antecedent condition doesn't really matter. You simply give the address. Getting there is the students' business.

But to advance thinking, you need some sense of its present condition. Thought can only grow by being stimulated in, and led to advance from, that condition. There was a college freshman composition teacher who insisted that all high school graduates had learned sentence diagramming. She demanded that her students diagram, while adamantly refusing to explain the process. A few students who had not in fact learned sentence diagramming managed to pass the class but maintained they hadn't the foggiest notion what that ritual was about, or why they were engaged in it. The teacher had clearly sparked thought, but it is questionable whether highly tuned survival mimicry was the kind she had in mind.

Granting that it's useful to determine the condition of your students in respect to your instructional goals, how does one take such an inventory? You can do it quite casually, as long as you remain very attentive. If your chief content emphasis will be on X, Y, and Z, inquire what your students think about, or can tell you about, X, Y, and Z. In their responses, do they address without prompting what you consider important characteristics of those topics, or do they seem oblivious? When it comes to key processes, methodologies, or techniques you intend to exercise and develop, ask "What if" questions that would tend to spark some use or mention of those processes by those familiar with them.

Suppose, for instance, that you plan to engage your students in some fairly demanding employment of scientific method. "What if," you ask, "someone comes up and tells you that unless you do something about it, the ozone layer will disintegrate in 5 years, and you'll be starving in 10?" The replies might cluster around something like, "I'd tell him he's talking to the wrong man. I (don't know; can't do; don't care) anything about it." Or they may gravitate toward, "I'd ask him what his evidence was. If it was compelling, I'd ask him if he had any suggestions. If he proposed a solution, I'd ask him how he devised it." In either case, you have a bit more data that could be of use in targeting instruction.

An economics teacher might ask, "What if someone told you that with the strangle hold farmers have on our economy, food prices will double in 4 years?" The point of such questions is to gain a glimpse of what the students bring. If they appear to bring what you thought they would, fine. Sometimes, however, they surprise you, as when a teacher from an English department asked, "What is the point of putting words in pretty packages called poems?" and got the reply, "They aren't pretty packages. They cut like razors."

That example will likely raise an objection to this entire review process. You will come away from the process, not with a unified view of where the class stands, but with some complex sense of a *range* of student abilities and content familiarity. You will probably find some students remarkably lacking in skill or information, or both, others remarkably endowed, and the rest spread out between. How can such a mess illuminate your instructional plan?

It isn't uniformity that you need to guide your lesson planning. You need two things. First, you need to touch the actual diversity within this clutch of students. Take heart if what you find is not all vanilla; you will be able to concoct much more with 31 flavors. Second, you need a feel for the center of gravity in your class, a kind of sense of its modal stance respecting your objectives. In aiming at that modal point, you will of course be aiming too high for some students and too low for others. But you will be on for the majority, and you will find that you haven't really missed the extremes, either. You will develop them, too, but in reference to the modal group. However, you will run into trouble if you significantly miss the modal point. Though your instruction may strive for good things, it will then tend to imbalance and fragment the class rather than resolve and knit it around your objectives.

Let's stop here and remind ourselves why we need to be concerned about such issues, which may seem far afield from subject matter instruction. Once you have included thinking skill development in your instructional goals, you have committed yourself to molding your class into a distinctive kind of miniature society. That society has to sanction and support activities not required in a class that has no mission to develop thinking skill. There must, for instance, be room in this society for student thinking to emerge openly and, however devoid of grace, find itself welcome. It must be the kind of society that accepts and is not cowed by your exposing, pointing to, and modeling your own thinking as instructor. Above all, it is a society in which the thinking that students produce is one of your *prime instructional resources*, to be used by you in improving the thinking they produce next. Building that kind of society needs very much to be an object of your instructional planning, and so you strive to assess your students just as you would any other instructional resource.

This doesn't immediately strike many of us as good news. We wonder if we couldn't develop student thinking *sub rosa*, somehow, without letting it intrude upon the classroom. Perhaps we could teach our subject matter in some clever format that would send students silently back to their nooks, crannies, and CRT stations where they can quietly nurture thinking themselves. What we have here, unfortunately, is wishful thinking. We know of no way to develop thought while comfortably banishing it. Remember that you do still have the option of just harnessing the skills students bring and not trying to develop them at all.

If you persist, however, the diversity you find in your students will actually serve as an asset. With the goal of developing thinking skill in mind, it is never a bad thing to have *some* students in your class below and some above your instructional aim. It is, in fact, a distinct advantage for the sensitive thinking skill instructor. First, the thinking produced by both extremes provides a useful counterpoint as you strive to advance the majority. The superior student helps you set a benchmark for the majority, just as the majority sets a benchmark for the poor. The superior student grows more precisely conscious of her strengths as she witnesses and perhaps helps the majority strive for them, just as the majority grasp their capabilities better in light of the efforts of the poor. As he addresses the development of the poorer students, the instructor can call on the full gradation of ability in the rest of the class. He will and should commit better students to help those less skilled – it's a contract that pays dividends to both parties.

In short, the variations you find among students will provide points of leverage that, used astutely, can help you elevate the whole bunch. Your student inventory is partly an attempt to preview those variations. You then begin to plan how that student's analytic bent, or this one's precocious analogies, or that one's ignorance, and the other's stout indifference can be harnessed to advance the operations of the whole.

At this point you may be prompted to reflect that this business of pursuing some kind of student inventory is not simplifying things. Remind yourself that it was not proposed as a way of making instructional planning *easier*, only *more effective*. If easy is what you want, abandon hope, all ye who enter here.

Additional benefits can be drawn from a casual inventory. For instance, students see in your questions a set of clues about where you are going to take them. It won't hurt to have them attend you with some speculation, perhaps even alarm. Once they begin speculating about where you are going, you can convey your objectives with a precision they would have otherwise ignored.

Your inventory could be more structured. If you have real use for the possible insight, you could ask students for a few paragraphs about where they think the class is going or should go, or even devote a period to letting students propose and defend a course design. You needn't adopt the course design, but the *assumptions* and *processes* students reveal in shaping one are very telling. Whether casual or more structured, the main purpose of this inventory is to help you plan in light of your real starting point.

Template #3: Learning Problems. As you evolve your plan of instruction, include an intent to openly address learning problems in class, regardless how extensive your institution's remediation, rehab, or counseling resources might be. Referrals are fine but make certain your students understand that you refer to implement your concern, not divest yourself of it. Among many reasons for doing this, we'd like to tack on one especially suited to thinking skill instructors: Few things will more quickly amplify your understanding of how students think, and how their actual thinking compares to your classroom aspirations, than access to student learning problems.

After working through Templates 1 and 2, you should have an improved sense of where your students stand respecting your course goals. Consequently, you will have a sharper notion of the difficulties they will likely encounter in striving to achieve them. Blend your experience of the toughest challenges they will face in gaining the mastery you want with your insight into their condition and give them a preview of the problems they are likely to encounter. An honest map of what they face is only fair warning, but that is not your motive for providing it. You discuss tough spots ahead, peculiar quirks of the discipline, and your own special demands because you want to sanction the students' learning process, whatever its hurdles and difficulties, as a proper and welcome classroom topic. As students set forth in your course, they *are* setting out on a problematic path; you acknowledge that fact and condone it as one of the course's open concerns. By doing so, you sanction both your own and your students' access to student thinking skill concerns.

As you point out the problems you foresee, however, do not append solutions, even if you've tried to build some into your pedagogy. Ask the students how *they* propose to deal with them. And (goodness forbid you should tip your students off to this) as soon as they begin proposing ways to respond to these foreseeable difficulties, plan yourself a small celebration. You've won a staggering victory. The students have given you token sign that they still hold title to their own learning problems. If you had pointed out both problems *and* solutions, many might have left the driving to you.

As your students begin dealing operantly with the difficulties you foresee for them — suggesting approaches, calling up resources, etc. — respond, in a spirit of helpfulness, with refinements and suggestions. Fairly quickly, their proposals will come to look very much like the solutions you would have offered. But they remain *their* proposals, bolstered and tuned by a very considerate teacher who might even have suggested some special resources or approaches to help at critical junctures.

If it seems we counsel deception here, the case is quite otherwise. We are discretely fending off deception. The deception we want to avoid is that it is the teacher's role to soothe the pains and resolve the kinks of learning. Teachers are not so obliged. They are obliged to awaken in learners the resource and motive to overcome those pains and resolve those kinks. You are telling them your course is a place where they can deal with this responsibility openly and consciously.

Sustain your concern for student learning problems throughout the course. If student performance suggests there are problems, be quick to surface them and keep the implication alive that you are interested in what the students plan to do about them. You are willing to support their effort, but *they* must do something about it. Even when there are no apparent problems, ask students how their learning is going, and yourself whether a few comments or a little course tuning by you might enhance that learning.

Template #4: Data Seeking. If your course is typical, it will require your students to command large quantities of new information. Remember that minds tend to grasp information for which they have need and context. Information that finds neither tends to be shed. It pays, whenever you can, to build need and context for the information you dispense before your dispense it.

The mind demonstrates that it has both context and need when it embraces an appropriate question. A question *is* an expressed need, and the satisfaction of that need sets a context for relevant information. However, you would miss a critical point if you concluded from this that all you need to do is ask questions. Asking questions of students is easy. The hard part is getting those questions embraced. It doesn't take much living to convince us that most questions we encounter are intrusive, aggravating, irrelevant from our perspective, and best avoided. We tend to begrudge the commitment that makes a question our own.

There are, however, ways that commitment can be enticed. The following is a basic strategy that can be employed usefully in many contexts. Say you have some information you want your students to retain. Behind any piece of information, there lie situations that the information, by definition, *informs.* Aim to engross your students, not in the information, but *in a situation it informs.* If you do this effectively, students will quite often not only embrace, but themselves devise, questions that set an appetite for your information.

All information has such a tie to some situation it resolves; it's just a question of tracing it. If there is one piece of information I am usually content to remain without, it is my mother-in-law's birthdate. But as Easter passes and the bloom leaves the dogwood, a compulsion grows and drives me to seek that date. My mother-in-law is a kind and thoughtful woman who never fails to remember my birthday. Her fellow feeling stimulates its counterpart in me, and that situation gives meaning to an otherwise dispensable piece of data.

The skilled lecturer who wants information to stick has always sensed this need to first sketch a situation that heightens the value of the information — that gives the information power to resolve or illuminate. Suppose you wanted your students informed about Edmund Burke's distinctive notion of liberty. Consider two ways of bringing a class to that topic:

Version 1: "For next period, Class, you have two readings by Edmund Burke, who lived from 1729 through 1797. Burke was a member of the British Parliament and an essayist whose writings and political activities did much to set English public opinion in his day against the French Revolution. His works are considered by many to be masterpieces of political thought. As you study the readings, I want you to pay particular attention to his ideas about liberty, and we'll have a discussion of those when we meet next time."

Version 2: "We have next a puzzling man, unless you can make some sense of him. He is Edmund Burke, an acclaimed champion of liberty, and he pursues a vigorous political life in Britain during a time when that nation has to respond to two great revolutions. History views both these revolutions — the American and the French — as monuments to man's thirst for liberty.

On one hand, this Burke works, speaks, and writes in support of the American colonists, arguing against the imperial policies of his own government. On the other, he fights tooth and nail *against* the revolution that is to set free the common man in France, earning the praise of imperial forces throughout Europe and the enmity of many who stood by his side on the American issue. He claims his notion of liberty held rock solid despite these apparently conflicting stances of his. Maybe, after you read your assignment, you can explain it to me. What could he have possibly meant by 'liberty'?"

Version 1 introduces the topic. Version 2 sketches a situation, and the reader can decide which is more likely to dispose the student's mind — inquisitively, attentively, and retentively — to Burke's conception of liberty. If Version 2 gets your vote, we think it is because that version sets forth a situation the student cannot resolve without the target information, whereas only the teacher's will sanctions the information in Version 1.

You haven't time to sketch situations for every piece of information you wish to dispense, but if you chose several key pieces carefully, you can awaken an appetite that will then feed itself; students will begin to uncover on their own situations in the discipline that need to be informed. Acknowledge and encourage that appetite wherever you can. Remember that every time you spark a resolving search for data, you've cornered a student mind. To win free, that mind must attend selectively, analyze, analog, suspend closure, and reassess. Information gained this way is not so likely to be discarded, nor are the skills that were called on to make the gain.

Template #5: Skill Priming. For every target skill you wish your students to develop and employ, see if you can take these four steps:

1. Find antecedent forms of the skill, or precursor skills, which you can be sure your students have employed.
2. Get students to exhibit those antecedent or precursor skills, so they fully recognize they possess them.
3. Either demonstrate by yourself, or otherwise evidence, some task completion that employs your target skill.
4. Constrain students to devise a path that would lead them from the kind of performance in step 2 to the kind exhibited in step 3.

With a slight qualification about step 4 that we'll make in a moment, these steps outline a process discussed on pages 131 thru 137 in Chapter 8. It is, put simply, a process of launching students toward new skill acquisition equipped with a consciousness of their own appropriate resources for the task and informed by a clear view of what they aim to achieve. As instructor, you will actually conduct step 4. You will devise assignments and exercises that harness present student capabilities in ways that produce desired ones. But it wouldn't hurt to begin by letting your students take a stab at step 4. If, with a little help from you, they can themselves piece together what it will take to reach your goal, there will be less balking and confusion on route.

As is true of all these templates, this one outlines a theme, and excellent variations can be played on any theme. A given teacher might find it closer to his art to begin with step 3, perhaps by demonstrating the target skill in a particularly intriguing way. With that example fresh in their minds, the instructor can then point out to the incredulous students how that performance is rooted in their own capabilities. Whatever sequence you elect, the point of these steps is to bring students to see the desired skill not as the preserve of some remote kind of genius, but as an extension of their present capabilities.

Your next priority in skill development is to in fact get the students to extend their present capabilities. Remind yourself that you can always and easily short-circuit this process by extending student capabilities quickly yourself. All you have to do is *train* students to the target skill. First show them exactly what to do, when to do it, and how to do it. Then just practice, practice, practice.

When you do this, however, you turn your back completely on one of your richest thinking skill development potentials. Good thinking seldom pays greater dividends than when it unveils a better way to do something, and you are depriving your students of an opportunity to earn that dividend. If, instead, you can get your students to see the unique demand your subject makes and themselves fashion a suitable response, they are using the skills at hand to articulate new ones.

Suppose, for a moment, that you've taken the considerable trouble to do this. Let's even say it works, but is the gain worth that trouble? Think about your own field for a moment. Is anything done differently in your field today than it was 20 years ago? If so, it is because some minds broke training and heeded a higher imperative to seek a better way. Their performance is close kin to the kind you've just exacted from your students. In both cases there is a thoughtful search, based on established capabilities, for new ones.

As you coach your students toward your target skill, ask yourself how they are making skill gains. Do they make gains simply by following your instructions, or through efforts you've constrained but they've composed? If you see them concentrating, analyzing, analoging, suspending closure, and reassessing, you probably have them on the latter path.

When you put them on that path, don't be surprised should you discover that they employ some of those generic skills poorly. If you do make that discovery, and on-the-spot coaching doesn't seem to resolve the problem, you have other options. If the problem appears specific — say, no tendency to analog, or suspend closure — shamelessly go all the way back to Chapter 4 and skim the "It's like" and "Another way" exercises outlined for elementary students. Versions of these suitable to your instructional level will easily suggest themselves. Suspend your syllabus for a day and tell your class openly you want to exercise some capabilities you feel they haven't been calling on sufficiently. Get them gaming in ways that showcase the skill they aren't sufficiently using. You can even let a little fun creep in.

If the malaise is more general, throw a few IQ type questions at them and run a mini ETSI, just so they can resurface and untangle their basic skills. You aren't attempting to develop these skills in these brief encounters; you're simply highlighting and recalling them. Silly as it seems, we sometimes just misplace or fail to recollect available tools.

Finally, if the thinking capabilities you wish to develop in your students involve a complex medley of skills unfamiliar to them, keep in mind the strategies of modeling and gaming. These let you confront your students with simplified challenges that marshall those skills in rudimentary ways, eventually grading up to the level of performance you have targeted. Recall the discussion on pp. 137–139 in Chapter 8. Pages 224–227 in Chapter 12 are also relevant.

Template #6: Protocols.   The prior templates in Set I will have led you to a course plan that makes noteworthy demands for skillful student thinking. This last template in Set I asks how you intend to both glimpse and capitalize on that thinking.

Remember that the actual thinking your students do is a prime resource in improving that thinking. The problem is that you must capture it before you can use it. You need accessible protocols and products of your students' thinking. The point to remember is that you can view student thinking in a range of ways. Within reason, the tendency that should guide you here is the *more varied* your glimpses, the more encompassing your view of a student's thinking and the greater your potential for directing it.

Some version of the paired problem-solving team can give you your most detailed and sustained views of raw student thinking protocols. These are hard to beat when diagnosing student generic skill employment. But don't forget that notes evidence thinking protocols and dispositions, as do various recordings — taped or written — of task processes and problem solvings. And, of course, written work in all its possible variety is hard to surpass as evidence of a student's more composed thinking.

There are two reasons it isn't wise to concentrate exclusively on one or two of these alternatives. First, the different alternatives capture the mind doing different work. A set of notes cannot reveal the same aspects of operant thinking that the course term paper can, and vice versa. Second, students sometimes form a distinct facility with one type of operant performance and experience trouble with others. Viewing student processes through a variety of assessments increases your odds of spotting points where performance falters and warrants distinct attention.

Whenever you set about developing a particular thinking skill, make it a habit to ask yourself how you plan to catch it under way. You can't lay your hands on it directly. The overt protocols produced by vocalization are perhaps as close as you can get. When these are not convenient — and they frequently aren't — aim for products of student thinking that will best reflect those thinking processes and allow you to infer them most sensitively. As you plan your instruction, this entails formulating an "en route" assessment strategy that has as its purpose not assigning grades, but informing your own insight to better guide student thinking performance.

You will have done most — perhaps all that is needed — of this before even picking up this template, but here is your chance to concentrate exclusively on whether the "window" you have built on student thinking processes promises the view you require.

Do be clear on one thing at this point. At best, you can prompt only random gains in student thinking skill unless you *do* come to grips with student thinking protocols. And the protocols themselves will be absolutely useless in stimulating thinking gains unless you employ the information they provide in *modifying* student thinking performance. What the protocols reveal lets you formulate growth-prompting demands of students, and that is what leads to better thinking behavior.

INSTRUCTIONAL PLANNING TEMPLATES — SET II

Having shaped your course as best you can to awaken operant thought, you need to view your product through a few more templates with Challenge B in mind. Recall that Challenge B entails putting those operant skills to work in the discipline or subject field you teach. Your aim here is to encourage in your students the kinds of task consciousness and task-composing skills that characterize the competent thinker in your field.

One reason we separate this set of templates from the other is that it addresses a different challenge, but there is another reason that we save until you've looked at them.

Template #7. Recollection. This template asks you to examine your plan of instruction in light of a special set of moments in your own intellectual career.

If you were to unroll your personal classroom learning history, it would probably reveal long stretches devoted to meeting course work challenges placed before you. You graduated, which means you handled those challenges competently enough. Your style in doing so was probably distinctive; you were pegged as rebellious, cooperative, neutral , antagonistic, or supportive, or various combinations of these at various times. But whatever your style, odds are that long durations of your time in school found you responding to compulsions imposed by the teacher.

Since you've presumably pursued education longer than you absolutely had to, it is also likely that at some point there was a significant shift in this learning dynamic. We can pinpoint the character of the change, though its quality and occasion are distinctively yours. It could have been a dramatic, once-and-for-all change. More probably, it was hardly noticed at first, perhaps impermanently coming and going. Maybe it still does. With a little luck it might have settled in you as a fairly stable disposition.

In any event, at some point in your learning history you found yourself pursuing inquiry in response, not to some external compulsion, but to one you devised for yourself. You were seeking insight not to satisfy some assignment or teacher, but a hunger of your own. If that hunger happened to wake in the arena of some discipline — like English Lit., math, some science, history, or language — it wasn't long before you discovered that you had put your foot on a perpetual treadmill. Every gain in insight revealed more cause for inquiry. Maybe you even began to sense a changing relationship with others working in your field of interest, the ones who wrote the books and articles you sought. You attended them more actively, hunting for and prizing their insights, even questioning and debating their views. You had staked out a cognitive venture of your own. Though you mightn't have put it this way, instead of just existing under a discipline's pall, you began to take part in its life.

Do your best to recall moments like this in your own intellectual career. Have you any notion what sparked them? As you reconstruct, could it have been something a teacher did? If so, can you do something like it for your students?

Whatever comes to mind, carry it immediately to a reflection on your course plan. Here are some of the things this exercise calls up when we do it:

We all know there are a host of ways students can intrude unjustifiably on the personal affairs of the teacher. But there is one kind of intrusion we think is defensible. Students often need a view of your personal relationship to your discipline. They witness your manifestations as a teacher and wonder why. Why is she in this? Why is he doing this? Whether you love your subject intensely or are just infatuated, find ways to share your affair openly with your students. Whatever delights, fascinates, or entrances you about your subject is liable to ensnare others if seen by them aright.

One way to focus your own delights more sharply is to concentrate on what disturbs you about your students. Frequently what disturbs you about your students is something that disables them, that keeps them from grasping what you esteem in your subject. They are too sloppy, too shallow, too unconcerned to see the point. Yet even teachers who are disturbed this way are often embarrassed to reveal their own intimate ties to their field, sometimes going to considerable lengths to disguise them. Reflect that it is just those ties you have that foster *your* dissatisfaction with your students. Perhaps if they had such ties, they too would be dissatisfied. If you fear students simply wouldn't understand, you will be correct as long as you deprive them of the chance to try. Since lots of bombast and false cheer sells poor beer, what might exposure to the honest attractions of an active mind sell?

Sometimes we love our discipline but don't like the introductory course we're forced to teach. After all, whatever early attractions such courses held for us have long waned and our interests are now far beyond them. Not really. Those early interests seeded your present sophistication. Cavorting in the branches, you now disdain the root. You owe it to your students to recollect how those seeds matured and resurrect the process for them as best you can. It will take some empathy—but not much—to translate your present passions into a context that will reach beginners.

A real danger exists that we design our course so that it will throttle any impulse the student might have to advance under his or her own steam. It is popular today to set a course tempo that is unfriendly to self-motivated student ventures in the discipline. In our anxiety to insure that students leave the course having achieved its objectives, we channel their progress into little cumulative steps. Each day has its instructional unit with its clear subgoal and appropriate short-range exercises. Oh, some allowances are made so the precocious student can forge ahead—skip units or leave lectures for extra CRT time—but the average student has little choice. It is safer and easier to lock-step and be pressed forward with the rest.

This is not a risk-taking learning environment. It is an actuarial plan to insure course outcomes. Getting a student to reach into the discipline—there to compose activity of his own under your watchful eye—is the premier risk you want him to take if your aim is to stimulate thinking skill. Prefabricate too much of the student's classroom behavior, and you leave neither room nor occasion for the more expansive and complex sweeps of operant thought that growth in thinking skill requires.

So try to remember what cut you loose and then look at your instructional plan. Remove from it any barrier that prevents your students from touching your own active life within your subject field. Make sure you have space to model that life, and that your students have space to venture into it.

There is an obvious corollary to this injunction. If you sport no passion for or share no active life of thought with your course subject, you will be hard pressed to encourage either in your students. You still have an option, as long as you enjoy an active life of thought respecting *some* subject. If you don't, it might be well to reconsider your career choice. But if you do, you know the moves such a life takes. Start openly cultivating an interest and a commitment to the subject matter, right there in class with your students. After all, it is no more than you ask of them. But do it openly so they can see what it takes. If you can't embrace your subject matter at least to this degree, perhaps it would be better to reconsider your commitment to develop thinking skill in that course context.

Template #8: Student Focus.   Suppose you've effectively modeled your own active life with your subject and in other ways drawn students toward composed activity in its arena. You've sparked interest, and they've taken their first tentative steps. This is a critical point for you as an instructor.

What has brought them this far is more likely the attraction of *your* commitment—the appeal of *your* love affair—than any firm attachment of their own to the subject. They may be drawn more by your involvement than by the object of that involvement. They tentatively consider that if it means so much to you, perhaps, just perhaps, it could come to mean that much to them.

Don't be disappointed. The attraction and the student response are natural — everyone seeks and is drawn toward fulfilling commitment. The problem is what to do next.

Sometimes teachers in effect do nothing next. Imitation, someone mistakenly said, is the highest form of flattery, and a class sprinkled with students imitating your interests and commitments can pleasantly flesh out a whole semester. But there is work left in this Eden that badly wants doing.

Your students have not yet been elevated to the most demanding plane of thought, which, as you know, the discipline itself provides.

Your criteria — shaped in service to the discipline — are not yet theirs; their performance still draws its motive from you. You want the demands of the discipline to set motive and shape criteria. It is the task you want them to embrace, not your love of it.

If you are competent in your subject matter, you have at hand the means to effect real student involvement with that discipline. First we approach what you need to do fancifully, and then we examine it practically.

Think of patterning your approach around the strategy of the shrewd jewelry salesman. You are interested; otherwise you wouldn't be standing in his shop. He does not thrust everything that meets your glance at you. You discuss a stone, perhaps even its pedigree, guarantees, and price, while it lies in the case. At this point, a simple nod from you would let you move on, but you abide. You ask if you might see it. He places the stone in your hand, so you can turn it, inspect its facets. This is the point where your appetite is liable to fix and your desire bond.

Let's suppose your own commitment has attracted students to your subject. In effect, they now stand in your shop, and you've brought them to the point where they've asked if they might see the jewel. What you need to do now is place the discipline in their hands and give them a feel of it. Sometimes we leave the jewel in the case and prattle on about lay-away terms. Students learn they can get their hands on the discipline after such-and-so requirements and conditions have been met. Many may nod here, and bid farewell.

You need to give the disposed student real, demanding work in your subject field. No matter how cleverly devised, no collection of itty-bitty programmed learning increments will sum to the full-bore challenge of disciplinary thought. And it takes that full-bore challenge to entice and hold the task composing and executing abilities that reflect the highest recursions of thinking skill.

We are still speaking too fancifully. What do we mean by a "full-bore challenge?" We don't mean a grandiose one. It can be a very pedestrian task appropriate to the subject field, like writing an essay or delivering an analysis, just as long as it demands that the student compose the product. The thing that makes it "full-bore" is your response to it. You must respond to it maturely, which means in light of the true prevailing criteria of your discipline.

Your student has tried to produce in light of your discipline. Let that discipline now speak to him honestly; that is the only way he will ever get his hands on it. Praise and even grade your student's effort in reference to any context you see fit ("Outstanding job for a freshman;" "That's junior level work, and you're only a sophomore"), but don't fail to introduce him to the real context the discipline sets for skillful thought.

To push our jeweler's analogy a bit further, you owe students a real touch of the jewel. They must see that its facets are complex, precise, hard, sharp, and do not readily yield. That's the price of the sparkle.

Too often we go no further than the pseudo-standards that are set around the anticipated mean of student performance. These are practical, and we must use them, but it is a profound error to set student aspiration in their terms. Perhaps it will help if we see both kinds of standards at work.

Ms. Kosinski has responded to your "See Me" note and is discussing her paper on the Hegelian dialectic with you in your office. You are about to deliver two paragraphs, the first in response to standards that prevail over class performance.

"A first-rate effort, Ms. Kosinski. A remarkable advance over your last paper and clearly the best in the present batch."

So much for prevailing class standards.

"Too bad about your reference to "church aristotelianism." You'll note I circled that on page 4. It was not an observation essential to the theme you developed. You might easily have avoided making it, but because you *did* make it, I have to take exception. The view of Aquinas as an aristotelian befuddled by theology has had proponents, but no credible ones. Whatever you might think of his work in present terms — assuming you actually examined some of it — he managed a brilliant synthesis of two of the most powerful and antagonistic ideologies of his day. That hardly sounds like an example of what Hegel's thought made obsolete. What about trying to align those two men a bit more carefully in your next paper?"

The first paragraph may justify Ms. Kosinski's "A" on her assignment. Too often our assessment and feedback stops here, and when it does, we've shown the student too little. Students can — all too many do — confuse the demands of the class with the demands of the discipline. Having excelled in meeting class demands, they are allowed the false conclusion that they excel in the discipline. They don't see that what even the best class asks is mere preface to the task-mastery exacted by the field. Perhaps Ms. Kosinski will decide she is totally content to settle for her high grade and has no wish to address the discipline's challenge. But we owe her that real choice, rather than the false presumption that she's satisfied both. The second paragraph challenges that presumption and asks a good deal more of Ms. Kosinski.

Now our summary point for this template. Each product—and only those products—that a student actually composes for you offers a distinct opportunity to improve his or her orientation toward subject mastery. But you must return feedback that defines *mastery*, not just class placement. As you strive to provide guidance, keep the stable aspects of task in mind. How well does the student grasp the task's context, motivating purposes, goal, applicable techniques, and resource requirements? What insights can you spark that will move that grasp toward the norms acknowledged by your discipline?

That concludes our two sets of templates, and very nearly this chapter. What remains is a final observation that applies particularly to the two templates in Set II. We promised an additional rationale for setting them apart, and here it is.

As they stand, the last two templates are in one sense the most difficult to apply in the context of a subject matter course. Fortunately, the sense in which they are difficult is not the most critical sense.

Considering the last two templates carefully can sharpen the aspirations you bring to your course planning and execution. Since this is the most important sense in which they should apply, that's good. But the priorities of subject matter instruction make it difficult to introduce these themes as conscious elements of your course. More likely you will have to snatch occasions for them on the fly.

Of course, you could, if you chose, socialize your class around these last two templates to varying degrees. You could elicit and examine thinking protocols in your class that highlight the self-motivated learning that is the heart of Template #7. Under your guidance, students might lead an analysis of already-graded student products in class, this time from the vantage of the discipline's normative standards. That could amplify Template #8's theme. But notice that the more of this you attempt to do overtly in class, the more your class will come to look like some of the extended ETSI sessions we explored in the preceding chapter. There, extended ETSI sought to develop task consciousness. These last two templates commend you to develop task consciousness specific to the subject field.

It is helpful to realize that our two approaches to thinking skill development—one in the pursuit of subject mastery and the other an extension of explicit thinking skill instruction—inevitably converge. Pushed to their logical extreme, the two approaches finally become indistinguishable. What motivates extended ETSI is the insight that better thinking is finding ways to build better constructs; more effective ways of configuring our world and our affairs. What else has a discipline in mind? Building better constructs is precisely every discipline's aim. That these two approaches meet is no more than we should expect.

THE FILE

THE FILE

THE FILE

CHAPTER 14

NOTES ON EVALUATION AND EXPERIMENT

Forethought

If you are firming up your commitment to a thinking skills course or program, you will want to know which instrument(s) you should use to evaluate it. Should it be Thurstone's Primary Mental Abilities Test, perhaps bolstered by some California Test of Mental Maturity subtests? Maybe the Key Math Diagnostic Arithmetic along with the J & J Wide Range Achievement. How about the PSAT, or the good old Watson–Glazer, or any of the hundred or so others, validated or otherwise, that could be called to active duty?

One thing this guide cannot do is select instruments for you. This is so primarily because every evaluation has to be tailored to the case at hand. Any assemblage of instruments needs to be suited with extreme *care to your specific skill development objectives. Even that isn't enough. The instruments have to be re-examined in light of the use you intend to make of the data they supply. An evaluation battery that will serve one purpose might very well fail at another.*

Remember that evaluation is a task like any other. It has (1) context, (2) purposes, (3) goals, (4) factors it has to influence, and (5) resources it consumes. You need a clear view of all five of these elements before you set your evaluation plan and finally fix your instrument battery.

Selecting evaluation instruments is not easy, although there is a healthy review literature on available instruments, and capable evaluation specialists can be found to assist. But picking your instruments is the least and almost the last of the problems you need to confront in evaluating your thinking skill effort. What we can do is alert you to some of these prior problems, especially those the evaluation literature infrequently explores.

We can imagine a reader reaction at this point that would spark our sympathy — even admiration: "Why must they always make evaluation sound so difficult? All I want to do is show people what's really happening. I'm not a shyster. I'm not trying to cover anything up. Just give me the tools that will reveal what's there!*"*

We wish we could, but we simply can't. Working within reason, the mind can't just reveal *the truth. If it could, and if the truth in its pristine virtue immediately overshadowed falsehood, truth would by now have come to reign in human affairs. The best the mind can do is propose and evidence the truth. Truth is what we try our best to build a case for.*

Evaluations are a particularly difficult form of this composing effort because they point emphatically at themselves and openly assert that they are building a case for the truth. They consequently attract a good deal more critical attention and scrutiny than do other forms of composed assertion. And they do this while balancing on the edge of an unkind principle.

We don't defend this principle here; we just describe it so you can consider it and play with it if you like. In doing so ourselves, we find it ironclad. It's a principle that serious theory-builders have uncovered. Willard Van Orman Quine describes it in the observation that truth is "underdetermined" by evidence.[19]

Assemble the most comprehensive and sweeping body of evidence you care to in support of a given theory. Perhaps it is a theory about general relativity, or one about why and in what way your thinking skill instruction is a success; "My approach works because. . . , etc." Let's say the evidence does, in fact, support your theory. Unfortunately, an unlimited number of distinct and incompatible theories can be devised around which your evidence will also array as support. In short, evidence alone does not exclusively and unequivocally sustain any given theory.

It may at first seem that this principle threatens and dissolves the basis of all knowledge, but this is not so. In a quirkish way it really underpins and promotes knowledge-building. We acknowledge theories — any assertions, for that matter — not because they alone fit the facts, but because they do so most plausibly. *It's another case of the "best fit" principle. Some other theory may fit all this evidence, but so*

---

[19]Quine, W. V., *Word and Object*. A version of Quine's argument begins around p. 22.

far this *theory fits this evidence—and all else I know—better. If even the best theory at hand doesn't fit well enough, we try to devise a superior one. But demonstrating what, in light of present consider- ations, appears the* most suitable *theory or assertion is the best that constructive thought can achieve, in or out of evaluation.*

So you can't simply reveal the truth about what's going on in your classroom. But you can, if you're willing to expend unusual care and precision, build a case for what most plausibly is going on there.

When you begin to see how demanding evaluation is at heart, you also begin to see how important it is to scrutinize its purposes and occasions with care.

VINDICATION VERSUS ILLUMINATION

There are roughly two overarching justifications for engaging in evaluation. We evaluate to vindicate and we evaluate to illuminate. Any given evaluation can try to do both, but a joint attempt is fraught with all kinds of peril, even when conscious of its two totally different goals. Be sure you sort the two out carefully before you address either.

EVALUATION TO VINDICATE

The effort to vindicate is sparked by a doubting audience. You've either proposed or done something with which the audience is unfamiliar, or of which it tends to disapprove. If you need the audience's support, your task is now to justify what you've done.

Guess who sets the criteria for justification. You? Not hardly. The audience sets the criteria, which is whatever it decides will win its support.

Many who work in academic communities make the mistake of assuming they know what will win that audience's support: dispassionate rational evidence, of course. What makes the error doubly tragic is that this audience will agree with you. Some of its members will do their best to hold to this criteria, even assisting you to achieve it. But remember the nature of your task, which is to evidence that what you've done is a highly plausible thing to do; perhaps even the most plausible thing under the circumstances. Now think of your doubting audience. All any member of it has to do is announce an alternate, but also plausible, interpretation of what you've done that inhibits his or her support. There is no shortage of such alternatives, and many of them can be far from complimentary. If your argument is tremendously convincing and hard to dislodge on its own ground (a rarity), a doubter can always invoke a new criterion, one that you had not addressed, around which a case can be made for withholding support.

What we've said should be enough to suggest that evaluation that seeks to vindicate is a highly political enterprise. The political activity mostly involves the business of arbitrating criteria: the criteria you can and should address and the criteria the doubters will invoke. Finally demonstrating how you meet a given set of criteria is actually the easy part. Getting criteria clear, fixing consensus on them, and keeping them from squirming loose is the tough part.

Avoid evaluation that seeks to vindicate whenever you can. If you must engage in it — and often the life of your venture demands that you do — proceed with your eyes open. What you should see first is that the odds are theoretically against you. Your position is vulnerable; the doubters' is secure. For every obstacle you surmount, they can — in good faith or bad — concoct a dozen more. This is simply the case, and there are no good grounds to view the case rebelliously or with resentment. Have you never, despite a fair amount of evidence to the contrary, withheld your support?

With your eyes calmly open, there are some things you should do. Try your best to fix the criteria your audience agrees to apply well before you design your vindicating evaluation. When you *have* designed it, explore with that audience precisely how your design invokes and attempts to address those criteria. Nine times out of ten, this will reveal discrepancies between what your significant audience said it wanted and what it thought it said it wanted. Arbitrate those discrepancies until you *share* an understanding of what you are talking about and what both parties expect.

If you can, try to establish any evaluation that aims to vindicate on the following grounds: Assure your doubting audience of your willingness to demonstrate that students who engage in your innovation will do *at least as well* as students in any established program your innovation might stand to as an alternative. At least as well in what respect? Any reasonable respect in which that audience chooses to evaluate students from the standard program. You first promise that much and then add that you will also present information about additional gains you feel will be distinctive for students in your program.

This is a sound approach to evaluation that tries to vindicate for several reasons.

To grasp these reasons, it helps to realize a peculiar truth about educational evaluation that is seldom brought to our attention. The most poorly evaluated enterprises in the field of education are, contrary to what might be supposed, the fully established and sanctioned ones. This observation isn't meant to be shocking; in our terms it is quite reasonable. Entrenched practices have already won the support of significant audiences;

they do not need to evidence themselves. If you doubt this, look at the evidence marshalled by any given department for any of its major instructional practices — say, for example, the large lecture program designed to serve incoming college freshmen. You probably, but not certainly, will find some evidence used to support the program. If, however, you were to suggest that you want to defend an innovation solely on *equivalent* evidence, ask yourself if you would not be laughed from the room.

Again, you shouldn't take offense. The laughter would be justified. Because it is you that insists on change, the onus of proof is yours. And besides, the situation can be turned to your honest advantage. When you set the criterion that your students will do *at least as well* as students in the established program, you have the advantage that the established program really knows very little about how well its students are doing. It will seldom have more to offer than student performance on a few standardized tests.

Now, whatever achievements you covet for your students, you probably do owe them performance on standardized tests at least equivalent to what other students are achieving. Despite your possible apprehensions, it turns out that this is seldom an insurmountable, or even an intrusive, handicap to sound innovation.

What can happen next makes this approach truly beneficial. Even if classic evaluation design did not require you to establish a control group, there are other good reasons you should. As your innovation gets underway, you will be examining your students in light of your evaluation battery. You will also be examining student performance in the established program in light of much of that same battery. Comparing these two views is what, of course, advances your insight. You now begin to see some of the distinctive effects your instruction is having on your students. Too often, not enough is made of the obvious corollary. You will also see, with greater precision than is usually available, what is distinctive about the effects of the established program.

Totally apart from your concerns for your own program, you now have illuminating insights about the established program. If you treat these seriously and objectively, you are likely to find more in them than a litany of the established program's shortcomings. More probably, you will find good effects in the established program, and a sufficiently detailed view of their causes to suggest how they might be enhanced. You have the wherewithal to advance your various audiences' insight regarding the established program, at no real expense to your own.

This is a kind of vindication much to be desired. You've vindicated not simply your own innovation, but the broader enterprise of instructional experimentation. You've given established practice a new sense of itself that it can achieve no other way.

EVALUATION TO ILLUMINATE

To the degree that evaluation strives to illuminate, it isn't concerned with audiences. With some purpose in mind, it wants to achieve a clearer and more precise view of what is going on. Usually, the purpose is to enable us to do something better, like decide, or comprehend, or achieve, or improve.

This sounds easier than winning the support of an audience, but in many respects it is a great deal more difficult. So much inhibits our gaining a significantly clearer and more precise view of things. Here are just a few stumbling blocks:

1.   Our guiding theory about what is going on may be too simplistic to sustain a better view. Or perhaps the theory is ill founded. In that case, it will systematically obscure rather than advance insight.

2.   This is actually a corollary of our first point, but so powerful it warrants mentioning on its own. The *language* we've so far developed to describe what is happening may be too crude to segregate and affirm a better view. We may need new signs and symbols, and new ways of manipulating them, before we can catch evidence that slips unnoticed through too coarse a system of meanings.

3.   If 2 happens to be the case, it follows that available evaluation instruments and techniques — based on available language — may also be too crude. Even if suitable language exists, the techniques and instruments available may not employ or reflect it, and consequently those instruments and techniques won't capture the distinctions a more precise view requires.

This list could easily go on, but already we see that evaluation that truly wants to illuminate has to worry about and tinker with theory, possibly devise strictures for and extensions of language to handle new meanings, and critically assess evaluation techniques and instruments, perhaps devising new ones. That's a tall order, and very little actual evaluation or even research attempts it. Most efforts to illuminate are satisfied to do so in terms of established benchmarks.

Instead of striving for a new level of insight about thinking skill achievement in your course, we settle for a view of what has happened to your students *in terms* of their Watson–Glazer scores, or *in light* of their incoming profiles on the MMPI, or as compared to any of a hundred other invokable standards. Efforts to do this do advance our view of what is going on. They also happen to respond to the needs of an identifiable audience — the research and evaluation establishment — and thereby, as a kind of bonus, assure you of some degree of vindication.

There are really only two shortfalls to this approach. First, your view of what is going on will tend to be limited by the sensitivity of the benchmarks you select, and that sensitivity can be quite narrow. If you stop there, much of what is happening will pass by you unnoticed. This is a handicap when you want to illuminate, but it seldom is when you need to vindicate. It usually requires only small amounts of data responsive to an audience's terms to resolve its support. Outlandish ventures can win a school board's support by producing a small rise in the SAT. Audiences bartering support generally get nervous and restless when given more information than they wish to see, whereas someone seeking illumination can seldom get enough.

This brings us to our second shortfall, which is that evaluation by established benchmark simply cannot supply the thinking skill instructor with the illumination required, not to evaluate instruction, but to guide it. You need a much better view of what is going on in your class and with your students than established instruments alone could ever provide. Consequently, you have to sustain an ongoing process of illumination entirely by yourself.

ILLUMINATING INSTRUCTION

You need to follow several simple steps to really see what is going on in your classroom. We hasten to add that these steps do not expose a secret path to insight. We've been too disparaging of recipe approaches to try to stick you with one now. What these steps mainly do is make conscious and explicit what good teachers tend to do implicitly. In this case, it happens that there are astonishing gains in being explicit. Taking the steps consciously lets you accumulate a history of your performance. Examining that history greatly enhances your ability to guide future steps. Let's examine the steps and then see what they comprise.

1. First you define a student outcome toward which you plan to instruct on a given day. For the thinking skill instructor, this is usually some enhancement of ability to think, or growth in insight regarding the thinking process. By "define," we mean you clearly set forth what will indicate to you that the outcome has been achieved.

2. On evidence available to you, you plan an intervention — a sequence of instructional activity — that you perceive has the best chance of prompting the outcome defined in step 1.

3. You instruct, and you do so by constraining your activity as closely as possible to the plan for instruction you established in step 2.

4. You now do your best to capture *actual* student outcome. You examine student performance in light of the indicators you established in step 1. The following steps all hinge on your care in this assessment.

5. If the student outcome is *exactly* what you intended it to be, you are, at least in respect to that outcome, an instructional genius. Time now to define a new outcome and repeat the process.

6. More likely, you are only a masterful instructor, in which case the actual outcome will deviate — in a range from slightly to significantly — from what you intended. Now you array all the evidence at your disposal about this intervention of yours and ask yourself:

a. Could the deviation be traced to some element of your instruction? Perhaps you departed significantly from your intended plan. If so, your planned intervention was not well tested. Perhaps you executed the plan faithfully but now see that reshaping elements of it might enhance the odds of achieving the outcome.

b. Could the deviation stem from a fault related to the targeted outcome? Perhaps you now see the outcome was not defined as well as it need be. It may have revealed itself to be more complex than it appeared. Student difficulties in achieving the outcome might suggest that your goal is premature. Perhaps intervening outcomes need attention before this one can be addressed.

7. Whatever you decide in step 6, you adjust either your instruction or your target, or both. *Note* those adjustments and repeat these steps again in light of your refined view of the task.

There is nothing new for us, as teachers, in reflecting on our behavior and our purposes in class. All our actions in class tend to be devised, in the sense that we perform them in light of consequences we hope they will have. But when we plan and examine our actions as consciously and explicitly as these steps admonish us to, we engage a process that has a name. It is called the experimental method. And yes, instruction that strives to assess its consequences and reshape itself in light of them is inherently experimental. The process illuminates instruction in several critical ways.

First, the experimental method builds an increasingly sensitive and articulate view of the objective — a better *conception* of the instructional goal. We see the goal anew in light of efforts to achieve it. In this regard, misses are often more instructive than hits. They uncover unwarranted or overly facile assumptions about what we expect to achieve, forcing us to redefine and reconceive our aim. We distinguish our objective more carefully on such evidence. Overthrowing old assumptions forces us to frame new and hopefully more suitable ones. We can't help it: We theorize.

Second, it illuminates what is inept or disruptive about our instruction. The experimental method highlights outcomes we don't want or did not expect and counters our tendency to ignore these. We're forced to examine our methods and techniques in light of their effects. Again assumptions are called to question, and we begin refining, revamping. We reconstruct method and technique.

Third, guiding instruction in accord with this experimental process illuminates the dark recesses of instructional research in ways that make that great body of effort pointedly useful. You will start carrying very specific questions and needs to that store of accumulated insight. You'll soon surprise yourself with how active and adept you become at this commerce: this gathering, assessing, selecting, and employing of the fruits of accomplished experimenters and researchers.

And if you maintain this commerce—in service to issues you yourself uncover in your classroom—for no more than a year, you will make a further surprising discovery. You will find that you are no longer traveling to the frontiers of research for insight; you're working *at* the frontier. You aren't reading about the state of the art, you're shaping it.

It is important to understand how this can be. No matter your degree of intelligence, it won't be your superior wisdom that takes you to the leading edge so quickly. Nor is your quick advancement due to some poverty in educational research. It may be true that there are considerable quantities of bad educational research, but there are considerable quantities of excellent work as well. No, your rapid rise comes from your special vantage regarding a very special environment: the classroom. There simply is no other environment so redolent of minds under a *controllable* variety of pressures to function. Day in and day out, you are witness to minds coming to various terms with this pressure as you apply it. No laboratory could give you a less fettered view of intelligence engaging or avoiding development, and there you sit in the catbird seat.

There is another way to consider the benefits of this experimental approach. Look again at the seven steps we propose you use to illuminate your instruction. Let's say that your course is up for a final and exhaustive evaluation. The most sophisticated, expert, professionally managed evaluation design imaginable cannot do more than invoke processes embedded in those seven steps.

That evaluation effort will apply an impressive panoply of instrumentation to the task, but it will execute only once. You, as someone who approaches instruction experimentally, execute these processes each day you instruct. For you, evaluation has grown recursive. You constantly tune effort to effect and effect to effort in light of a deepening daily view of consequent student performance. Small wonder that this should carry you quickly to the leading edge of instructional insight.

Recollect also our discussion of those things that inhibit the formation of clearer and more precise views of what is going on. As an instructor who proceeds experimentally, you will grapple with all of them. Normal evaluation, we said, often avoids this grappling by basing its view on established benchmarks. But you will be trying theory for its adequacy; noting weaknesses and entertaining modifications. You will be adopting, discarding, and reforming meanings and ways to express them. You'll be pushing assessment practices for more insight, again modifying and devising. You will do what much educational practice avoids doing, and you'll do it as long as it promises to better illuminate the task.

It's from this perspective that the following assertion doesn't seem so absurd: If you instruct experimentally, and do so conscientiously, your own classroom can teach you more about developing thinking skill than can the finest degree program at the finest institution of the land.

If you want to develop an experimental approach to instruction, it helps immeasurably to do so in collaboration with one or more like-minded colleagues. Collaboration lets you reap all the benefits we've ascribed to the paired problem-solving teams. You'll be *vocalizing* your instructional objectives and techniques, and nothing else will quite so sharpen your perception of both, because you will see them in light of feedback from a concerned coprofessional. Even if you and your colleagues differ in course goals and approaches, sharing will multiply everyone's experience of this process of instructing experimentally.

As an aside, you can often tell when you and your colleague(s) are instructing experimentally by the shocked, or otherwise odd, looks you receive on certain occasions from others not so engaged. Teachers who pursue their instruction experimentally end up socializing in ways that seem peculiar to teachers who don't. You might, for instance, rush to the faculty lounge, find a fellow experimenter, and eagerly begin debriefing with something like, "Sue, you know that sequence I planned to get my class producing like Impressionists? Man, what a *fiasco*!" Teachers not inclined to address instruction experimentally don't tend to expose performance that might call their competence to question. Teachers who do instruct experimentally repeatedly call their own performance to question. For them, competence requires it.

There is a tendency—and you may need to fight it—to shy away from sound evaluation and experimentation, partly because of the considerable work they entail, but mostly because of ill-formed preconceptions about them. Experimentation conjures the apparent drudgery of the lab, and evaluation seems anticlimactic—the clean-up work you do after you finish the job. Try to remember that you don't have a "job" until you evaluate. You don't know what your product is until you thump it, wiggle the parts, and give it a few trial runs. Evaluation is the climactic act of the creative process, the one that keeps you from fostering a shiny pile of junk. Experimentation *is* that creative process, gone careful and self-conscious.

You might discover, as you experiment and evaluate, that the considerable work involved seems to lighten as you go on. You can grow accustomed to the point where engaging in experimentation and evaluation seems natural, and you wouldn't think of launching a venture without invoking them. That may be because both evaluation and experimentation are special cases of the mind's most seminal work, which is to assess. Thought can neither direct action nor advance itself without assessing something in light of something else. So doing evaluation and experimentation really is doing what comes naturally.

THE FILE

THE FILE

THE FILE

CHAPTER 15

THEORY, AND OTHER CONCLUDING ISSUES

Forethought

We haven't tried to systematically expound a thinking skills theory in this guide, although there is one that underpins the practices it recommends. We've pointed to some of this theory's features from time to time where doing so might help explain practice, and we add a few observations about it in this concluding chapter. But a systematic development would expand to a book considerably beyond the size of this one.

In keeping with the purpose of this guide, there really is a more important issue concerning theory that we need to consider. That issue is how a thinking skill instructor ought to relate to theory — not just the theory implicit in this book, but any theory that seeks to inform his understanding of thinking skill and its development.

This issue has a kind of contemporary urgency because of the perceived state of the thinking skills movement. Educators striving to come to grips with thinking skill issues often express a certain frustration. They find progress difficult because they seem to be picking their way through a snarl of unrelated, if not conflicting, theories about the enterprise. Assertions come to us from a bewildering array of sources. The path is crowded with positions that beckon our attention, from Cognitive Mapping to Right Brain–Left Brain through Multiple Intelligence. Frequently the theory sustaining these positions remains implicit and is not easy to uncover. Sometimes theory is simply skirted, and the position tries to advance itself on technique alone. It's difficult to sort it all out.

In light of this difficulty, there is a species of advice to newcomers that appears to be on the increase. Often it is triggered when someone expresses confusion while trying to integrate different skill listings or instructional priorities. "The labels don't matter," comes the advice. "It isn't very important what you call the skills, or even which ones you strive for when. All you have to do is pick a set that seems to make sense and get at it. Underneath the terminology, we're all really striving for the same thing."

This is, in effect, counsel not to do anything about the theoretical snarl. Oh, perhaps someone else should worry about it, but the proper thing for us to do with the theory problem is ignore it, and get on with the work at hand.

Could that advice be sound?

THEORY AND YOU

Theories are assertions that selectively organize and sustain whole rafts of other assertions about what is and is not so. They are inescapable, in the sense that not one of us can make so much as an observation without at least implicitly invoking theory. "I want this area left just as it is," you tell the man from the nursery, "except for that tree. I'd like it taken out." The words make no sense apart from a set of basic assertions that both you and the nursery man share, one of which affirms that trees are individual organisms, separable from their surrounds.

We adopt most of our theories unconsciously and hence uncritically. This isn't much cause for alarm, since most of these theories work well enough. They are the dues we pay and the gifts we gain as members of a society. We take them in like mother's milk, or its carefully formulated equivalent. Then there are a smaller set of theories we consciously adopt. Here a good deal of alarm is justified, because conscious adoption does not require demonstration. We can embrace a theory without ever asking for, let alone examining, its credentials. We adopt it simply because we like it; it satisfies some need, simplifies things, stokes coveted feelings, or sanctions some desire. Theories of racial supremacy or of other forms of supposed privilege, with no hope of adequate demonstration, have never been shy of advocates. Minds have grown numb trying to count the costs of devotion to baseless theory.

Finally, we come to that tiny set of theories we make accountable to evidence. We do this when our present theory-bolstered views prove stubbornly inadequate; when they fail to resolve nagging anomalies and can't clarify troublesome ambiguities. We finally come to insist, regardless what we might want or might like to see, on a more penetrating, more enabling view of what is really going on. In such cases, when a theory presents itself as proposing a better view, we sometimes take the trouble to check the claim.

There are many things we do to check a theory's credentials. We look for internal consistency. We count the cost of adoption; what old theory do we send packing by adopting the new, and what does the exchange cost us in capability? How much of the furniture of established knowledge does it rearrange, and is the disruption worth the gain? But most importantly, we try to see if the theory works.

Roughly, our confidence begins to grow in a theory when what it says will happen, happens. It doesn't grow much, because other theories might predict the same outcome. But when a theory accounts for something other theories can't, or don't, we gain respect. If we find it accounts for — reveals — more than other available theories, we have good reason to plunk for it.

So the process of testing a theory can grow quite complicated. But whether simple or complex, we can't even begin the process until one requirement is met. We must understand just what the theory is asserting. We need to master its propositions and their meanings. At the point where these grow unclear, they are, ipso facto, uncheckable. In effect, where a theory ceases to discriminate usefully, it ceases being a theory at all.

That is why, and in what sense, terminology always matters. Terminology is the vehicle that theory uses to fix its meanings on events, and so a theory whose terminology "doesn't matter" is a theory that doesn't matter. The only way to see if it in fact does matter is to take its terminology seriously.

When you have trouble fitting pieces together from the thinking skills literature, resist advice to set the trouble aside because it "doesn't matter." As aggravating as it might be to do so, push to discriminate and make clear. At times the effort will show you that the differences really don't matter. This happens when sources you are trying to reconcile have pinned different labels to meanings that really don't compete, very probably stemming from theories that really don't compete. If this proves to be the case, you know you are playing with the third string. Don't waste time on theories that haven't the spine to compete.

But often, the effort to discriminate will reveal different meanings behind the different terminology. When you determine that your sources are, in fact, asserting different things about thinking skill, take heart. Your sources *are* competing, and now you have the advantage of being able to compare them in harness, gauging which does better at what. You can call on them to face identical tasks and see how they perform. And keep an eye out for that special case that often arises between competing theories: occasions when they use the same terminology to convey quite different meanings.

Why should you bother with all this? We point to two reasons. The first is that there's an unfortunate parody in the image of a thinking skill instructor *not* bothering with it. You are teaching people to think, and the principle purpose of thinking, we have argued, is to build a better case—a better comprehension, a surer insight, a sounder resolution. It is difficult to make sense of teaching other people how to build better cases while standing pat on shaky ones about thinking. If there is no point in you, the teacher, advancing beyond the theory and practice about thinking skill that has been handed you, where is the point in students ever advancing beyond what is handed them?

The second reason could get out of hand. It could challenge some current research practice in education and stand much of that practice on its ear. But we won't carry it that far. Our second reason is simply that *no* one occupies a more suitable position to build a better case for thinking and its development than the practicing classroom teacher who deliberately sets out to do so. There is no better evidential source of insight than the classrooms you enter day after day. If better understanding and more potent theory about thinking skill comes, it will trace to someone in shoes like yours.

The classroom grind is what will best sharpen your grasp of everything in this guide. If you grind with your wits about you (i.e., instruct experimentally as outlined in the prior chapter) you can soon outstrip this guide or any other in your discrimination about thinking behavior and attempts to guide it. You have *exampled* insight in your hands, and that is just what it takes to test, to adjust, to reconstruct, to advance theory.

The really tough question isn't why you should bother with theory. It's why you shouldn't.

THEORY AND US

Theories exist to serve you, and not the other way around. They are tools intended to enhance your insight, and you should hold them accountable on grounds of performance. You owe them careful scrutiny, never awe or devotion. If one comes along that performs more usefully than others, give it your allegiance but make even that grant tentative. You never know when you might encounter, or find cause yourself to build, a better one. Be especially suspicious and demanding of any you do build yourself. Parenthood tends to be just as blind here as elsewhere.

Take this hardheadedness with you as you move through the thinking skills literature. In doing so ourselves, we found much in that literature that was interesting, even intriguing. Unfortunately, try as we might, a good deal that was interesting and intriguing did not seem to us useful. We could coax from such positions no significant advance in our comprehension of thinking skill and its development. Bear in mind that this failure could as well be ours as that of the positions in question. We might not have had the wit to see properly. You will have to decide when you look yourself. Whatever the case, it doesn't alter the fact. We failed to find use, and consequently warrant, for some of the positions advanced.

We found multiple intelligence theories extremely intriguing. But since we can't fruitfully imagine any intelligence, however many we might have, functioning without exercise of the generic skills — without attending selectively, without discerning, without analoging, without suspending closure, or without reassessing — we could not locate the force of the distinction. An acknowledgment that the mind deploys the generic skills in distinctive ways with distinctive classes of tasks seemed to us just as discriminating and does not require reifying new species of intelligence.

Cognitive mapping and newer approaches to detailing the learning propensities of students are clearly interesting and do give us a sense of the great assortment of ways the mind can approach things. But these efforts are often coupled to an assumption whose merit escapes us. The assumption is that once we understand a student's distinctive learning style, we ought to adapt instruction to suite it. Why ossify existing propensities? Why not challenge them and make them flexible? Liberating students from predisposed learning modes strikes us as at least as promising as reinforcing those modes. A few analysts of cognitive style do seem inclined this way.

Right brain–left brain theory is a champion in its own domain. The research faces a few little problems but on the whole is imposing and definitely illuminating. Some educators have attempted to apply these neurophysiological insights to instructional practice, and we worry about the great extent and relative lack of control of their leap. The problem is that the units of analysis appropriate to these two domains — brain synapses and classroom techniques — are so disparate. It's like trying to understand driving skill in terms of clutch design.

Occasionally we came across terminology that irritated because it tended to obscure more than it revealed. The term *metacognition* seems to enjoy great currency. As best we can tell, its various uses appear to reference "thinking about thinking." The notion roughly seems to be that most of the time we go around thinking about things, but on special occasions we can or should think about thinking. When we do so, we are engaging in metacognition.

First, we question the need for the term. We've engaged in and pursued considerable thinking about thinking in this book without encountering a compulsion to use it. But more important, you can't fix such an ostentatiously learned label to a set of thinking behaviors without making them seem quite remote and lofty; very *special*. The term intentionally smacks of something like "metaphysics;" an enterprise *above* and *beyond* physics. We get the feeling that metacognition is a form of thinking *above* and *beyond* normal thinking.

High among those things a thinking skill instructor wants to establish in her students is the notion that critical reflection on one's own thinking is a normal, natural, common, and unexceptionally useful thing to do. It's just a phase of healthy thinking's recursiveness.

So in that sense, we think *metacognition* connotes unfortunately. But it doesn't stop there. The term goes on connoting in all the wrong directions. It sponsors an established view of what thinking involves that might be better disestablished. The notion that most of the time we go around thinking about things and occasionally preoccupy ourselves with the processes and products of the mind is clinically incorrect, and almost the inverse of what, as best we can tell, actually happens. In an odd but more accurate sense, we *usually* think about thinking and only rarely think about things.

The closest we ever get to thinking about things is when we actively worry about how well our constructs apprehend them, (i.e., when we think critically). The rest of the time, we are content to stay a comfortable distance from things, dealing instead with the handy signs and symbols we've devised for them. It's a shorthand all of us use so consistently that we have no trouble buying the convenient illusion that we are dealing with things. Commonly, our thinking is with, about, and in terms of socially sanctioned products of thought; the coined meanings that thought has fixed to established signs and symbols. Remember that concepts and other mental constructs are distillations of our thinking about things, so in that sense most of our thinking engages products of thought. This is as much the case when we "think about thinking" as when we think about anything else. If any brand of thinking deserves the prefix "meta," it is the relatively rare kind that tries to shape meaning so that it couples more closely with events; that strives anew to move past available constructs toward what events might be in their own right — critical thinking about *things*. Anyone at any time can, of course, "think about thinking," but that by itself is not noteworthy. It is how we think about it that counts. When we try to surmise, on the basis of carefully weighed and scrutinized evidence, what kind of *thing* thinking is, then the effort is noteworthy.

We've recollected dissatisfying moments in our personal tour of the thinking skill literature. We haven't mentioned the many moments that were very satisfying, because pages of praise would not so clearly illuminate the nature of the trip you yourself need to take. You must make your own trip, not as sightseer, but as a picky and demanding professional, intent on coming away with your own strengthened, informed, and hence *demonstrable* vision.

A GESTURE TOWARD SOURCES

Short of an annotated bibliography the size of this book, we resist providing you with a reading list, although we do reluctantly explore some sources in the Appendix. It is difficult to be selective without a thorough knowledge of the reader. To the degree that backgrounds differ, so will the constructive value of readings. What gives us scintillating new insight may prove old hat to you, and vice versa. The best we are willing to risk in the Appendix is mention of a few points in our own history of reading and searching that were pivotal in forming our views.

The key to our theory of thinking skill and its development lies, as should now be clear, with the perception that thought is constructively rather than predeterminedly representational. The mind, we are convinced, selectively builds purposive models — paradigms — of events, using these to govern and increase its purchase on experience. Looking at how it does this, we've been forced to conclude that the mind is a reluctant builder, often preferring, for good reason and bad, the tools at hand to the arduous work of shaping better ones. We see the shaping of better constructs as the *distinctive* capability of human thought. We already have machines that outstrip us in simple manipulation. We think that education must grow less and less content with a view of its mission as primarily one of dispensing constructs and techniques. We think it needs to emphasize the skills of devising and assessing constructs and techniques, the skills of thinking. Consequently, we are especially drawn to the kind of instruction that ratifies and fosters the operant mind, the mind that is, at heart, a maker.

Regarding the Appendix, which points to some sources that helped form these views and appetites, we apologize to those not mentioned there whose insight might equal or surpass those mentioned.

BEYOND SUCCESS

One last flight of fancy. Suppose you use this guide. As you apply its suggestions, tailoring them to suit you and thereby almost certainly improving and enhancing them, there will likely come a time when you step back, survey your work calmly, and pronounce it good. You have helped students achieve new thinking skill and insight. The evidence is there, and despite your intense modesty you can no longer avoid it. You've initiated a process that works. Not only are you confident that you can sustain the process, but you see exciting ways it might be improved. Ahead of you lies that pleasant, fulfilling walk into the sunset, with accompaniment. Flower petals, triumphant music, applause — pick one or mix and match.

We love happy endings, and we'd like to leave you with one, but don't count on quite that kind of walk. You might take the following inconsequential event as a deeper parable. There were belated introductions to a notable colleague at the same large institution. At first she responded with a blank look, but then the brows knitted and she said, "Oh yes. You're the one that's doing that thinking skills business. I've had some of your students. Disruptive. Keep gumming things up with questions."

Not everyone will ecstatically embrace your accomplishments. Assuming you've developed more skillful thinkers, and not just assertive poseurs, those thinkers will leave you for environs that do not expect them and often don't know what to do with them. Such environs can include the next scheduled class.

If you've developed an appropriate sense of task within your students, you have helped mitigate the problem for them. They should be able to distinguish their own expectations from those that others will have of them. But you are a more stationary target. There you sit, turning out capabilities many of our systems may not be prepared to harness.

It is less than consoling to realize that the problem doesn't stop with your environs. The world at large is often not as ravenous as it claims for skillful thinkers. An engineering friend wanted to share the cleverness of a small spindle-like automotive part. "See," he said, noting a protruding cam, "with this, not even an idiot can assemble it wrong." When asked how much of his time was devoted, not to designing a working part, but to designing one an idiot couldn't misuse, his estimate was well over a third. Mass production components could hardly be handled otherwise, but one wonders how much of our societal design is dedicated to arranging things so that even an idiot must get it right. If the trend exists and persists, what role might their be, eventually, for great numbers of nonidiots? Perhaps we misperceive, but aren't there signs of idiot-proofing in education? Outlandish, isn't it: the thought that some of our more capable minds should strive not to enhance capability, but to arrange things so that it ceases to be a factor.

There could—it is conceivable—come a day when a commitment to developing thinking skill is not buoyed up on the crest of popularity. There might even come a day—just barely conceivable—when commitments to develop thinking skill have to be made despite what the world wants, because it would be good for the world, because the world needs the firm check of good thinking, and because, whereas poor thinkers multiply chaos, only good thinkers can disrupt it.

Fortunately, whether the social clime is hostile or friendly ought not matter much to the thinking skill instructor. This professional commits to the individual—not the many—and concern about society's stance isn't finally relevant. A hunger to enable drives the true thinking skill instructor, not a hunger to preach, lead, or indoctrinate. That hunger abates only when actual growth is catalyzed in an individual, and someone has in fact become more able. That is the thinking skill instructor's proper appetite.

We will count it worth the effort if this guide helps strengthen such an appetite. If it does, some readers may resolve to persevere, and we all know success crowns perseverance.

Good fortune to those who persevere, and should any knocks come to you as you develop minds, may they be light, though heavily instructive.

BIBLIOGRAPHY

Chickering, Arthur W., & Associates. (1981). *The American College*. San Francisco: Jossey–Bass.

Gregg, L. W., & Steinberg, E. R., (Eds.). (1980). *Cognitive processes in writing*. Hillsdale, NJ: Lawrence Erlbaum Associates.

Keeley, Stuart M., Browne, N. Neil, & Haas, Paul F. (1976, November). *Cognitive activity in the classroom: A comparison of three kinds of raters, using the Cognitive Activities Ratings Scales (CARS)*. Unpublished report to the CUE Center, Bowling Green State University, Bowling Green, OH.

Martinelli, Kenneth J. (1987, January). Thinking straight about thinking. *The School Administrator, 44,* No. 1, American Association of School Administrators, Arlington, VA.

Marzano, Robert J., & Hutchins, C. L. (1985). *Thinking skills; A conceptual framework*. Aurora, CO: Mid-continent Regional Educational Laboratory.

Quine, W. V. (1969). *Ontological relativity and other essays*. New York: Columbia University Press.

Whimbey, Arthur, with Linda Shaw Whimbey. (1975). *Intelligence can be taught*. New York: E. P. Dutton.

Whimbey, Arthur, & Lockhead, Jack. (1982). *Problem solving & comprehension* (3rd ed.). Philadelphia: The Franklin Institute Press.

Vygotsky, Lev Semenovich. (1966). *Thought and language*. (Edited and translated by Eugenia Hanfmann & Gertrude Vakar.) Cambridge, MA: The MIT Press.

APPENDIX
. . . A PathTaken

The following bibliographic notes will seem a long way from contemporary on-line thinking skill literature. Their only purpose is to give you some sense of the sources that underlie many of the key assertions in this guide. They also shape much of the screen through which this author sifts that on-line literature.

A. Fundamental statements of a relativistic epistemology, which characterize what kind of job knowing is and thereby constrain what skills are to be seen as generic.

   1. Dewey, John. *The Quest for Certainty*. Dewey touches on the enervating consequences of assumed objectivity in all his works, but on that subject, this is his tour de force.

   2. Beyond this first book, the list grows endless. From Wittgenstein to Teilhard de Chardin, Polanyi to Schrodinger, Pierce to von Bertalanffy, there are pertinent and probing analyses of the function of mind, and all of them point to a fundamental need to impose purposive system on experience, rather than to reflect innate essences.

B. Scientists and students of science, on the relativism of scientific knowledge. Particularly, the primacy of *constructive* versus merely perceptive and receptive skills in producing scientific understanding.

277

1. Koyre, Alexandre. *Metaphysics and Measurement*. Particularly interesting in that a physicist explains why common sense tends to be medieval and Aristotelian and consequently resists relativity.

2. Heisenberg, Werner. *Physics and Philosophy*. Also, (a) *The Physical Principles of the Quantum Theory*, (b) *The Physicist's Conception of Nature*. This is the man who was compelled to reject not only scientific claims to the sanction of objectivity, but the very division of the world into subject and object — strong argument for the skills required to "make" rather than simply find meaning. There is, of course, an exhaustive literature here, including works by Einstein and Infeld, Pierre Duheim, Toulmin, Hempel, and so forth.

3. Kuhn, Thomas S. *The Structure of Scientific Revolutions* bears special mention because it so cogently establishes how much the productivity of higher order capabilities depends on and devolves from social enterprise and maintenance of a social context.

4. The works of various anthropologists such as Claude Levi-Strauss (e.g., *The Raw and the Cooked*) provide an important transition. They evidence that the dynamics of forming scientific knowledge are kin to those afoot in forming primitive myth and language.

C. Linguists and logicians, on language systems themselves as optional and limited constructs — models — of experience, rather than labelings of an objective order. Again, the emphasis is on constructive skills (skills that underpin building language systems).

1. Quine, Willard Van Orman. *Word and Object*. A classic proof that languages do not reflect objective referents but rather construct meanings for experience. Demonstrates the "nontranslatability" of the semantic systems that underpin radically different languages. The writings of Benjamin Lee Whorf add excellent support.

2. A superior anthology edited by Joseph H. Greenberg, *Universals of Language*, presents work by Uriel Weinreich, Charles Osgood, Joseph Casagrande, Stephen Ullman et al., all of which decry the objective referent as a dependable source of linguistic universals.

3. The constructural alternative to objective referents is approached in another anthology entitled *Structuralism*, edited by Jacques Ehrmann. Scheffler, Nodelman, Levi-Strauss, and others disclose our propensity to devise explanatory and predictive approximations of the real, with again some implications for what skills are generic in our encounter with the world.

D. Developmental psychologists and genetic expistemologists, on the emergence of "generic" skills.

1. Here we have the endless roster of Piagetian works and commentaries. I would particularly nominate *Six Psychological Studies* as good access to Piaget's insight and method. The entire developmental sequence is sketched there, and his treatment exhibits his admirable view of the interdependence of cognitive and affective maturation. Reason enough for his thought to be renown.

2. Piaget should not be embraced without the corrective of Lev Semenovich Vygotsky's *Thought and Language*. More than does Piaget, Vygotsky suggests why the developmental sequence is (a) not preordained, and (b) not homogeneous. An individual *need* not develop all the skills in the sequence, and the emergence of a higher order skill does not preclude extensive and continuous employment of lower order ones. Vygotsky also illuminates the recursive quality of higher order skill maturation: Higher order skills tend to be made up of lower order ones operating on their own products.

3. Perhaps a minor footnote, but Quine, in his *Ways of Paradox*, speaks of the manner in which concepts are formed as a process of *legislative postulation*, establishing again that the currency of thought is made up of constructs, not givens.

E. Finally, there is the current thinking skill literature itself. We can't begin to assess it in this space, so we leave with you the delights of discovery. However, if you come to this literature fresh, do be sure to visit Arthur Whimbey's *Intelligence Can Be Taught*, Benjamin Bloom and Lois Broder's *Problem-Solving Processes of College Students*, Albert Upton and Richard Samson's *Creative Analysis*, Upton's *Design for Thinking*, and D. N. Perkins' *The Minds Best Work*. These are important touchstones early in your tour, but given your special needs and interests, there are many others you may come to rank more highly.

TOPICAL INDEX